"In this excellent book, Webster considers nun
freshing way. Of particular importance is the co
communication method of articulating the gospel
and resistance, and its relevance to today's world. Jesus told the truth slant. The book
includes a very helpful appendix spelling out how to preach the parables. This is a book
to read with your Bible open."

—Graham A. Cole,
Dean and Senior Vice President of Education
and Professor of Biblical and Systematic Theology,
Trinity Evangelical Divinity School

"With the heart of a pastor and the mind of a scholar, Doug Webster explores the parables
of Jesus as 'truth slant' — everyday stories that draw hearers in through their familiarity,
but then, 'like time bombs that only explode when they have penetrated our hearts,'
transform them into true disciples. This engaging volume will inspire and motivate those
'with ears to hear' the subversive values of the kingdom of God."

—Mark L. Strauss,
University Professor of New Testament,
Bethel Seminary of Bethel University

"Jesus did some of his most important teaching in parable form. Two thousand years
later, many of us have become so familiar with this pedagogical approach that we no
longer fully appreciate its significance—not only for our understanding of the nature of
the triune God, but also for the ways we serve in our own ministries.

"In *The Parables: Jesus's Friendly Subversive Speech*, Douglas D. Webster defamiliarizes the
familiar to help us read these ancient stories with new eyes. Scholarly insights and honest
reflections on his own ministry come together in a thoughtful exploration of the parables'
indirect—but powerful—confrontations of the religious status quo, and of how Jesus
not only teaches us *what* message to communicate, but *how* to communicate it best."

—Rebecca Poe Hays,
Assistant Professor of Christian Scriptures – Hebrew Bible/Old Testament,
George W. Truett Theological Seminary of Baylor University

"We are told in the Gospels that Jesus never taught without using parables, so their
importance to his teaching cannot be overemphasized. And yet, Jesus's parables are often
overexplained by those who teach them. I'm thankful for this pastoral and practical work
from Doug Webster. His keeping the bigger picture in view, and thereby the point of
following Jesus intact, is refreshing and needed. The next time I preach on the parables
this will be a really great resource."

—Cole Huffman, Senior Pastor,
First Evangelical Church

THE
PARABLES

JESUS'S
FRIENDLY
SUBVERSIVE
SPEECH

DOUGLAS D. WEBSTER

The Parables: Jesus's Friendly Subversive Speech

© 2021 by Douglas D. Webster

Published by Kregel Academic, an imprint of Kregel Publications, 2450 Oak Industrial Dr. NE, Grand Rapids, MI 49505-6020.

The Greek font, GraecaU, is available from www.linguistsoftware.com/lgku.htm, +1-425-775-1130.

ISBN 978-0-8254-4690-0

Printed in the United States of America

21 22 23 24 25 / 5 4 3 2 1

Dedicated to
David and Brenda Mensah

CONTENTS

INTRODUCTION

Jesus reached a communicational impasse following the Sermon on the Mount. At every turn, serious opposition confronted Jesus's straightforward message. Whenever he opened his mouth, the cultural and religious elite were there to ridicule him and challenge his message. They made it their mission to bully and intimidate not only Jesus but anyone who showed interest in his teaching. The narrative pace quickens in Matthew's gospel. Miracles are performed, people are healed, and the disciples are sent out on a mission to proclaim that the kingdom of heaven has come near (Matt. 10:7). Jesus's momentum is building, but so is the ugly opposition. The religious leaders have dedicated themselves, allegedly for the good of the nation, to bring down this nonconformist Galilean rabbi. The Pharisees accuse him of working for the devil. They ask him for a sign to prove his authority. Jesus answers, "A wicked and adulterous generation asks for a sign! But none will be given it except the sign of the prophet Jonah" (Matt. 12:39).

Even Jesus's immediate family attempted an intervention. Their actions reflect bewildered embarrassment and a guilty sense of familial responsibility. When his mother and brothers show up to speak to him, Jesus ignores them. He points to his disciples and says, "Here are my mother and my brothers. For whoever does the will of my Father in heaven is my brother and sister and mother" (Matt. 12:46–50; see also Mark 3:21).

In the face of growing opposition, Jesus's communicational strategy hit the wall. Straight-up authoritative teaching was becoming counterproductive. This is why I think Jesus switched to parables. Through the medium of *story* he was able to communicate to the crowds without giving his enemies a clear target. The general audience hung on his captivating stories—stories they could hear superficially, almost as entertainment. Or they could hear Jesus's stories provocatively as world-upending stories. The disciples knew full well that Jesus was doing more than telling simple stories, and he invited their questions. I suspect the scribes and Pharisees also knew that Jesus's parables were operating at a deeper level, but this indirect mode of communication offered little leverage for their campaign against Jesus. Parables provided just the right genre to extend Jesus's teaching ministry. He was able to keep the crowd with him, frustrate his enemies, and invite his disciples to embrace the meaning of the gospel.

Matthew's gospel narrative makes it pretty clear that Jesus switched to parables because of his enemies' intensity and the crowd's naivete. But personally I didn't see Jesus's new pedagogical strategy for a long time. I had to hit the wall myself with my own communicational strategy before it dawned on me why Jesus used parables. I was teaching four consecutive Wednesday nights on the Sermon on the Mount at a church about an hour away from my home. Fighting heavy traffic to get there made me more tense than I wanted to be. The people were good-natured and friendly, but they seemed unfamiliar with basic Christian truth and they didn't seem all that interested in changing. After a long day they were tired, too. They were fairly quick to write off Jesus's Sermon on the Mount teaching as overly idealistic and impractical. They rated their subjective interpretation of the Sermon as more important than anything I could say. They had no qualms about wrapping the Sermon on the Mount around their sentimental opinions and suburban expectations. Nice people, but we might as well have been discussing an op-ed piece in *The New York Times*.

Each evening I left a little more discouraged than the week before. On the last night, I concluded our session on the Sermon on the Mount with the story of the two builders, one who built his house on the sand, and the other who built his house on the rock. I said my goodbyes and walked to my car in the dark. I felt pretty discouraged. After thirty-some years of pastoral ministry, I felt defeated, with nobody to blame but myself. My current calling is to help seminary students preach and teach effectively and faithfully. Had I wasted people's time for four weeks trying to teach the Sermon on the Mount to people who seemed to think it was out of date and irrelevant? It sure felt like it. As I was walking to my car, it suddenly hit me: *This is why Jesus told parables.* I even said it out loud. It was a breakthrough moment for me. The parables were not just an alternative teaching method. They were a communicational necessity. Jesus turned to parables to penetrate people's defenses, circumvent the opposition, extend his gospel ministry, and creatively train his followers. If I had read my audience better, the way Jesus did, I would have switched to parables—simple, yet provocative, stories that invoke the truth implicitly or indirectly, causing hearers who have ears for meaning to dig deeper.

TELL IT SLANT

> Tell all the Truth but tell it slant—
> Success in Circuit lies
> Too bright for our infirm Delight
> The Truth's superb surprise
> As Lightening to the Children eased
> With explanation kind
> The Truth must dazzle gradually
> Or every man be blind—
>   —Emily Dickinson

A combination of hard-hearted resistance and popular messianic fervor triggered the need for parables. Jesus chose parables to get around these obstacles of resistance and resentment. He used a communicational strategy that proved effective. He introduced the gospel by means of earthy, secular stories about sowing seed, finding treasure, and casting a net.[1]

---

1 The study of parables is an interesting case study in biblical scholarship. New Testament experts tend to approach the subject in the abstract. They debate the interpretation, analysis, and classification of parables as a whole. They discuss whether parables may have one, two, or three points and argue

His characters were farmers, merchants, and fishermen. He chose metaphor over syllogism and the poet's terse art over the philosopher's elaborate abstraction.[2] Parable comes from the Greek word *parabolē*: *para* = "beside" + *ballo* = "to throw." Jesus used simple stories to set up a comparison between life as we know it and the life made possible by the gospel. He juxtaposed these stark realities to create a positive tension and reveal the gospel. Jesus's stories, like a good joke, turn on a "sudden perception of incongruity."[3] It is that twist of plot that unsettles the complacent and shakes the soul. Jesus knew that "the soul is like a wild animal—tough, resilient, and yet shy," and he knew that "when we go crashing through the woods shouting for it to come out so we can help it, the soul will stay in hiding."[4] Jesus knew how to approach the soul. He juxtaposed the invisible truths of the gospel with the everyday images of ordinary life. He drew out the meaning and significance of faithfulness by picturing a wise and faithful steward. He highlighted prayerfulness by picturing a persistent widow. He captured the joy of salvation in the homecoming of a lost son. He compared the worldly strategy of a shrewd manager to the kingdom strategy of a faithful disciple. He used a proud Pharisee to illustrate self-righteousness and a remorseful tax

---

over an allegorical versus analogical interpretation. Lectures on the parables can miss the impact and the meaning of the parables altogether.

2 Kenneth E. Bailey, *Jesus through Middle Eastern Eyes: Cultural Studies in the Gospels* (Downers Grove, IL: InterVarsity, 2008), 279.

3 C. S. Lewis, *The Screwtape Letters* (San Francisco: HarperOne, 2001), 54.

4 Parker Palmer, *The Courage to Teach* (San Francisco: Jossey-Bass, 1998), 151.

collector to show true repentance. Jesus intentionally chose the medium of parables to separate the admiring crowd from his faithful disciples. He accommodated those who only had ears for a moralistic tale, but he penetrated the hearts and minds of those who were open to the gospel. "Whoever has ears, let them hear" (Matt. 13:43). Parables are time bombs that only explode after they have penetrated our hearts. Their purpose is to turn admirers into followers. Jesus was the master of telling truth slant.

Jesus didn't invent parables. They were used by the prophets to effectively penetrate people's defenses. The prophet Nathan told a parable when he confronted King David. He reported to the king an account of two men; one man was very rich with a very large number of sheep and cattle, and the other man was very poor with nothing except one little ewe lamb. David thought he was hearing the day's news, but Nathan was making up the whole thing. "Now a traveler came to the rich man, but the rich man refrained from taking one of his own sheep or cattle to prepare a meal for the traveler who had come to him. Instead, he took the ewe lamb that belonged to the poor man and prepared it for the one who had come to him" (2 Sam. 12:4). David was outraged. His verdict against the unjust rich man was decisive: "As surely as the Lord lives, the man who did this must die." But then with perfect timing, Nathan jumped from parable to truth. He said in a tone that we can only imagine, "You are the man!"

The story of the little ewe lamb did exactly what a parable should do by casting truth in a new light. Parables use familiar situations, sayings, or stories to highlight meanings that lie below the surface. The hidden point embedded in the parable is not obvious on the surface of the discourse. The saying or the story remains simple, but the underlying truth is either obscured or revealed depending on the listener. Getting past people's defenses is not easy. This is why Jesus said repeatedly, "Whoever has ears, let them hear."

TYPOLOGY AND PARABLES

Parables appear deceptively simple on the surface, as if Jesus was making it up as he went along, pulling the strategy out of thin air. But their "spontaneity" is an artistic feature concealing the fact that parables belong to a genre deeply embedded in salvation history. Parables prove that "no content comes into our lives free-floating: it is always embedded in a form of some kind."[5] Jesus's "stories with intent" are not new inventions but Spirit-inspired elaborations, rooted in prophetic ministry, reverberating throughout salvation history.

Jesus does in the parables what the Spirit has been doing throughout salvation history, using story and images to teach the invisible truths of the gospel. Hughes Oliphant Old explains: "The typologist takes the concrete and amplifies the abstract, harnesses the visible so as to vivify the invisible, makes use of the earthly to mirror the heavenly, and engages the here and now in an effort to elucidate the then and there."[6] The

---

5 Eugene H. Peterson, *The Pastor* (Grand Rapids: Eerdmans, 2012), 33.
6 Hughes Oliphant Old, *The Reading and Preaching of the Scriptures in the Worship of the Church* (Grand Rapids: Eerdmans, 2010), 7:359.

typological correspondence between promise and fulfillment serves as a precedent for Jesus's use of parables. A type and a parable are poetic techniques, the former rooted in salvation history, the latter created out of ordinary human affairs, but both designed to reveal the meaning of the gospel.

There is a parabolic dimension throughout biblical revelation that is evident in recognizable biblical types (lamb, altar, circumcision, Passover, exodus, tabernacle, temple, etc.). This is also true of biblical images, "visual aids" that instruct us in what it means to fear God and follow the Lord (a shepherd's staff, an easy yoke, jars of clay, a thorn in the flesh, etc.). Wherever we turn, the ultimate referent is the Incarnate One. T. S. Eliot called this connection in the Psalms the *objective correlative*—that is to say, the person and work of Jesus is the ultimate focus of the Psalms.[7] The longer we live in the Word of God, the more we experience that the revelatory purpose of every type, figure, image, and parable is Christ. Jesus is essentially who and what the Bible is all about. Jesus said as much

---

7 James W. Sire, *Praying the Psalms of Jesus* (Downers Grove, IL: InterVarsity, 2007), 31. T. S. Eliot's phrase "objective correlative" comes from his essay "Hamlet and His Problems" (1919); see https://www.bartleby.com/200/sw9.html. Eliot writes, "The only way of expressing emotion in the form of art is by finding an 'objective correlative'; in other words, a set of objects, a situation, a chain of events which shall be the formula of that *particular* emotion; such that when the external facts, which must terminate in sensory experience, are given, the emotion is immediately evoked." Eliot related the phrase to psychology and the artistic build up to an inevitable emotional reaction. I'm relating it to theology: "The only way of expressing *truth* in the form of *theology* is by finding *the* 'objective correlative.'" All the biblical types, images, and parables lead to the crucified and risen Messiah.

to his disciples, when he said, "Everything must be fulfilled that is written about me in the Law of Moses, the Prophets and the Psalms" (Luke 24:44). Jesus is the true connection and correlation between petition and prophecy, promise and fulfillment.

The typographical significance of parables lies in the fact that their surface meaning organically serves the deeper gospel meaning. Truth's significance is hidden from those who reduce the metaphor to a moralistic fable or a clever tale, but for those who receive the truth, it resonates with the whole counsel of God. We hear echoes of the Father's love in the parable of the lost sons, otherwise known as the parable of the prodigal son, and celebrate the promise of the wedding feast of the Lamb in the parable of the wedding banquet. There is an organic connection between promise and fulfillment in biblical prophecy, biblical types, and biblical parables. Jesus wasn't just making things up as he went along.

THE FOUR GOSPELS AND PARABLES

I trust the Gospel writers. They framed Jesus's parables correctly. Their placement in the narrative context provides the key to their interpretation. Our focus will be on the parables found in Matthew and Luke. Matthew collected Jesus's parables around certain broad themes: the advance of the kingdom of heaven (Matt. 13:1–52), the true nature of salvation and discipleship (Matt. 18:10–14, 21–35; 20:1–16), the rejection of the good news of the kingdom by the very people who should have eagerly embraced the gospel (Matt.

21:18–22, 28–32, 33–46; 22:1–14), and faithfulness to the end (Matt. 25:1–13, 14–30, 31–46). Matthew used Jesus's stories to graphically show the difference between faithfulness and faithlessness. His editing of Jesus's extended analogies not only drew a picture of the Christian life, but they prepared the followers of Jesus for the world's resistance and rejection.

Mark included key parables like the sower and the soils (Mark 4:3–8, 14–20), the mustard seed (Mark 4:30–32), the wicked tenants (Mark 12:1–11), and the fig tree (Mark 13:28–29), but not to the same extent as Luke. Mark's fast-paced action narrative used parables sparingly. Matthew grouped Jesus's parables around significant themes, and Luke leaned into Jesus's parables on numerous occasions to illustrate the meaning of the Master's teaching. Key themes such as social justice, gospel-rich hospitality, and the inclusion of women, the poor, and the disabled are reflected in Luke's use of parables.

John's gospel has only a few parables, yet his work unites type and gospel in a way that harmonizes well with how the other gospel accounts use parables. To Nicodemus, Jesus says, "You must be born again," adding, "Just as Moses lifted up the snake in the wilderness, so the Son of Man must be lifted up, that everyone who believes may have eternal life in him" (John 3:14–15). Instead of identifying Jesus with great figures of Israel's past, like Jacob and Moses, John highlights Jesus's implicit connection to objects that have parabolic significance. In dialogue with Nathaniel, Jesus recalls Jacob's dream at Bethel (Gen. 28:10–17). He says, "You will see heaven open, and the angels of God ascending and descending on the Son of Man" (John 1:51). Jesus compares himself, not to Jacob, but to the ladder that connects heaven and earth. Once again, in dialogue with the woman at the well, Jesus does not compare himself to Jacob but to Jacob's well flowing with living water (John 4:14). Similarly, Jesus does not compare himself to Moses, even though he is the one greater than Moses, but to the bronze serpent (John 3:14) and to the manna, the bread from heaven (John 6:32–35).[8]

Like the parables, these indirect comparisons require reflection. Their Old Testament typological rootedness bears New Testament fulfillment in Jesus. These references call us to go deeper and pick up on the meaning of the analogy and the purpose of the type. They show John to be a pastor-poet, artistically and strategically using metaphors that are deeply embedded in salvation history. Jesus is the living water (John 4:10–13), the bread of life (John 6:35), and the kernel of wheat that falls to the ground and dies (John 12:24). John's parables of the good shepherd and the vine and the branches climaxes with Jesus being the explicit objective correlative: "I am the good shepherd" (John 10:11), and "I am the vine; you are the branches" (John 15:5).

John saved the full force of his parabolic technique for the book of Revelation. Like his Lord, John used indirect discourse built on metaphor and symbol to keep his hearers' attention and

---

8 Robert A. J. Gagnon, "The Bible and Homosexual Practice: Theology, Analogy, and Genes," *Theology Matters* 7, no. 6, (Nov/Dec 2001): 1–13, specifically 2–3.

reveal the meaning of the kingdom of God. Jesus drew from ordinary daily life to shatter his hearers' preexisting understanding. His stories about farmers and seeds, servants and masters, sons and fathers turned everything upside down to reveal a radical new counterculture: the kingdom of God. On the surface, parables may appear to be quaint moral stories designed to make people nicer, but Jesus worked their obvious hiddenness to open up the secrets of the gospel. He used the common stuff of daily life to teach the extraordinary truths and subversive message of the gospel. He challenged his hearers to interpret the metaphors, to look beyond the surface meaning. This is why Jesus says, "Whoever has ears, let them hear" (Matt. 13:43).

The apostle John was tutored in the power of metaphor from the Master, but instead of drawing on ordinary everyday things, John shaped his parables from the extraordinary complexity of the cosmic realm. He drew his metaphors from the stars instead of seeds and monsters instead of masters. He exchanged an agrarian world of wicked tenant farmers for the cosmic war between God and the devil. He transposed Jesus's everyday world into the end of the world. He merged the parabolic style of Jesus with an in-depth understanding of the prophets and brought the message home, not with stories drawn from everyday experience, but with horrific scenarios of global war and ecstatic scenes of rhapsodic worship.

MESSIANIC CONSCIOUSNESS

Jesus did not invent parables, but he used them in powerful new ways to reflect his own self-understanding. He was naturally drawn to Old Testament symbols for God as a means of communicating his own messianic self-understanding. Philip Payne concludes, "Here in the parables, the most assuredly authentic of all the traditions about Jesus, is a clear, implicit affirmation of Jesus's self-understanding as deity. His sense of identification with God was so deep that to depict himself he consistently gravitated to imagery and symbols which the Old Testament typically depict God."[9]

Jesus is the embodiment of God-in-person. He took on our humanity to show us God, and he took on the stuff of our humanity to give concrete expression to the gospel. The metaphor and the message are rooted in salvation history, and the messenger is none other than the Incarnate One. Jesus freely used an incarnational technique to convey his message—a strategy embedded in his very being. He refused to engage in the pedantic style of the rabbis, who were in the habit of supporting their teaching with a ponderous recital of sources. Instead, he proclaimed the truth with such authority and wisdom that people questioned how he could be so learned without having received formal education (John 7:15). It is critically important to remember who is creating and delivering the parables.

First-century rabbis used parables as well, but the dramatic twist in Jesus's parables was how he used them to reveal his identity. He implicitly designated himself as the sower, the director of the harvest, the rock, the shepherd, the bridegroom,

---

9 Philip B. Payne, "Jesus's Implicit Claim to Deity in His Parables," *Trinity Journal* 2 (Spring 1981): 3, 9.

the father, the giver of forgiveness, the vineyard owner, the lord, and the king. Each of these images represents a significant association with God and his work, which is clearly evident in the Old Testament and in all likelihood familiar to many of Jesus's listeners. For example, when Jesus drew an analogy between obedience to his words and building on the rock in the parable of the two houses, he used one of the most common pictures of God in the Old Testament. The parable implies that "response to Jesus and his words is tantamount to response to God."[10] Other biblical allusions are also obvious (Isa. 28:16; Ps. 118:22; Matt. 21:42), leaving the distinct impression that Jesus is purposefully selecting an image that reflects his messianic consciousness.

We need pictures. Have you ever bought bookshelves or a cabinet from IKEA? Your purchase comes in a heavy box that doesn't look like anything resembling the floor model. You get it home and pull out a stack of panels and a bag of nuts and bolts. You'd be foolish to begin without looking at the step-by-step sheet of instructions. We need the picture to put it together. Again, I don't know anyone who tries to make a jigsaw puzzle without looking at the picture on the box. We need pictures. Jesus told parables to help us visualize the gospel. He gave us a mental picture of what it means to receive the gospel.

To highlight the importance of mental models, Charles Duhigg compares pilot reaction on two international flights,

---

10 Payne, "Jesus's Implicit Claim," 3, 9.

Air France Flight 447 and Qantas Airways Flight 32. On a flight from Rio de Janeiro to Paris, the Air France pilots became disoriented when ice crystals froze the airspeed indicators and automatically turned off the auto-flight system. If they had done nothing, the plane would have continued to fly safely, but they panicked. Instead of taking a step back, assessing the overall picture and gaining perspective, the pilots became fixated on an emergency procedure that is used to abort a landing. The pilot at the controls maximized the plane's thrust and raised the nose of the plane. At thirty-eight thousand feet, the air is so thin that it only increased the severity of the stall. Psychologists call this cognitive tunneling. It led to reactive thinking dooming Flight 447. They were unable to picture what was happening.[11]

One year after the crash of Air France Flight 447, Qantas Airways Flight 32, flying from Singapore to Sydney, sustained massive damages when an oil fire led to an explosion that ripped apart an engine turbine. The plane's computers responded to the ensuing catastrophic systems failure by giving step-by-step instructions, but there was no way to keep up with the cascading data. Duhigg reports that the captain shouted, "We need to stop focusing on what's wrong and start paying attention to what's still working." As another pilot began ticking off what was still operational, the pilot imagined that he was flying a little single-engine Cessna. He took control of his mental model.

---

11 Charles Duhigg, *Smarter, Faster, Better: The Secrets of Being Productive in Life and Business* (New York: Random House, 2016), 71–88.

Instead of being inundated with information overload, he was able to focus on flying the plane instead of reacting to the stream of data. Duhigg writes, "To become genuinely productive, we must take control of our attention."[12]

The parables do that for us. They show us what it means to follow Jesus. Like the Air France pilots, it is easy to be inundated by all the data streaming at us from a myriad of sources. Jesus's parables cut through the forest of theological concerns, ethical controversies, religious debates and the cacophony of worldviews. Parables rescue us from the chaos of social media by providing a simple and compelling picture of Christian discipleship. The Australian pilot rescued a dire situation by imagining that he was flying a little Cessna. Parables are an antidote to cognitive tunneling. That is why Jesus told them and that is why we study them. We need Jesus's parables because they give us a picture of Christian discipleship.

THE LAYOUT

We begin with Matthew's Sermon of Parables. Matthew groups seven parables into a collection to show how Jesus navigated between enemy hostility and popular hype. In the parable of the sower, Jesus offers an analysis of people's responses to the word of God, negative and positive, and concludes with a theology of hope. The parable of the wheat and weeds follows. Jesus pictures a kingdom-growth strategy free of coercion and judgmental worry. In the parables of

---

12 Duhigg, *Smarter, Faster, Better*, 102.

the mustard seed and yeast, Jesus prepares the disciples for the gospel's surprising high-impact growth from minuscule beginnings. The parables of the hidden treasure and the pearl celebrate the incomparable joy of the kingdom of heaven. Finally, in the seventh parable, the parable of the net, Jesus describes the climatic eschatological judgment, separating the wicked from the righteous. In Matthew's Sermon of Parables the crowds get their entertaining stories, and the disciples get their gospel truth. Everybody hears Jesus, but only those with ears to hear *really* hear.

Instead of grouping parables into a body of work as Matthew did, Luke scattered Jesus's parables as illustrative material throughout the course of Jesus's teaching and preaching. Both methods—grouping the parables together in a series, or strategically placing them in the narrative flow of Jesus's teaching ministry—demonstrate their useful flexibility. They can be studied and preached as a group or individually. We will explore Luke's fourteen major parables to show how Jesus leveraged his context to give us a clear picture of the gospel. This is followed by Matthew's version of Jesus's Passion week parables and the climax of his teaching ministry. Finally, in an appendix I reflect on the importance of preaching the parables. This could also be a good place to begin.

❀ 1 ❀

THE SOWER

MATTHEW 13:1–23

O n the same day that the Pharisees accused Jesus of possessing demonic power and his family sought to carry out an intervention, Jesus went out of the house and "sat by the lake" (Matt. 13:1). A large crowd gathered around him and "he told them many things in parables" (Matt. 13:3). In the midst of a cultural storm he sat down in a boat. There is a cove near Capernaum that provided a natural acoustical setting. His voice amplified off the surface of the water. His body language was a picture of composure and calm engagement—an example to believers today of how to engage the world in the midst of resistance and rejection. When speakers sit, they naturally limit their voice volume and animation. The focus narrows to what is being said rather than how it is being said. Jesus's simple style corresponds to his simple parables. But the simple content of the story is a fiction, a calculated cover for profound truths and a not-so-subtle invitation to the listener to go deeper. The preacher of the Sermon on the Mount has shifted genres. The Sermon of Parables was designed to stymie the opposition, keep the crowd listening, and draw the disciples deeper into gospel truth. Jesus diverted an early end to his public ministry by his friendly, subversive speech.

"HOLY SEED"

Those with ears to hear will understand even before Jesus quotes from the prophet Isaiah that Jesus's simple story of the sower invokes the deep meaning of salvation history. When he begins with "A farmer went out to sow his seed" (Matt. 13:3), he telegraphs to his audience that this story should be understood on a deeper level than a carpenter's son's commentary on farming. Isaiah spoke of "the holy seed" sprouting from the "stump in the land." The seed signified the early growth of the kingdom of heaven (Isa. 6:13). The Isaiah reference linked the sower's seed to the word of God in Jesus's audience. The promise of a fruitful harvest suggests the fruitful productivity of the word of the Lord: "It will not return to me empty, but will accomplish what I desire and achieve the purpose for which I sent it. You will go out in joy and be led forth in peace; the mountains and the hills will burst into song before you" (Isa. 55:11–12). If someone listened to Jesus closely, they would have anticipated the positive conclusion of the parable of the sower: "the seed falling on good soil refers to someone who hears the word and understands it" (Matt. 13:23).

There is little mystery as to who the sower is in Jesus's parable. The word "sower" is unusual. The normal word to use back then was "farmer." But Jesus chose "sower" to give the hearer another clue. The parable wasn't about farming. It was about the proclamation of the word of the Lord. Jesus himself is the sower. The refrain "Whoever has ears, let them hear" implies that there is something more to be understood than the surface meaning. The deep meaning of the parable of the sower is related to the prophecy of Isaiah.

The liberally sown seed fell in four places, on a hard-packed footpath, on rocky ground with a thin layer of soil, on a thorny patch of earth, and on fertile soil producing a fruitful crop. The sower scatters seed everywhere. He is unconcerned about wasting seed. Later, when the disciples get Jesus away from the crowd, they ask him, "Why do you speak to the people in parables?" They are aware that Jesus changed his communication strategy, and they want to know why. In other words, they ask, "Why do you teach them so cryptically? Why not spell things out for them?"[1] The question implies a change in Jesus's teaching method, a change that must have impressed them as unusual.

Jesus answered their question indirectly. His response did not focus on method (why are you choosing to speak in parables?), but on meaning (explaining what God was up to). His strategy is in response to what God was doing, rather than in how he could change his method to reach people. Reception, Jesus insists, is in the hands of God, not humans. Instead of changing methods because of consumer demand, Jesus insists on a deeper reason. Understanding, like grace,

---

1   R. T. France, *Matthew: New International Commentary* (Grand Rapids: Eerdmans, 2007), 510.

is a gift of God, lest anyone should boast. The disciples are privileged by God to be given "the secrets of the kingdom of heaven"—the crowd is not; the religious leaders are not. The synergy between a human response ("Whoever has ears, listen!") and God's sovereignty ("The knowledge of the secrets of the kingdom of heaven has been given to you, not to them," Matt. 13:11) cannot be explained in an equation or measured in percentages. Jesus lifts the preaching of the gospel above competing ideologies and the eloquence of human wisdom (see 1 Cor. 2:1–4).

ISAIAH'S OPEN SECRET

Jesus described the gospel as "the knowledge of the secrets of the kingdom of heaven." The Greek word for "secret" is "mystery," a word we tend to associate with what we find vague, inscrutable, and puzzling. The apostles used the word "mystery" for the truth of God *revealed*. Truth is not unknowable and beyond our grasp, but neither does it originate with us. We are not the clever creators of truth. The source of universal truth is in God alone. Redemptive truth, absolute truth, is received, not achieved. This truth can only be known by the revelation of God (1 Cor. 4:1). The secret of the kingdom of heaven is that Jesus is God's revelation in person. This is the open secret that the disciples are privileged to hear and understand. This is the truth that the crowd fails to comprehend. *Mystery* is the revelation of God, previously hidden, now made known. The privilege of reception is not a problem but a blessing, and the gift received increases in abundance.[2] Both reception and rejection of "the secrets of the kingdom of heaven" are orchestrated by the sovereign will of God. Theologian Carl Henry offers a line worth remembering: "Human reason is a divinely fashioned instrument for recognizing truth; it is not a creative source of truth."[3]

Jesus attributes his reason for using parables to the hardness of people's hearts. The crowd's willful refusal to receive the truth undoubtedly has many reasons and excuses, but ultimately reception belongs to God. Jesus is neither surprised by the rejection nor filled with sorrow. His courage and conviction is reflected in the words of the prophet Isaiah. The prophet was called to preach the word of God to his own people who heard it clearly enough, but refused to accept it. They hardened their hearts, closed their ears, and shut their eyes.

Ironically, Isaiah's calling reinforced the people's failure to comprehend the truth. The better the prophet preached, the more resistant the people became. The Lord commissioned the prophet to make the truth plain and the people's rejection complete: "Be ever hearing, but never understanding; be ever seeing, but never perceiving. Make the heart of this people calloused; make their ears dull and close their eyes. Otherwise

---

2 Frederick Dale Bruner, *Matthew: A Commentary*, vol. 2, *The Churchbook*, Matthew 13–28 (Grand Rapids: Eerdmans, 2007), 10. Bruner writes, "This is hard. But the sentence cannot be explained away. And we will accept it as it stands only if we are prepared to let God be God. The God of Jesus of the biblical writers is not a God caught by surprise by the response of people."

3 Carl F. H. Henry, *God, Revelation and Authority*, vol. 1 (Waco, TX: Word, 1976), 225.

they might see with their eyes, hear with their ears, understand with their hearts, and turn and be healed" (Isa. 6:9–10).

How did the prophet do this? He did this by presenting the truth with such clarity, simplicity, and sincerity that each successive refusal to respond to the grace of God made it that much more difficult for the people to receive the message. Isaiah was a straight-talking prophet who did everything he could to convince the people of the truth of God, yet because of his effectiveness, he only drove them further from the truth. Isaiah "faced the preacher's dilemma: if hearers are resistant to the truth, the only recourse is to tell them the truth yet again, more clearly than before. But to do this is to expose them to the risk of rejecting the truth yet again and, therefore, of increased hardness of heart. It could even be that the next rejection will prove to be the point at which the heart is hardened beyond recovery."[4]

Isaiah was actually criticized for making the truth simple and straightforward. His critics asked, "Who is it he is trying to teach? To whom is he explaining his message? To children weaned from their milk, to those just taken from the breast?" In today's theological circles, Isaiah sounded like the simple believer who embraces the reality of the incarnation and the necessity of Christ's atoning sacrifice on the cross. Isaiah believed and proclaimed the word of God plainly, yet boldly, and critics mocked him for it. They ridiculed his message: "Do and

---

4   J. Alec Motyer, *The Prophecy of Isaiah: An Introduction and Commentary* (Downers Grove, IL: InterVarsity, 1993), 79.

do, do and do, rule on rule, rule on rule; a little here, a little there" (Isa. 28:10 NIV 1984). Can you imagine dismissing the prophet Isaiah with "yada, yada"? Given such an unbelievably hard challenge, Isaiah naturally asked, "For how long, O Lord?" The answer he received was not easy! "Until the cities lie ruined and without inhabitant, until the houses are left deserted and the fields ruined and ravaged, until the LORD has sent everyone far away and the land is utterly forsaken" (Isa. 6:11–12). Not only did Isaiah present the truth clearly and compellingly but he did it for more than fifty years with the same discouraging result. The substance and style of his ministry of the word was matched only by his endurance.[5]

Understanding is a gift.[6] God opens eyes and ears to the truth otherwise concealed by our depravity and hardness of heart. Jesus frames the rejection of the crowd and the understanding of the disciples in the big picture of salvation history. The disciples were privileged by God's amazing grace not only in their reception of the truth but in their timing. In Jesus, the

---

5 Eugene H. Peterson, *The Jesus Way* (Grand Rapids: Eerdmans, 2007), 140. Peterson writes, "Isaiah is the greatest preacher to be represented in our Scriptures. He is also our most conspicuous failure. . . . He preached powerful, eloquent, bold sermons. Nobody listened. He preached repentance and the salvation of Jerusalem and Judah. The people did not repent and were taken into exile."

6 Robert Farrar Capon, *Kingdom, Grace, Judgment: Paradox, Outrage, and Vindication in the Parables of Jesus* (Grand Rapids: Eerdmans, 2002), 59. Capon writes, "Jesus thinks about the obtuseness he sees all around him— about the unlikelihood of anybody's getting even a glimmer of the mystery, let alone a grip on it—and the passage from Scripture pops into his head as the perfect summary: 'Isaiah really had it right,' he thinks, and then he simply recites the verses out loud." Thankfully it wasn't all obtuseness. Jesus believes the Father is revealing the secrets of the kingdom to the disciples.

revelation of God had reached its critical, redemptive climax (1 Peter 1:10–12; Heb. 11:13–16).

JESUS'S INTERPRETATION

We are used to expositions coming before illustrations. But here we have the reverse: an illustration first that anticipates exposition. The parable functions as a riddle, designed to provoke thought. For the crowd, the parable conceals; for the disciples, it clarifies. Jesus himself entitled the parable: "Listen then to what the *parable of the sower* means" (Matt. 13:18, emphasis added). We may be inclined to change the title to the parable of the soils, because much of our preaching focuses on the various ways we reject the word of God. But it is best to follow Jesus's lead. He keeps the focus on the sower and the sower's assessment of the four soil types.

The sower's analysis of rejection does not discourage as much as warn. The ratio of rejection to reception is three to one. The fate of the seed (the gospel) is negative 75 percent of the time. Although, as we will see, the abundant yield of the good soil makes up for the rejection (Isa. 55:11). But Jesus's description of these three forms of rejection serves as a warning to his followers. Jesus doesn't want the disciples to be surprised by the rejection rate. One of the big secrets of the kingdom of heaven given to the disciples involves a radically new understanding of the Messiah. Instead of the political triumph of a popular messiah who defeats Rome and ushers in a new Davidic kingdom, Jesus calls for a righteousness that surpasses the righteousness of the scribes and Pharisees. The kingdom ethic outlined in the Sermon on the Mount promises persecution, not power.

The three forms of rejection all have to do with people who hear the good news of the kingdom. So even when the seed falls on the beaten path, the gospel has been heard. They may even be part of the church, but when it comes to the word of God, it goes in one ear and out the other. "The first-soil hearer *lets* the devil steal the Word of God from his heart because he does not want to know or do the will of God."[7] Like seed on a hard-worn footpath, there is no soil in which the gospel can germinate. The secular and religious idols and ideologies of the world have hardened the soul and enthroned the self.

The people represented by this type move along the path of life with such speed and distraction that the loss of meaning and significance is not even noticed. They are sufficiently thoughtless that even nihilistic despair can be laughed off as a joke. Sex, fame, power, and adventure are sufficient goals in the secular age to inspire those who race along the well-worn path. The sexualized, secularized self does not realize that the good news of salvation has been snatched from their hearts by the evil one. They are oblivious to the power of evil and the seduction of the soul. The tragedy of the first-soil hearer is no respecter of persons. It is shared by the corner-office master of the universe and the homeless street person whose night shelter is made of cardboard.

---

7   Bruner, *Matthew*, 2:18.

The second-soil hearer accepts the gospel enthusiastically, but the seed has fallen on rocky ground. It springs to life in the warmth of community, in the inspiration of worship, in the joy of being a part of something bigger than themselves. But no sooner does it sprout up than the pressures and persecution of the world choke the life out of it. The church received them warmly but may have failed to prepare them for suffering. Their optimistic faith was no match for the world's resistance. The gospel never had a chance to take root and bear fruit. Like flowers in the desert, they sprang to life only to shrivel in the noonday heat. There are biblical examples that fit this type, such as the disciples who were shocked when Jesus said, "Unless you eat the flesh of the Son of Man and drink his blood, you have no life in you" (John 6:53), or the high-achiever disciples who enthusiastically said, "Lord, Lord," only to be told by the Lord, "I never knew you. Away from me, you evildoers" (Matt. 7:21–23).

The third-soil hearer accepts the gospel. It takes root and grows. But the thorny competition of the world chokes the life out of it. The third soil-type represents the hearer who believes the gospel is true. In a philosophical argument, they agree on behalf of the word of God, but in their day-to-day living, "the anxiety of the age," and the pressures of money put a stranglehold on the word of God. Dale Bruner writes, "These neutralized believers are about as unbelieving as complete pagans, even though they stay right in the church."[8]

---

8   Bruner, *Matthew*, 2:22.

Two of the three soil-hearers who end up rejecting the gospel often stay in the church. Bruner continues, "Only one of the four who hears the Word stands under it, yields to its authority, obeys it. Armed with this 'three-out-of-four' truth, the scandal of un-Christian Christians can be overcome, for we know that this scandal is not proof against Jesus—he *predicted it.*"[9]

GOOD-SOIL UNDERSTANDING

The fourth-soil hearer *understands* the word. The key word for the reception of the gospel is grace-induced *understanding* (Matt. 13:13, 14, 15, 18, 23).[10] Derived from the Old English, it means to take our stand at the center of the gospel. The person who *understands* makes the gospel message his or her own. It means "standing under Jesus's teaching in obedience."[11] This is not a purely intellectual grasp of the truth. It is a life commitment framed by the Sermon on the Mount. It involves taking up our cross and following Jesus.

The parable calls for our response—not the accomplishing of a work, but the bearing of fruit.[12] The good-soil hearer is productive. Being a fruitful hearer of the word of God shows itself in the fruit of the Spirit and a transformed life (Gal.

---

9 Bruner, *Matthew*, 2:22.
10 The etymology of the verb "to understand" is derived from Old English *understandan*, meaning to "comprehend, grasp the idea of," probably literally to "stand in the midst of." The prefix "under" in Old English conveyed the idea of "between, among."
11 Bruner, *Matthew*, 2:18.
12 Cappon, *Kingdom, Grace, Judgment*, 74.

5:22–26; Rom. 12:1–2). This soil is beatitude enriched; it is the state of grace that makes the greater righteousness possible. Good-soil understanding takes its "stand against the devil's schemes" and "puts on the full armor of God" so you may be able "to stand your ground," having done everything to stand (Eph. 6:11, 13). This is the *understanding* of freedom in Christ that says, "Stand firm, then, and do not let yourselves be burdened again by a yoke of slavery" (Gal. 5:1). The parable of the sower challenges all believers to understand the gospel and to grow in the grace and knowledge of the Lord Jesus Christ (2 Pet 3:18).[13]

Jesus concludes the parable of the sower on a high note. Those who hear and understand the gospel are productive. They have a salt-and-light impact in a world that desperately needs preservation and illumination. They let their light shine before others, that others may see their good works and glorify their Father in heaven (Matt. 5:13–16). This grace-inspired, beatitude-based understanding of God's redemptive provision bears abundant impact *organically*. Jesus's organic models of growth counter modern church-growth experts with their

---

13 Thielicke, *Waiting Father*, 59. In his sermon on the parable of the sower, Helmut Thielicke, the German pastor-theologian who resisted Hitler and went on to teach and preach in postwar Germany, observed: "There are certain times in our life and there are certain levels in the self in which we are hard ground, rocky ground, thorny ground, and fertile soil all in one." Thielicke continues, "We dare not leave this grim hour of admonition without resolving to enter into judgment with ourselves and sternly asking ourselves: to what birds, what thorns, what superficiality am I exposing the Word of God in my life; what are the threatening forces and the roots of peacelessness in my life?"

marketing strategies and target audiences. Jesus seems to relish the miracle of growth resting in God's hands rather than ours. However, Jesus's growth strategy is no excuse for sloth. As planters and harvesters, we are part of the process, but the real growth remains a divine mystery rather than a human endeavor. The advance of the kingdom does not lie in our initiatives, methodologies, and budgets but in God's blessing. We pray for the seed of the gospel to take root and produce a crop, "yielding a hundred, sixty or thirty times what is sown" (Matt. 13:23).

2

THE WEEDS AMONG THE WHEAT

MATTHEW 13:24–30

Exposition without illustration can be boring, but illustration without exposition can be confusing. On the surface, these simple, nonthreatening parables come across as riddles in search of meaning. Some in the crowd must have wondered why Jesus was talking about wheat and weeds. What did the farmer do to deserve an enemy who went to all the trouble of sowing weeds in his fields? Most likely the crowd didn't catch on that Jesus saw himself as the owner of the good seed. They heard the parable as a moralistic tale about bad neighbors and self-control. They didn't come close to hearing Jesus's parable of the weeds among the wheat as the Son of Man's kingdom strategy. But that's what it was, his kingdom strategy, even if the crowd didn't get it.

The parable begs for an explanation, but instead of explaining it to the crowd, Jesus gave two more parables in rapid succession—the parable of the mustard seed and the parable of the yeast. Jesus introduced each parable with "the kingdom of heaven is like . . . ," but the crowd failed to see how the kingdom of heaven is like a farmer with a nasty neighbor or like a tiny mustard seed that grows as big as a tree. Jesus's new method of communicating in parables was provocative to the Pharisees, entertaining to the crowd, and intriguing to the disciples. You can almost hear some in the crowd saying, "We came all this way to hear about farming!" Others hung on every word.

Jesus had become something of a celebrity, and the crowd may have been more into his popularity than his teaching. In our day, a big game or a hyped concert may be the excuse for excitement, but there is always more going on than the game or the music when one hundred thousand people crowd into a stadium. Events that draw a crowd are an experience, a spectacle, a mix of celebrity, excitement, and theatrics. Jesus's presence had become an event that attracted crowds of admirers and spectators. His parables were entertaining to the crowd and provocative to the religious leaders. Jesus's rabbi-like status, coupled with his critical edge against the religious establishment, may have added to his popularity. Jesus's shift in strategy from straightforward teaching to storytelling left everyone wondering what Jesus was doing, although I imagine the crowd picked up on the fact that Jesus was calling out the Pharisees in his parables. He identified the religious leaders of the day with disgruntled workers, wicked tenants, and lazy wedding guests. If the crowd didn't get it, the scribes and the teachers of the law did.

MUSTARD SEEDS AND YEAST

Jesus's proposed three-to-one rejection rate in the parable of the sower does not appear to have discouraged the disciples. Jesus precedes to tell two little *local* stories: the mustard seed and the leaven. The kingdom of heaven is like a mustard seed; it starts small and grows big. If you want to illustrate something small and insignificant that becomes big and unstoppable, the proverbial mustard seed will do. Around the Lake of Galilee, the mustard seed can grow into a ten-foot shrub. The little-to-great ratio illustrates the power of Jesus's little gospel to go global. Likewise, a small amount of old fermented dough (leaven or sourdough) mixed into roughly sixty pounds of flour will make enough bread to feed a hundred people.

The gospel flies under the radar. As Dale Bruner says, it "will rarely be front-page news; its standard method of operation will be barely visible to the eye of publicity."[1] The parables of the mustard seed and leaven were meant to fill the disciples with confidence, so that they wouldn't "despise the day of small things" (Zech. 4:10) nor impatiently expect the kingdom to appear in its fullness right away (Matt. 11:3). Bruner continues, "The gospel goes out as seed, little but alive, and it comes back with big things like food, shade, and shelter for the nations." Apart from faith in the Lord Jesus, Bruner insists, "we will be tempted to distrust the little gospel we bear when we compare it with contemporary 'powers.'"[2]

---

1   Frederick Dale Bruner, *Matthew: A Commentary*, vol. 2, *The Churchbook*, Matthew 13–28 (Grand Rapids: Eerdmans, 2007), 37.
2   Bruner, *Matthew*, 2:34.

ECHOES OF ASAPH

Matthew wants the reader to know that Jesus's parables are a matter of fulfilled prophecy. They reflect the post-resurrection teaching of Jesus: "Everything must be fulfilled that is written about me" (Luke 24:44). Matthew traces Jesus's strategy back to Psalm 78, where the psalmist Asaph chronicles Israel's resistance to God's unforgettable acts of redemption. The thrust of Asaph's sermon is that the people of God must not repeat Israel's sad history of disloyalty, faithlessness, rebellion, unbelief, and hypocrisy. He begins with an impassioned plea: "My people, hear my teaching; listen to the words of my mouth. I will open my mouth with a parable; I will utter hidden things, things from of old." Matthew sees in Asaph's psalm echoes of Jesus's strategy.

Asaph's redemptive epic is a parable wrapped in history. He links history with parable in order to tell the truth slant. Asaph uses Psalm 78 to set up a comparison between history and meaning. History as a record of dates and events yields little, but when history is the medium for God's revelation, namely, "the hidden things," then salvation-making meaning is communicated. This is why "parable" (Hebrew *mashal*) has come to mean "wisdom." The plural form of *mashal* is the title of the book of Proverbs. The comparison of life and revelation yields life-transforming meaning.[3] So, alongside the miscellaneous

---

3 Calvin, *Psalms*, 227–28. Calvin concludes that the reference to using parables "denotes grave and striking sentences, such as adages, or proverbs, and apophthegms." Calvin implies that a degree of sophistication and eloquence lies behind this effort: "The inspired penman affirms that it is his purpose to utter only striking sentences and notable sayings." This interpretation of the term may distort his understanding of Christ's reason

ins and outs of history, Asaph boldly tells the "the praiseworthy deeds of the LORD" (Ps. 78:4). He presents the "decreed statutes for Jacob" (Ps. 78:5) and testifies to the established law of God. This is not breaking news, but it is good news. Asaph is not revealing anything new that the people of God did not already know. But it is precisely these unforgettable actions and commands of God that Israel's ancestors have rejected and forgotten along the way because they were a "stubborn and rebellious generation" (Ps. 78:8). Asaph's purpose for writing was to remind the people of God to be faithful and obedient to the steadfast covenant love of the Lord.

Asaph's communicational strategy meant presenting Israel's life and meaning, history and revelation, with a dynamic twist designed to get the attention of the hearer. This precedent-setting strategy was used by Matthew to explain Jesus's use of parables. Matthew says that Jesus "did not say anything" to the people "without using a parable," adding, "So was fulfilled what was spoken through the prophet [Asaph]: 'I will open my mouth in parables, I will utter things hidden since the creation of the world'" (Matt. 13:34–35; see Ps. 78:2 LXX). Both Jesus and Asaph "make the past hold up a mirror to the present" in order to reveal the truth of salvation history.[4]

---

for speaking in parables. Calvin writes, "Christ's object in doing so, was to prove that he was a distinguished prophet of God, and that thus he might be received with greater reverence. Since he then resembled a prophet because he preached sublime mysteries in a style of language above the common kind, that which the sacred writer here affirms concerning himself, is with propriety transferred to him."

4   Derek Kidner, *Psalms 73–150: An Introduction and Commentary* (Downers Grove: IL: InterVarsity, 1973), 281.

Simple parables reveal profound truths of the kingdom of heaven. *Good-soil understanding* is not popular, but amazingly fruitful. *Good-farming patience* allows the seed of the gospel to grow in spite of persistent weeds. *Good-kingdom growth* begins hidden and small but grows by the power of God exponentially. These truths remain hidden to the crowd because they are satisfied with Jesus's parables simply as stories. The disciples are drawn from the same cultural milieu as the crowd. They have the same education, the same Bible background, and the same hardscrabble existence, but instead of being satisfied with an entertaining story or a maxim to live by, the disciples know that Jesus's story is about something far more. The contrast between the crowd and the disciples who follow Jesus into the house seeking an explanation ought to challenge our readiness to embrace the meaning of the gospel. Do we really want to know the truth, "hidden since the creation of the world" (Matt. 13:35), or are we content with our own perspective of how things are?

Many people seem satisfied with a shallow reflection on the meaning of life. Jackson Brown's *Life's Little Instruction Book* offers practical advice for daily living. Five hundred and eleven random one-liners distill a father's wisdom for his college-bound son. Much of Brown's advice is common sense. It never hurts to be reminded to "Compliment three people every day" or "Watch a sunrise at least once a year" or "Remember other people's birthdays." No one is going to go wrong if you "overtip breakfast waitresses," and give people "a firm handshake." But life reduced to little proverbs to live will only take you so far. Life is too complicated for simple one-liners. Meaning is too great for fortune-cookie maxims.

JESUS'S EXPLANATION

In the house, away from the crowd, the disciples ask Jesus for an explanation (Matt. 13:36). They need his interpretation of what the parable means in order to understand it—not because the story is complicated, but because an illustration without exposition leaves the meaning up for grabs. The interpretative key lies in the explanation of Jesus, not in the disciples' imagination. Jesus obliges by giving them the deeper meaning. The sower of the good seed is the Son of Man. Jesus doesn't need to add, "That's me," because Jesus had already identified himself as the Son of Man ("Foxes have dens and birds have nests, but the Son of Man has no place to lay his head," Matt. 8:20). The field is the world, not the church. The good seed stands for the people of the kingdom of heaven. The weeds stand for the people of the evil one. The burning of the weeds is the final judgment. It is ordered by the Son of Man and executed by the angels.

Jesus tells the story in such a way that the Son of Man is still sowing good seed. His sowing continues past his ascension and into the present. Dale Bruner writes, "The Sower Parable taught us that the source of fruit is God's Word; the Weed Parable teaches us that the goal of fruit is God's world."[5] Jesus locates the mix between believers and

---

5   Bruner, *Matthew*, 2:41.

unbelievers *in the world*, not in the church.[6] "The weeds are the people of the evil one, and the enemy who sows them is the devil" (Matt. 13:38–39).

When Jesus told the story to the crowd, he explained that the owner's servants came to him and asked, "Sir, didn't you sow the good seed in your field? Where did the weeds come from?" But when he debriefed his disciples on the meaning of the parable, he identified the devil as the enemy. The devil is depicted "as a spiteful enemy," "a spoiler" who is out to destroy the harvest. Under cover of darkness, while the servants of the owner slept, the devil sowed his weeds. The weeds in question are darnel (*Lolium temulentum*, which comes from the Latin word for "drunk"), described as wheat's evil twin because it looks so much like wheat. It is poisonous and in small amounts it has an intoxicating effect.[7] Jesus's original audience was undoubtedly impressed by the despicable nature of the enemy's attack and its ruinous effect on the harvest.[8] But the owner takes it all in stride and simply responds, "An enemy did this" (Matt. 13:28). The servants offer to pull up the weeds, but the owner responds with an

---

6 R. T. France, *Matthew: New International Commentary* (Grand Rapids: Eerdmans, 2007), 533.

7 Craig S. Keener, *Matthew: The IVP New Testament Commentary Series* (Downers Grove, IL: InterVarsity, 2011), 242. See Sarah Laskow, "Wheat's Evil Twin Has Been Intoxicating Humans for Centuries," *Atlas Obscura*, March 22, 2016, https://www.atlasobscura.com/articles/wheats-evil-twin-has-been-intoxicating-humans-for-centuries.

8 Laskow, "Wheat's Evil Twin." Laskow writes, "When darnel was grown for its intoxicating properties . . . it likely would have been somewhat analogous to cannabis today—planted, gathered and processed under the cover of more acceptable crops, or kept secret."

emphatic "No!" because it would mean pulling up the wheat with the darnel. The owner's good servants must be patient and wait. The parable illustrates the theme of willed passivity that runs throughout salvation history. The people of God surrender and submit to the will of God and refuse to take matters into their own hands. The Lord is sovereign over salvation and judgment, and history is allowed to play out.

The calm resolve of the Son of Man, the great seed sower, must have impressed the disciples. Jesus declares the world is not the enemy; it is the mission field of the gospel. The evil one is the enemy. He is in the world. Patient endurance is called for, because he that is in us is greater than he that is in the world (1 John 4:4). Luther got it right in his great hymn "A Mighty Fortress": "The prince of darkness grim, we tremble not for him; his rage we can endure, for lo! his doom is sure, one little word shall fell him." The devil is our enemy. To deny his existence and belittle his impact is a mistake. But it is also wrong to make too much of the devil. In Ephesians, the apostle Paul describes the devil as the ruler of the kingdom of the air, suggesting that the immediate inspiration for evil is as close and as penetrating as the air that we breathe. Evil is pervasive. To preside over the "kingdom of the air" underscores the ethereal nature of the devil's being and work. Evil is the negative unreality of God's created good.

Jesus adds to the warning of the three-to-one rejection ratio (the parable of the sower) by preparing disciples for the mix of wheat and weeds growing together *in the world* ("the field is the world") and *in his kingdom* ("they will weed out of his kingdom everything that causes sin and all who do evil"). Two spheres are identified, the world and the church; both require the believer to be patient and resilient. The Son of Man asks his disciples to live in the tension of belief and unbelief without anger and resentment. The world has nothing to fear from Christians who are committed to demonstrating God's goodness. We are to love our enemies and pray for those who persecute us (Matt. 7:44). We will not fight the world with the weapons of the world (2 Cor. 10:4).

Karl Barth described Jesus-style militancy this way:

> The militant revolt demanded of Christians—and this distinguishes it from all kinds of other revolts—is not directed *against* people: not even against the host of unbelievers, false believers, and the superstitious . . . nor even . . . against the wicked. . . . In terms of their commission—even though they will sometimes clash with all kinds of people in discharging it—they rebel and fight *for* all men, even, and in the last resort precisely, for those with whom they may clash.[9]

Jesus warned us to expect opposition from the world. The advance of the gospel inspires the devil's resistance and the

---

9 Karl Barth, *The Christian Life: Church Dogmatics* IV/4, *Lecture Fragments*, trans. Geoffrey W. Bromiley (Grand Rapids: Eerdmans, 1981), 210 (emphasis original), quoted in Douglas Harink, *1–2 Peter* (Grand Rapids: Brazos, 2009), 127.

world's antagonism. The old paganisms and the new messianisms fight against the church with everything they have. Missionary statesman Lesslie Newbigin writes,

> Wherever the gospel is preached, new ideologies appear—secular humanism, nationalism, Marxism—movements which offer the vision of a new age, an age freed from all the ills that beset human life, freed from hunger and disease and war—on other terms. . . . Once the gospel is preached and there is a community which lives by the gospel, then the question of the ultimate meaning of history is posed and other messiahs appear. So the crisis of history is deepened. Even more significant as an example of this development than the rise of Marxism is the rise of Islam. Islam, which means simply submission, is the mightiest of all the post-Christian movements which claim to offer the kingdom of God without the cross. The denial of the crucifixion is and must always be central to Islamic teaching.[10]

We are not surprised to find opposition in the world, but we are surprised to find it in the church. We have been warned that there is a mix of wheat and weeds in the church.

---

10 Lesslie Newbigin, *The Gospel in a Pluralistic Society* (Grand Rapids: Eerdmans, 1989), 122.

The parable of the sower lets us know that there are plenty of shallow Christians and distracted Christians. When Jesus said, "The Son of Man will send out his angels, and they will weed out of his kingdom everything that causes sin and all who do evil," we know that on this side of eternity "the enemy is within the camp" and in the world.[11]

A final judgment awaits "all who do evil," but in the meantime, disciples practice their faithful presence in the world without violence and with longsuffering patience, and in the church they deal with sin with great care and love (Matt. 18:15–19). The willed passivity of the cross-bearing disciple seeks to live out the gospel *in* the world, *for* the world, without being *of* the world. Jesus's strategy gives the Christian space to be positive in a negative world. We are encouraged to accept the weeds for the time being and to get on with a positive gospel witness. There is room in Jesus's kingdom strategy for the Christian to live at peace in a radically pluralistic world where the government sanctions sinful practices and where the ethos of the culture opposes the Christian.

Jesus used the parable of the weeds to remind his original and future disciples that it is not our job to "exterminate the evil in the world" by our efforts.[12] We are not in the business of calling down fire from heaven (Luke 9:54–55) or mounting

---

11 Bruner, *Matthew*, 2:43. France, *Matthew*, 532. France sees the mix of wheat and weeds in the church reflected in a number of passages in Matthew (7:15–20; 13:49; 22:10–13; 21:28–32; 25:1–12).

12 Helmut Thielicke, *The Waiting Father: Sermons on the Parables of Jesus* (New York: Harper & Row, 1959), 76.

a campaign "against the rulers, against the authorities, against the powers of this dark world and against the spiritual forces of evil in the heavenly realms" (Eph. 6:12). Instead, we let the word and wisdom of Jesus shape our willed passivity: "In this world you will have trouble. But take heart! I have overcome the world" (John 16:33).

In the household of faith, the nonsectarian disciple cultivates an openness to confessing believers, "for whoever is not against us is for us," and the discerning disciple exercises diligence and sensitivity so as not to cause any young believer to stumble (Mark 9:40–42). The apostle prayed that "[our] love would abound more and more in knowledge and depth of insight, so that [we] may be able to discern what is best and may be pure and blameless for the day of Christ, filled with the fruit of righteousness that comes through Jesus Christ—to the glory and praise of God" (Phil. 1:9–11).[13]

---

13   John Calvin, *Harmony of the Evangelists*, 16.121–22. Calvin writes, "The Church is burdened with the reprobate to the very end of the world; but Christ enjoins on us to exercise patience till that time, that we may not deceive ourselves with a vain hope. Pastors ought to labor strenuously to purify the Church; and all the godly, so far as their respective callings enable them, ought to lend assistance in this matter; but when all shall have devoted their united exertions to the general advantage, they will not succeed in such a manner as to purify the Church entirely from every defilement. Let us therefore hold, that nothing was farther from the design of Christ than to encourage pollution by lending countenance to it. All that he intended was, to exhort those who believed in him not to lose courage, because they are under the necessity of retaining wicked men among them; and next, to restrain and moderate the zeal of those who fancy that they are not at liberty to join in a society with any but pure angels." So far so good! But then Calvin said something I believe Jesus never intended. Calvin writes: "This passage has been most improperly abused by the Anabaptists, and by others like them, to take from the Church the

The mix of wheat and weeds in the world and in the church means that we live with a certain sense of ambiguity and unsettledness. This confusion leads believers to earnest prayer. We need discernment. Looking back over my pastoral ministry, I think there have been times when I failed to act. Instead of leading, I looked the other way. I have felt like the Old Testament prophets and kings who did not tear down the high places. People may not have been literally bowing down before an idol, but they were perilously close. I am referring to those gray areas in church life where right and wrong are difficult to discern and even more difficult to address: the person who uses "ministry" to satisfy his or her ego; the young families who forfeit worship so their children can play soccer or baseball on Sunday mornings; the crusader who fixates on a single issue; the "God and country" worshipers who equate their national pride with the kingdom of God. These are the type of problems that remind me of the golden calf experience.[14] The idolatry we contend with seems more subtle and elusive, but nevertheless real. I am comforted by Jesus's parable of the wheat among the weeds. He seems to be cutting us some slack, allowing us to let some things take their course. He's telling us to leave the "weeding" to God's

---

power of the sword." Calvin contends that Jesus is not removing the power of the sword from "the office of pastors or of magistrates," who must presumably execute their responsibility against "the polluted dregs of society." What is unusual here is extending the power of the sword to the office of the pastor.

14 Douglas D. Webster, *Living in Tension: A Theology of Ministry* (Eugene, OR: Cascade Books, 2012), 1:160–61.

judgment. When it comes to some of these sticky, intractable problems, it may be sufficient to pray earnestly and let God be God. I hope so.

Jesus does not shrink from describing the horror of hell. The sure destruction of toxic weeds in a blazing furnace on harvest day is analogous to what happens to those who refuse the gospel of the Son of Man. Jesus contrasts "the people of the evil one," who are weeping and gnashing their teeth, with the righteous, who are "shin[ing] like the sun in the kingdom of their Father" (Matt. 13:42–43).[15] Jesus finishes his explanation of the parable of the weeds among the wheat with the admonition to "Listen!" We are meant to take Jesus's commands to heart. The parable of the sower challenges us

---

15 Jesus on hell: a quick review of his teaching ministry captures the highlights. Jesus repeatedly promised that on the day of judgment, those who rejected the gospel would suffer a worse fate than Sodom and Gomorrah. Jesus stated it plainly: "There is a judge for those who reject me and do not accept my words; the very words I have spoken will condemn them at the last day" (John 12:48). "Repent or perish" was a refrain that ran through his ministry. Any generation that rejects the gospel is guilty of the blood of all the prophets. Jesus lashed out, "You snakes! You brood of vipers! How will you escape being condemned to hell?" (Matt. 23:33). To be ashamed of Jesus and his gospel was to identify with an "adulterous and sinful generation" and to invite a reciprocal response: "the Son of Man will be ashamed of them when he comes in his Father's glory with the holy angels" (Mark 8:36–38; Luke 9:23–26). Jesus warned, "Do not be afraid of those who kill the body but cannot kill the soul. Rather, be afraid of the One who can destroy both the soul and body in hell" (Matt. 10:28). Jesus described judgment in graphic and violent language. Hell is outer darkness, a place of weeping and gnashing of teeth. Jesus offers these words of condemnation at the final judgment: "Depart from me, you who are cursed, into the eternal fire prepared for the devil and his angels" (Matt. 25:41). On the theme of judgment, the language of Jesus and the language of the Revelation draw on the same truth.

to sow and harvest the good seed. The parable of the weeds among the wheat challenges us to be Jesus-like in our missionary endeavors.

3

THE HIDDEN TREASURE, THE PEARL, AND THE NET

MATTHEW 13:44–52

Matthew concludes Jesus's Sermon of Parables with a flurry of images. Like a two-minute movie trailer, Matthew's high-impact strategy hits home. Three quick parables are given to the crowd without interpretation, followed by an epigram meant for the disciples. The narrative distinction between the crowd and the disciples is ambiguous. Presumably the meaning of the parables was fairly obvious given the explanation of the parable of the sower and the parable of the weeds among the wheat. The disciples appear to be catching on, even though the crowd remains in a fog.

THE JOY OF THE GOSPEL

The parables of the hidden treasure and the pearl belong together. In meaning and message, they parallel one another.

They capture the joy of gospel discovery. A farmer happens to be walking through a field when he discovers a partially buried treasure. There is no indication that he was even looking for a treasure. He quickly hides his life-changing discovery, and "in his joy," he goes and sells everything he owns and buys the field. The disciples needed no explanation of the parable because they were already living it. They had found sufficient reason to leave their businesses and follow Jesus (Matt. 4:20, 22; 9:9). For them the object lesson of a priceless discovery had already materialized in their personal experience. The issue comes up again in Jesus's encounter with the rich young ruler, who refused to sell off his great wealth and follow Jesus. Peter was quick to remind Jesus, "We have left everything to follow you! What then will there be for us?" (Matt. 19:27).

The reference to a *treasure* was familiar to the disciples. In the Sermon on the Mount Jesus said, "Do not store up for yourselves treasure on earth, where moths and vermin destroy, and where thieves break in and steal. But store up for yourselves treasures in heaven, where moths and vermin do not destroy, and where thieves do not break in and steal. For where your treasure is, there your heart will be also" (Matt. 6:19–21). The theme of *treasure* is developed in the gospel narrative consistently. As R. T. France puts it, "Once the kingdom of heaven is truly understood, nothing else can compare with it in value."[1]

---

1   R. T. France, *Matthew: New International Commentary* (Grand Rapids: Eerdmans, 2007), 541.

The upper class merchant in search of fine pearls is on a mission to discover the pearl of great price. And when he does, like the farmer, he sells everything he has to obtain the prize. The implicit social diversity of the finders indicates that whether one is poor or rich the gospel is the one discovery that is worth everything we have. However, the point of the parable is not the cost of discipleship, nor is it about complete surrender, nor is it a call to "heroic action." Joachim Jeremias explains,

> When that great joy, surpassing all measure seizes a man, it carries him away, penetrates his inmost being, subjugates his mind. All else seems valueless compared with that surpassing worth. No price is too great to pay. The unreserved surrender of what is most valuable becomes a matter of course. The decisive thing in the twin parables is not what the two men give up, but the reason for their doing so; the overwhelming experience of the splendor of their discovery. Thus it is with the kingdom of God. The effect of the joyful news is overpowering; it fills the heart with gladness; it makes life's whole aim the consummation of the divine community and produces the most whole-hearted self-sacrifice.[2]

To discover the gospel is to discover a whole new orientation to life—a whole new way of living. Everything has

---

2   Joachim Jeremias, *The Parables of Jesus* (London: SCM, 1972), 201.

changed. Religious duty is swept aside in the wake of the gospel's privilege and joy. Meaning and mission are redefined. Missionary statesman Lesslie Newbigin writes, "Mission begins with a kind of explosion of joy. The news that the rejected and crucified Jesus is alive is something that cannot possibly be suppressed. It must be told. Who could be silent about such a fact?"[3]

Dale Bruner writes, "I conclude that few places in the NT as perfectly spell out the two main foci of the gospel (grace and demand), and put them in their proper order, as do the Gem Parables: first the jewels and then the selling; but without the selling there is no possession of the jewels."[4] Bruner parallels these twin truths with Jesus's invitation to "Come to me, all you who are weary and burdened, and I will give you rest" (grace and joy), coupled with "Take my yoke upon you and learn from me" (easy demand and slight cost). He also sees a parallel with the Sermon on the Mount: the Beatitudes (grace and joy) followed by commands (challenge and obedience).[5]

THE NET

The disciples did not need an explanation for the seventh and final parable, because it was a close parallel to the parable of the weeds among the wheat. They identified with everything

---

3 Lesslie Newbigin, *The Gospel in a Pluralistic Society* (Grand Rapids: Eerdmans, 1989), 116.

4 Frederick Dale Bruner, *Matthew: A Commentary*, vol. 2, *The Churchbook*, Matthew 13–28 (Grand Rapids: Eerdmans, 2007), 49.

5 Bruner, *Matthew*, 2:50.

about the parable from casting the big net to separating out the bad fish. At the outset Jesus called them to fish for people, and they immediately left their nets and followed him (Matt. 4:19). The parable of the net is a final judgment parable. It is about the ultimate separation of the bad from the good. The kingdom of heaven is like a big net cast into the lake that catches all kinds of fish.

Craig Keener reports that there were at least twenty-four species of fish in the Lake of Galilee. As experienced fishermen, some of the disciples knew firsthand the job of sorting through a big catch of fish and separating out the bad and keeping the good. They were experienced in throwing out the unclean and the inedible and keeping the clean.[6] The disciples must have found it amusing that in this parable, angels were tasked with that responsibility. Angels will be deployed to do that work in the final judgment and the disciples are compared to the good fish that are saved. France writes, "Until the final judgment there will be no separate existence for the true people of God: the wicked will be in the middle of them, like wolves among the sheep (Matt. 7:15)."[7] The final judgment of the weeds and the bad fish are the same. They are thrown into a blazing furnace of destruction where there is weeping and gnashing of teeth (Matt. 13:42, 50).

Matthew does not tell us how the crowd reacted to the parable of the net. They are not included in the picture, but he

---

6 Craig S. Keener, *Matthew: The IVP New Testament Commentary Series* (Downers Grove, IL: InterVarsity, 2011), 246.

7 France, *Matthew*, 543.

reports that Jesus asked the disciples, "Have you understood all these things?" "Yes," they replied. This prompts Jesus to add a mini-metaphor or epigram to his communication strategy. A third perspective is now applied to every teacher of the law who has become a disciple of the kingdom of heaven. Before we look at it, let's review the first two perspectives.

Jesus has already said that the disciples are unique and set apart because they have been given the secrets of the kingdom of heaven (Matt. 13:11). They have been blessed to see and to hear what "many prophets and righteous people longed to see but did not see . . . and to hear what [they] hear but did not hear" (Matt. 13:16–17). The Lion of the tribe of Judah, who is the Lamb standing at the center of the throne, has opened the seals and disclosed the gospel of the revelation of God (Rev. 5). To this first perspective, Matthew adds a second from Psalm 78, presumably based on Jesus's conversation with the disciples at some point, that emphasized that the gospel is the truth "hidden since the creation of the world" but now revealed (Matt. 13:35). That which was hidden is now being revealed in parables (1 Peter 1:10–12; Heb. 11:13–16).

NEW TREASURES

The third perspective likens the disciple to a homeowner "who brings out of his storeroom new treasures as well as old." Once again "the new wine in new wineskins" theme is sounded (Matt. 9:17). Bruner writes, "All teachers want good texts. Jesus tells his disciples that they have the best: the apostolic

Scriptures (the new) and the wisdom of Israel (the old), and in that order. The phrase 'new things and old things' seems most naturally to mean the new treasures of the gospel and the old treasures of the law."[8] Jesus has not come to abolish the old (Matt. 5:17), but to fulfill "things hidden since the creation of the world" (Matt. 13:35). For he is the Lamb who was slain from the creation of the world (Rev. 13:8).

We should pause here and reflect on the immense task before us in the household of faith.[9] The teaching responsibility of the gospel belongs to all disciples, to the priesthood of all believers. "Everyone who follows Jesus is commissioned to teach others ('Follow me, and I will make you fishers of

---

8 Bruner, *Matthew*, 2:54.
9 Robert Farrar Capon reflects on the responsibility of the householder, whom he describes as having been given "full authority over an incredibly rich castle." Capon writes, "Therefore, the bringing forth referred to here by Jesus is no rummage-sale unloading of junk; rather, it is a displaying of rare treasures for the fascination of the castle's guests. And there is a lesson in that for preachers. So often, whether because of thickheadedness, lack of study, scanty preparation, or just plain boredom, they unceremoniously heave the treasures of Scripture out of the pulpit as they were flopping out so many dead fish. There is no fascination in their monologues, no intrigue, no sense whatsoever that the ministry they have been given is precisely that of being majordomo [chief steward] over a house to end all houses. The most they ever achieve is a kind of monomaniacal enthusiasm for the one or two items that happen to suit their own odd tastes: hellfire, perhaps; or their sawed-off, humanistic version of love; or their short-order recipe for spirituality; or the hopelessly moralistic lessons in good behavior that they long since decided were more palatable than the paradoxes of the Gospel. . . . May God hasten the day on which they will stay in the castle storeroom long enough to get stark staring bonkers about the Word and hilariously drunk on Scripture" (*Kingdom, Grace, Judgment: Paradox, Outrage, and Vindication in the Parables of Jesus* [Grand Rapids: Eerdmans, 2002], 143).

others!'), even if it's one's own family in devotions and readings or one's office mates in Bible and other studies."[10]

Matthew frames Jesus's Sermon of Parables with an epilogue that confirms Jesus's rationale for choosing parables over explicit teaching. When Jesus finished these seven parables, he returned to his hometown Nazareth (Luke 4:16) and resumed his biblical teaching in the synagogue. Initially, the reaction of the people was positive, but their admiration quickly turned to skepticism (Matt. 13:53–58). They could not believe that someone who grew up in Nazareth was capable of such miraculous powers. How could a local person preach with such wisdom? Jesus stirred up controversy and provoked a lot of questions: Where did this man get this wisdom and these miraculous powers? Isn't this the carpenter's son? Isn't his mother's name Mary, and aren't his brothers James, Joseph, Simon, and Judas? Aren't all his sisters with us? Where did this man get all these things? The hometown crowd knew just enough about Jesus to balk at listening to him. They took offense at him. What they knew about Jesus and his family only served to reinforce their prejudice against him. Instead of being open to his message and testing it against the Old Testament Scriptures, they despised Jesus.

Was their reaction out of fear or envy? Did the town's people possibly feel they were being played or manipulated by Jesus? Matthew doesn't give us a full-blown account, but we know they took offense. Jesus was aware of their reaction and

---

10 Bruner, *Matthew*, 2:55.

his response sums it up: "A prophet is not despised (*atimos*, is the same Greek LXX translation of Isaiah 53:3) except in his own hometown and in his own family."[11] Jesus himself had become the issue, not the truth he proclaimed and the teaching he embodied. This is often the case in our churches and hometowns today. The age, background, race, family, and pedigree of the preacher becomes an obstacle to hearing the gospel, not because there is something wrong with the witness, but because of fear, envy, pride, prejudice, and bias. It is significant that Matthew frames this important collection of parables with an understanding of the power of culture to harden our hearts and make us blind to the truth. These are the reasons that led Jesus to choose a communicational strategy that satisfied the crowd, kept the religious leaders at bay, and instructed the disciple in the kingdom of heaven.

---

11   Bruner, *Matthew*, 2:61.

4

THE GOOD SAMARITAN

LUKE 10:21–37

Of all Jesus's parables, the parable of the good Samaritan may be the most famous. People who know very little about the Bible are familiar with this parable. Its popularity can be attributed in part to the shaping influence of Christianity on Western thought. Strangers who come to the assistance of those in need, such as helping a stranded motorist or assisting a lost child, are called "good Samaritans." Most states have "good Samaritan" laws that offer legal protection to people who might otherwise hesitate to help someone for fear of being sued. We hear the parable today in a culture that takes pride in helping the stranger in need and commends "first responders." The hero in the story is a despised minority, who without meaning to, challenges preconceived notions and stereotypes in the culture. What sounded offensive to Jesus's first hearers comes across as politically correct to contemporary ears. The parable of the good Samaritan impresses many today as a morality play. It makes a humanitarian appeal by commending the rescue of people in distress. This is widely recognized as a good thing.

You won't go wrong helping someone in need, and Christians should be in the vanguard of those who serve others in this way. But stripping down the meaning of the parable to social action on behalf of the needy misses the reason why Jesus gave this parable. It misses what Jesus taught the disciples about mercy over merit.

What happened along the road from Jerusalem to Jericho, an eighteen-mile descent from 2,500 feet above sea level to 770 feet below it, through desert and rocky terrain, can only be understood in the light of Jesus's journey to the cross. The ordinary, concrete realities depicted in this story deserve to be seen in the context of a much bigger story—God's redemptive story. This parable is a small story within a much bigger story. We respond better to stories than statements and pictures over propositions. We usually remember stories; we tend to forget statements. Vivid pictures evoke the emotions that aid the memory. Jesus told intimate, down-to-earth stories that we could easily identify with in order to reveal the epic story of the gospel.

Jesus chose the medium of parables to separate the crowd from the disciples. Today's popular humanitarian meaning of the parable fits with the original crowd's understanding: we have a responsibility to show compassion to those in need. The obvious meaning is there for all to see: show pity to the stranger. But there is more. The deeper meaning is hidden in the context of Jesus's teaching and in the scribe's question, "What must I do to inherit eternal life?" Mercy over merit fulfills the law. The parable is commentary on the fifth beatitude: "Blessed are the merciful, for they will be shown mercy" (Matt. 5:7).

It is a natural reaction to put ourselves in this parable and to identify with a character. To hear Jesus tell this story is to ask yourself, "Who am I in this parable?" Are you the man in the ditch in need of rescue? Are you the priest or the Levite who hastily passes by on the other side? Are you the good Samaritan who rescues the half-dead man? Few people, I imagine, identify with the priest and Levite, yet many of us feel guilty because of this parable. The story triggers our defenses. We feel guilty for ignoring the homeless person asking for money. The parable begs the question, Should we be more involved in social justice? Does Jesus expect us to befriend everyone in need, to rescue every street person on our way to work? If we live and work in a city, we encounter this dilemma everyday. We are surrounded by chronic, systemic human need. Who can hear this parable and not feel guilty or defensive? Before tackling this question, we need to let Luke set the scene of one of Jesus's most popular parables.

SETTING THE SCENE

Luke gives us the big picture. "As the time approached for him to be taken up to heaven, Jesus resolutely set out for Jerusalem" (Luke 9:51). Immediately, Jesus's journey to Jerusalem met with Samaritan resistance. His advance team of disciples were discouraged from entering a Samaritan village (Luke 9:51–55). The reason was "because [Jesus] was heading for Jerusalem" (Luke 9:53). This fits with the Samaritan insistence that Mount Gerizim was the true place of worship instead of Jerusalem. The Samaritans were an ethnic splinter group despised by the Jews. They were descendants of Israel's northern kingdom founded by Omri (1 Kings 16:21–24). In the spirit of Elijah (2 Kings 1), James and John, the sons of thunder, are ready to call down fire to destroy them. Jesus rebuked them, and they walked on to another village.

Mindful that he is on the way to Jerusalem to die on the cross, Jesus sends out the seventy-two with good news, "The kingdom of God has come near to you" (Luke 10:9). The Lord of the harvest gives specific instructions. In the light of our parable, one directive is particularly ironic: "Do not take a purse or bag or sandals; and do not greet anyone on the road" (Luke 10:4). The seventy-two are commissioned to go out as "lambs among wolves." We note the seamless line of authority from the Father to the Son to the disciples. Jesus said, "Whoever listens to you listens to me; whoever rejects you rejects me; but whoever rejects me rejects him who sent me" (Luke 10:16). To their surprise and joy, they meet with supernatural success, saying, "Lord, even the demons submit to us in your name" (Luke 10:17).

Finally, Luke sets the scene with the highest and deepest meaning of who Jesus is. The rule of God has begun through Jesus. Jesus tells the disciples, "I saw Satan fall like lightning from heaven. . . . Rejoice that your names are written in heaven" (Luke 10:18, 20). "At that time," Luke reports,

> Jesus, full of joy through the Holy Spirit, said, "I praise you, Father, Lord of heaven and earth, because you have hidden these things from the wise and

learned, and revealed them to little children. . . . All things have been committed to me by my Father, and no one knows who the Father is, except the Son and those to whom the Son chooses to reveal him." Then he turned to his disciples and said privately, "Blessed are the eyes that see what you see. For I tell you that many prophets and kings wanted to see what you see but did not see it, and to hear what you hear but did not hear it." (Luke 10:21–24)

The scene is set for the parable. Luke's passion narrative has begun, the orientation to the Great Commission has been given, and the eschatological rule of God has commenced. Luke frames the parable in the context of the Lord's unfolding revelation to the disciples. Luke distinguished between past expectation and present fulfillment. Salvation history had reached a critical turning point. Matthew distinguished between the crowd and the disciples (Matt. 13:11). In both cases, the disciples were set apart to receive what the prophets and kings longed to see, and what the crowd was not yet willing or ready to see. Whether you translate the opening phrase (Luke 10:25) as "on one occasion" (NIV) or "just then" (e.g., NRSV) the placement of the parable is intentional. The encounter with the expert in the law and the story to follow fits the sequence theologically. Jesus is the one to be listened to, and Mary will exemplify the importance of listening to Jesus (Luke 10:38–41). Did Jesus have to die to tell this story? The answer is yes. *Who* is telling the story is decisive for its interpretation. There is more here than a humanitarian appeal, as important as helping people in need and loving our neighbor may be. The crowd heard the parable one way, but Jesus intended the disciples to hear it another way.

WHOSE INTERPRETATION?

The early church was quick to relate this parable to the epic drama of the gospel. One of the early church's greatest theologians, Augustine (354–430), gave free reign to an allegorizing interpretation. The half-dead man, robbed and beaten, lying in the ditch, stands for Adam. He had fallen from the heavenly city Jerusalem. Robbers, symbolizing the devil, strip him of his immortality. The priest and the Levite stand for the law, which is powerless to save. The Samaritan, who shows him mercy and bandages his wounds, represents Christ who forgives sin. The inn is the church; the innkeeper, the apostle Paul.

As inflationary as Augustine's interpretation may seem, I favor it over the interpreters who reduce this parable to a *gotcha* moment. They claim that Jesus tells the parable to show the expert of the law that he cannot possibly comply with the law. They contend that Jesus tells this parable as a rebuke to the notion of salvation by works.[1] Since the impossible standard of absolute neighbor-love can only be met by Jesus, then only Jesus can fulfill the law. When Jesus says, "Do this and you will live," what he really means is "You cannot possibly do this!"

---

1   Ligon Duncan, "What Shall I Do to Inherit Eternal Life?," First Presbyterian Church, Jackson, Mississippi, https://www.fpcjackson.org/resource-library/sermons/what-shall-i-do-to-inherit-eternal-life.

As the argument goes, Jesus is not showing us how to love our neighbor as much as offering proof that we all fall far short of God's standard of love. "Jesus is the Good Samaritan because we cannot be."[2] Jesus says, "Go and do likewise," knowing that he is giving impossible spiritual direction. But he says this so that we will come to the end of ourselves and our effort and turn to him for his righteousness. Instead of emphasizing that this "going" and "doing" is empowered by God's grace and mercy, these interpreters see all effort, all obedience, as contradicting God's grace. This interpretative approach overlooks the positive tension between works righteousness, based on merit, and the work of righteousness, based on mercy. It fails to recognize that behavior flows from belief: to believe is to obey and to obey is to believe. These two dynamics, belief and behavior, are in synergy.

Contrary to those who challenge the call to obedience, Jesus meant what he said: "Do this and live." Jesus is not being ironic, much less disingenuous. The false path of works righteousness is a grave danger, but it must not be allowed to obscure what Jesus is saying and the truth of the gospel. The message of the parable is that we ought to love our neighbor, no matter who our neighbor is, even the neighbor who is beyond our help—but never beyond the help of God. The message is not that we cannot earn our way to heaven, which of course we cannot. We are saved by grace through faith and

---

2 Nick Lannon, "The Good Samaritan," *The Modern Reformation*, Sept/Oct 2010, 38.

it has nothing to do with our effort. The parable is about neighbor-love empowered by the gospel of Jesus Christ.

The only way the expert in the law could grasp the truth of what Jesus was saying and show mercy was if he accepted the authority of Jesus over the law. This also applies equally to the rich young ruler, who approached Jesus with the same question and received a similar response (Luke 18:18–30). The only way this young man would have given up his wealth and followed Jesus was if he was convinced that Jesus was the way, the truth, and the life (John 14:6).

THE EXPERT

This expert in the law was more like a biblical scholar than a lawyer, but his fixation with precise wording and cognition fits the profile of a legal professional or an academic theologian. We tend to buy into "a stunted pedagogy that is fixated on the mind." The result "is a talking-head version of Christianity."[3] The point of course is not that we retreat from the mind, but that we prioritize the soulful self over a "thinking thing." We are neither body-less souls nor soul-less bodies, but bodies and souls in community.[4] Love's formation takes in the mind and the heart. Person-as-thinker is fundamentally reductionistic, but person-as-lover is holistic, encompassing the whole self. In Luke's mind, the "expert" represents "the

---

3 James K. A. Smith, *Desiring the Kingdom* (Grand Rapids: Baker, 2009), 42–43.

4 John R. W. Stott, *Christian Mission in the Modern World* (Downers Grove, IL: InterVarsity, 2008), 47.

wise and learned" (Luke 10:21) who do not understand what God is doing (Matt. 13:13–15). God has not opened their eyes. They cannot fathom who Jesus is. They do not understand the coming kingdom and the rule of God. The expert sought to test Jesus. He wanted to confirm his suspicions and prove that Jesus was wrong.

But with a simple question, "What is written in the Law? How do you read it?" Jesus deflected the philosophical question and focused on the real issue, knowing God. The encounter "wonderfully illustrates Jesus's capacity for turning an abstract theological discussion into a discourse on real life issues."[5] The expert answered in two parts, drawing on Deuteronomy 6:5 and Leviticus 19:18. We are to love God with all our heart, all our soul, all our strength, and all our mind. Such love is as all encompassing as you can get, and such love embraces the neighbor as oneself. Brilliant answer! Jesus replied, "You have answered correctly. Do this and you will live" (Luke 10:28). End of discussion. Class over.

WHO IS MY NEIGHBOR?

Well, not quite. Jesus takes it deeper. The point of the parable is hard to miss: everyone is my neighbor. We can never again use God's love as an excuse for not loving someone, no matter how different they may be. But this love is not so much an emotional love as a practical love. It is not about feelings

---

5   Darrell L. Bock, *Luke: The NIV Application Commentary* (Grand Rapids: Zondervan, 2009), 299.

as much as it is about tangible love, practical compassion, and common sense concern. Jesus did not tell this parable to make us feel guilty but to make us truly grateful. Jesus, the storyteller, is the one who is absolutely critical to the meaning of the parable. Jesus's parable of the good Samaritan resonates with the apostle Paul's description of Christ destroying the dividing wall of hostility. God's purpose is "to create in himself one new humanity" (Eph. 2:15–16). Because of Christ and his cross, there is no basis for any person, group, race, tribe, or nation to feel superior. This one new humanity in Christ is not part Jewish and part Gentile, nor is it part black and part white. This new race is an act of creation, not a mixture of Asian and Arab, Latin and European.

The desire to justify himself betrays the expert's merit-based rationalization. His follow-up question, "And who is my neighbor?" may have been prompted by his observation that Jesus was more open to foreigners, to the demonized, to the diseased, and to the corrupt than most law-abiding Israelites were. He had heard Jesus say, "Love your enemies, do good to them, and lend to them without expecting to get anything back" (Luke 6:35). He knew that Jesus commended the Roman centurion with high praise: "I tell you, I have not found such great faith even in Israel" (Luke 7:9). He also knew the rumors that Jesus tried to reach out to Samaritans. The expert in the law may have wanted to ask Jesus his views on Samaritans even before Jesus referenced one. Presumably, the biblical scholar expected to challenge Jesus's view of the law. In Leviticus "neighbor" parallels "the children of your own people." The law reads:

"Do not seek revenge or bear a grudge against anyone among your own people, but love your neighbor as yourself. I am the LORD" (Lev. 19:18).

Leviticus qualifies love for foreigners in a significant way. They must "[reside] among you in your land" (Lev. 19:33) and comply with Old Testament law. In other words, foreigners who qualify as neighbors have accepted the law and Jewish culture. Thus, loving one's neighbor is consistent with the prophetic denunciation of Samaria. A case in point is the prophet Hosea's harsh verdict against Samaritans: "The people of Samaria must bear their guilt, because they have rebelled against their God. They will fall by the sword; their little ones will be dashed to the ground, their pregnant women ripped open" (Hos. 13:16).

The expert saw the love of God in tension with loving certain people who did not qualify for being one's neighbor. He assumed that some people, especially Samaritans, were excluded from neighbor-love. But Jesus's parable eliminates this exclusion by making sure that no one can turn loving God into an excuse for not loving one's neighbor.[6] We cannot limit love to the people we find loveable. The love of God is inclusive. No one is excluded.

---

6 Helmut Thielicke, *The Waiting Father: Sermons on the Parables of Jesus* (New York: Harper & Row, 1959), 163. Thielicke writes about Jesus's response to the rich young ruler's question, "It is really very awkward and annoying that spiritual things should be so simple, that they should have to do with ridiculous everyday life, with neighbors, friends, peddlers, or any insignificant, colorless employee who happens to come along. He inquired about the meaning of life; he presented a sublime subject for discussion—and here he is, sent to the servant's quarters! It's enough to make one weep, or laugh."

It is interesting to note that some church-growth strategies are similar to the rationale of the expert in the law. Church-growth experts argue that it is important to target your audience and determine the segment of the market you want to reach. One popular pastor defined his target audience as the people he would like to spend a vacation with. Many churches "discovered" that their market niche was the upwardly mobile, success-driven, child-centered professional. These churches catered to the religious consumer without asking if Jesus had a target audience or a defined market share.

It is difficult for a serious student of the Bible to think that Jesus used social rapport, income levels, and generational targeting to determine his mission. His market niche was the world. The nineteenth-century Danish Christian thinker Søren Kierkegaard exposed the rationale of the expert in the law. He distinguished between loving the people we actually see versus a high-flying love that is always waiting for the right person to love. He compared *airy* love to *actual* love. Kierkegaard reasoned that our duty is not to find "the lovable object" but to find the person before us lovable. Actual love, loving the person before us, is always concrete and often sacrificial. "Truth takes a firm step," says Kierkegaard, "and for that reason sometimes a difficult one, too." The opposite of actual love is a theory of love focused on the ideal. "Delusion is always floating; for that reason it sometimes appears quite light and spiritual, because it is so airy."[7]

---

7   Søren Kierkegaard, *Works of Love* (New York: Harper & Row, 1962), 158–61.

My hunch is that none of us need to look very far to find a challenging person to love. A day after re-reading Kierkegaard's meditation on love, I received an accusatory email from a church member. His criticism against me and others was deep-seated and mean-spirited. My immediate impulse was to fire back an angry email to set the record straight and to defend myself and others. But Kierkegaard's *intrusive* reminder to love as Christ loved was stuck in my mind. I remember wishing it wasn't. We never have far to look for a person to love who is impossible to love apart from the grace of God. Actual love is for the real people with whom we must deal with daily. Airy love is a fine-sounding theory filled with ethereal possibilities.

The expert in the law asked a follow-up question to justify himself. Jesus responded with a parable designed to reveal the meaning of mercy. Self-justification confronts its opposite in the profound, life-changing dynamic of justification by faith. Like most of Jesus's parables, this simple story has a surprise twist. The priest and the Levite are religious and represent compliance with the law. For whatever reason, they chose to avoid a social crisis. They saw a man in the ditch half-dead, but passed by on the other side. Whether they did so out of fear for their own safety or scrupulous concern for the law does not matter. Like many religious people, they are boring and uninteresting. Just as they passed by the man in the ditch, we pass them by and move on to the Samaritan.

Ironically, a person outside the tradition of covenant privilege and blessing—a Samaritan—took pity on the half-dead man and showed him compassion. Most of the story describes in detail what the good Samaritan did for the man. He saw him and went to him. He bandaged his wounds. He cleaned his wounds with oil and disinfected them with wine. He put him on his own donkey and brought him to the inn to take care of him. We are not told where the Samaritan was headed. We know the priest and Levite were heading to Jericho. The Samaritan may have been headed to Jerusalem.[8]

The priest and Levite bring to mind a religious tradition that ignores the practical command to love your neighbor, while the Samaritan quietly illustrates the angst and hope of the prophet Amos: "I hate, I despise your religious festivals; your assemblies are a stench to me. Even though you bring me burnt offerings and grain offerings, I will not accept them. . . . But let justice roll on like a river, righteousness like a never-failing stream!" (Amos 5:21–22, 24). His actions reflect the prophet Isaiah: "Stop bringing meaningless offerings! Your incense is detestable to me. . . . I cannot bear your worthless assemblies . . . stop doing wrong. Learn to do right; seek justice. Defend the oppressed. Take up the cause of the fatherless; plead the case of the widow" (Isa. 1:13, 16–17). Ironically, the Samaritan represents the tradition found in Hosea: "For I desire mercy, not sacrifice, and acknowledgment of God rather than burnt offerings" (Hos. 6:6). He reminds

---

8   The intentional choice of a Samaritan as the model of mercy, especially after the occasion of Samaritan opposition (Luke 9:51–56), points forward to the gospel's outreach. Jesus envisions evangelizing Samaritans (Acts 1:8) and the Samaritan Pentecost (Acts 8:4–8). On a further note, those who define their target audience as people like themselves will usually end up with a lead pastor like Simon the Sorcerer (Acts 8:9–25).

the reader of Micah: "He has shown you, O mortal, what is good. And what does the LORD require of you? To act justly and to love mercy and to walk humbly with your God" (Mic. 6:8). What we learn from the story of the Samaritan is that to believe is to obey, and to obey is to believe. Being and doing are all of one piece.

The conclusion to the parable of the good Samaritan has three parts: (1) The question: "Which of these three do you think was a neighbor to the man who fell into the hands of robbers?" (2) The answer: "The expert in the law replied, 'The one who had mercy on him.'" (3) The imperative: "Go and do likewise" (Luke 10:36–37). What is at stake here is not "a set of cognitive, heady beliefs: Christianity is not fundamentally a worldview."[9] As Kierkegaard says, "Worldly wisdom is very willing to deceive by answering correctly the question, 'where is the road?' while life's true task is omitted, that is, how one walks along the road."[10] Jesus makes sure that from now on no one can use the command to love God as an excuse for not loving your neighbor. We cannot limit love to the people we find loveable. John writes, "We love because he first loved us. Whoever claims to love God yet hates a brother or sister is a liar. For whoever does not love their brother and sister, whom they have seen, cannot love God, whom they have not seen. And he has given us this command: Anyone who loves God must love their brother and sister" (1 John 4:19–21).

---

9   Smith, *Desiring the Kingdom*, 216.
10 Kierkegaard, *Works of Love*, 161.

We show mercy to our neighbor because we are completely dependent on the mercy of God. The biblical meaning of mercy goes to the heart of the human dilemma. We need mercy—not random acts of human kindness, but radical divine redemption. Those who show mercy to others are people who have been transformed by God's mercy. We acknowledge our utter dependence upon God. We are conscious of our own unworthiness and guilt. Those who are deeply moved by the mercy of God have a deep affinity for those in need of God's mercy. This is why the apostle Paul challenges us "in view of God's mercy" to offer our bodies as living sacrifices (Rom. 12:1).

The grace of the Lord Jesus Christ makes justification by faith alone possible, liberating believers from works righteousness and any possibility of self-salvation. We are saved by faith alone, but saving faith is never alone. As a motto of the Reformers suggests, "Faith alone justifies, but not the faith that is alone." Early American pastor-theologian Jonathan Edwards framed the positive tension this way: we are not saved on account of our works, but we are not saved without works.[11] I heard the late J. I. Packer quip, "Holiness is no more by faith without effort, than it is by effort without faith." Klyne Snodgrass writes, "This is not a question of earning salvation; it is a question of being and identity that determines actions. It is not a question of whether we should work. We will work. The question is from what identity will

---

11   Jonathan Edwards, "Christian Graces Concatenated Together," in *Charity and Its Fruits*, The Works of Jonathan Edwards, vol. 8 (New Haven, CT: Yale University Press, 1989), 327–29.

we work. . . . This parable may not tell us how to love our neighbor as ourselves, but it creates a reality that challenges passivity and self-interest. Loving the neighbor as oneself is difficult, but no alterative is allowed for followers of Jesus."[12]

Faith and works go hand in hand. Faith takes the lead: "For it is by grace you have been saved, through faith—and this not from ourselves, it is the gift of God—not by works, so that no one can boast. For we are God's workmanship, created in Christ Jesus to do good works, which God prepared in advance for us to do" (Eph. 2:8–10).

Jesus emphasized this same truth in the parable of the sheep and goats. The Son of Man will commend those on his right *not* for performing great signs and wonders (cf. Matt. 24:24), but for giving food to the hungry, water to the thirsty, hospitality to the stranger, clothes to the needy, care for the sick, and friendship to the imprisoned. Moreover, they do this naturally. It is part of their routine. They are not asking, "Who is my neighbor?" They are asking, "To whom am I a neighbor?" Need-meeting in the name of Jesus is what they do. It is no pious big deal. They follow Jesus, and this is what disciples who are saved by grace through faith do with their lives. The gospel of Jesus Christ plays itself out in ten thousand ways in the daily routine of ordinary selfless acts of neighbor love. There is something beautiful about the ignorance of those on the right: "Lord, when did we see you hungry and feed you,

---

12   Klyne R. Snodgrass, *Stories with Intent: A Comprehensive Guide to the Parables of Jesus* (Grand Rapids: Eerdmans, 2018), 359, 361.

or thirsty and give you something to drink? When did we see you a stranger and invite you in, or needing clothes and clothe you? When did we see you sick or in prison and go and visit you?" (Matt. 25:37–39). This is an ignorance that runs contrary to the presumption of works righteousness. It fits with "so-that-no-one-can-boast" salvation by grace through faith. Because of Jesus Christ, the righteous care for the needy.

MESSIANIC EDGE

Jesus tells the parables with a messianic edge.[13] There is an implicit self-consciousness embedded in the parables that subtly reveals Jesus's messianic self-understanding. Ken Bailey suggests that Jesus sees himself in the Samaritan: "After the failure of the listeners' religious leaders, the saving agent

---

13   John Calvin, *Commentary on a Harmony of the Evangelists: Matthew, Mark, and Luke,* vol.17 (Grand Rapids: Baker, 1981), 62–63. Calvin's opposition to an allegorical interpretation impacts his Christology. He rightly criticizes "free-will advocates" who argue that the wounded man's "half-dead" state indicates that human nature is not totally corrupt and is capable of responding to God. He condemns as well the allegorical interpretation that, as he says, "has been so highly satisfactory, that it has been admitted by almost universal consent, as if it had been a revelation from heaven. This Samaritan they imagine to be Christ, because he is our guardian; and they tell us that wine was poured, along with oil, into the wound, because Christ cures us by repentance and by a promise of grace." Calvin does not distinguish between allegorical inflation and apostolic insight. True, wine and oil do not symbolize repentance and grace, but is it so inconceivable for the one who was to die on the cross to see himself in this story? Calvin resisted this deeper meaning, writing, "I acknowledge that I have no liking for any of these interpretations; but we ought to have a deeper reverence for Scripture than to reckon ourselves at liberty to disguise its natural meaning. And, indeed, any one may see the curiosity of certain men has led them to contrive these speculations, contrary to the intention of Christ."

breaks in from outside to save, disregarding the cost of that salvation. Jesus is talking about himself. The good Samaritan offers a costly demonstration of unexpected love. . . . Jesus is demonstrating a part of the meaning of his own passion."[14]

But we can take this a step further and see in the half-dead man, robbed and scorned, stripped and beaten, a picture of Isaiah's Suffering Servant. Jesus is not only the good Samaritan but also he is the suffering servant. The man in the ditch foreshadows the man on the cross: "He had no beauty or majesty to attract us to him, nothing in his appearance that we should desire him. He was despised and rejected by mankind, a man of suffering, and familiar with pain. Like one from whom people hide their faces he was despised, and we held him in low esteem" (Isa. 53:2–3).

So we see that Jesus is the good Samaritan. We are the helpless person in the ditch, and Jesus comes to us and cares for us. But Jesus is more than that. He is God in the ditch, who takes our place on the cross. He is both the good Samaritan and the suffering servant.[15] Humanity is in the ditch and in desperate need of salvation. We are not half-dead; we are

---

14 Kenneth E. Bailey, *Jesus through Middle Eastern Eyes: Cultural Studies in the Gospels* (Downers Grove, IL: InterVarsity, 2008), 297.

15 Klyne Snodgrass disagrees, "I see no justification in the parable for any such identification. . . . It is unfair to inject Jesus (and the rest of the salvation scheme) allegorically into the parable. It is one thing to say that the theology of the parable is also the theology that drives much of Jesus's actions but quite another to say that he intended a self-representation with the story. Nor is he identified with the victim. All attempts to find Jesus (or Israel) mirrored in the parable are illegitimate allegorizing" (*Stories with Intent*, 356).

all dead in our trespasses and sins. And God gets down into the ditch to rescue us and take upon himself the penalty we deserve. Remember what Jesus said, just before this encounter with the expert: "Blessed are the eyes that see what you see. For I tell you that many prophets and kings wanted to see what you see but did not see it and to hear what you hear but did not hear it" (Luke 10:23–24). Peter echoes this theme in his epistle when he says, "Concerning this salvation, the prophets, who spoke of the grace that was to come to you, searched intently and with the greatest care, trying to find out the time and circumstances to which the Spirit of Christ in them was pointing when he predicted the sufferings of Christ and the glories that would follow" (1 Peter 1:10–11).

Helmut Thielicke says it well: "All loving is a thanksgiving for the fact that we ourselves have been loved and healed in loving." Then, we "grow into all the mysteries of God when we pass on what we have received and when we learn by experience that a disciple of Jesus becomes not poorer but ever richer and happier in giving and sacrificing and that whatever of [our] feeble strength, [we] put at God's disposal. . . . For God is princely in his giving and incalculable in the abundance of his mercy."[16]

---

16 Thielicke, *Waiting Father*, 169.

❧5❧

THE FRIEND AT MIDNIGHT

LUKE 11:1–13

Matthew presents Jesus's Sermon on the Mount and his Sermon on Parables as two distinct units, but Luke juxtaposes themes from the Sermon on the Mount, such as prayer and justice, with select parables. Luke develops Jesus's "travel narrative" (Luke 9:51–19:44) chiastically. The parable of the friend at midnight (Luke 11:5–13) corresponds to the parable of the widow and the unjust judge (Luke 18:1–8). The parables play a supporting role in emphasizing Jesus's teaching. They offer vivid images that open up the hearer's imagination to the truth. These parabolic case studies picture what it means to be a disciple of Jesus Christ. The parable of the friend at midnight is an "interrogative 'how much more' parable."[1] Luke connects the Lord's Prayer, and especially the central

---

1 Klyne R. Snodgrass, *Stories with Intent: A Comprehensive Guide to the Parables of Jesus* (Grand Rapids: Eerdmans, 2018), 437.

petition, "Give us each day our daily bread," with the friend's late night request for bread.

MIDNIGHT REQUEST

Jesus knew when he told this parable that he had the people's attention. Eastern hospitality makes it inconceivable for a friend to answer a friend's late night plea for bread to feed his guests with, "Go away. Don't bother me!" It would be utterly inconceivable. You can almost hear the crowd say, "What a jerk!" The interrogative, "Who of you can imagine someone—a friend—turning down a request for bread, even in the middle of the night, even with your kids asleep?" Jesus asks the crowd to imagine the unthinkable. Who could possibly refuse this man's request? If the sleeper didn't get up and give him bread out of friendship, he would have done it anyways out of practical convenience, just to get his neighbor to go away.

Scholars debate the nature of the persistence of the neighbor-in-need. The translation of the Greek word *anaideia* as "shameless audacity," with a negative connotation, is consistent with how the word is used elsewhere to describe a person who has no sense of shame. Such a person is willing to stoop to demeaning and offensive tactics that no self-respecting person would do in order to get his way.[2] In Jesus's story the man is rude and obnoxious, and he will not let up until he gets his bread. Thus, the clash of the two characters conveys

---

2   Snodgrass, *Stories with Intent*, 443.

a break with Middle Eastern custom on both sides, the man who refuses to get out of bed and the man who refuses to go away. The two sides are at loggerheads. In the showdown of wills, who will blink first?

A friend needs bread, not for himself, but for a guest who arrived very late. The occasion is rare and the request unique. It probably had never happened before. The "insider" hears the simple request, but he refuses to be bothered. "Don't bother me," he says. He explains that the door is locked, the children are in bed, and he can't get up. Of course no self-respecting Middle Easterner could possibly do this, but he does. The incongruity between friendship and inconvenience, revered custom and inexplicable reaction is striking. No one hearing the parable could imagine the "insider" being so selfish and rude. But even this ornery neighbor will get up and give bread to his persistent friend just to get him to go away. Jesus compares this recalcitrant insider to the gracious and responsive God who is eager to meet our needs. Jesus offers his hearers a "how much more" argument. If the insider reluctantly does the right thing after all, how much more will the loving and sacrificial God be gracious and give us every good gift.

GLOBAL NEIGHBORS

I imagine some of my African brothers and sisters can identify with the neighbor-in-need. They approach the church in the West like the friend in the parable in search of bread with shameless audacity because the need is great, even desperate. The parable captures the disparity between the haves and the have-nots, between an unresponsive wealthy church and a struggling poor church. Whether they are rude in their persistence or not, they are made to feel like a nuisance by a church rich in resources that cannot get out of bed. Their humble circumstances lead to humiliation rather than rejoicing.

A second parable pictures parental generosity (Luke 11:11–13). If a child asks for a fish, will his father or mother give him a snake instead? If he asks for eggs for breakfast will he be given a scorpion? Of course he won't. The contrast is between parents who come through in spite of their weaknesses and the Lord who gives good gifts. The meaning of these parables and our understanding is not left to chance. Right in the middle, Jesus spells it out: "So I say to you: Ask and it will be given to you; seek and you will find; knock and the door will be opened to you. For everyone who asks receives; the one who seeks finds; and to the one who knocks, the door will be opened" (Luke 11:9–10).

These two parables correspond to Jesus's teaching on prayer drawn from the Sermon on the Mount (Matt. 6:26–34 // Luke 12:22–34). There is no comparison between our ability to meet needs and God's capacity to answer our prayer. "If God cares about birds and flowers, will he not care about you? If a friend will get up and give a person bread because he needs it, will not your heavenly Father? . . . The parable teaches the certainty of a God who hears prayer and responds."[3]

---

3 Snodgrass, *Stories with Intent*, 442, 447.

HOW MUCH MORE!

Why are we so reluctant to ask? Perhaps we have been conditioned not to ask. Like the two-year-old toddler who insists on doing it himself, we are steeped in our individualism and in our vain notions of self-sufficiency. Or perhaps we are we too polite to ask. The myth of self-sufficiency dies hard. Good friends of ours were driving through town and they stopped by to have dinner and to spend the night with us. Around 1 am the smoke detector in our upstairs guest room began to beep, indicating a low battery. Our friend fiddled with the battery but to no avail. They put pillows over their heads and tried to sleep, but nothing blocked the persistent beeping noise. They even switched to another room upstairs but they still could hear it. Instead of waking me up to change the battery, they suffered all night long. They didn't want to disturb us! In the morning over breakfast they told us. We felt badly and truly wished that they had gotten us up. It would have been easy to change the battery and go back to sleep.

The fact that they didn't wake us up probably says something about our friendship. If we were really close friends, they would not have hesitated. Is our reticence to "ask, seek, and knock" a commentary on our relationship to the Lord? The Lord is not disturbed by our requests! God never sleeps and God always cares (Ps. 121:3–4).

The climax to these two "how much more" parables comes in the promise of the Holy Spirit: "How much more will your Father in heaven give the Holy Spirit to those who ask him!" (Luke 11:13). We sense that Luke has Pentecost in mind and the outpouring of the Spirit (Acts 2:1–13). The gifts we have in mind to request may have more to do with health and wealth than advancing the gospel and the kingdom of heaven. The Holy Spirit is described as the quiet member of the Trinity who comes alongside (the Paraclete) for the sake of the gospel. In the upper room, Jesus explained the work of the Spirit this way: "When he comes, he will prove the world to be wrong about sin and righteousness and judgment: about sin, because people do not believe in me; about righteousness, because I am going to the Father, where you can see me no longer; and about judgment, because the prince of this world now stands condemned" (John 16:8–11). The Spirit of truth strengthens the fellowship of disciples by inspiring biblical insight, ethical discernment, and faithful obedience. The fullness of the Spirit has more to do with making disciples locally and globally than inspiring a spiritual high.

Since Jesus's how-much-more parables emphasize the Father's responsiveness to our prayer requests, I want to end this chapter with an encouragement to pray the Psalms. The Psalms of Ascent (Pss. 120–134) are a good place to begin. They teach us that distress is a catalyst for devotion. We have set out on a journey of faith in the company of the Lord Jesus, who is our daily guardian, protector, and keeper. The apostles grasped this truth as well and reassure us that nothing shall separate us from the love of Christ (Rom. 8:35–39).

I lift up my eyes to the mountains—
where does my help come from?

My help comes from the LORD,
the Maker of heaven and earth.
He will not let your foot slip—
He who watches over you will not slumber;
indeed, he who watches over Israel
will neither slumber nor sleep.
The LORD watches over you—
The LORD is your shade at your right hand;
the sun will not harm you by day,
nor the moon by night.
The LORD will keep you from all harm—
he will watch over your life;
the LORD will watch over your coming and going
both now and forevermore.
                    —Ps. 121:1–8

Salvation and shalom are bound together. They are the gifts from God for the people of God, "so that no one can boast" (Eph. 2:9). The promise of answered prayer does not imply a trouble-free life. The psalmist offers the Lord's practical daily assurance of sure-footed grace and shade-protected companionship. But the promise of protection does not stop there. The Lord promises personally to be our "keeper" in every facet of life. Although we do not come close to meriting his loving attention, the Lord in his mercy promises to care for everything about us. The Lord promises to watch over our "coming and going both now and forevermore." This means there is no time or place outside of his loving protection. "This is our God; this is the God of our pilgrimage. This is the God of unfailing, unending watchfulness and keeping grace, the Father, the Son and the Holy Spirit, Creator, Redeemer, and Companion."[4]

---

4 Alec Motyer, *Journey: Psalms for Pilgrim People* (Nottingham, England: InterVarsity, 2009), 36.

⟡6⟡

THE RICH FOOL

LUKE 12:13–34

Luke focuses his attention on the values of the kingdom of God. In a unique sequence of parables, Luke highlights Jesus's teaching on wealth with three provocative parables: the rich fool, the unjust steward, and the rich man and Lazarus. These parables share a common interest in the subject of money and the kingdom of God. Jesus's communicational strategy speaks to the crowd, maybe even entertains the crowd, but his primary purpose is to instruct his small community of disciples. On the parable of the rich fool, New Testament scholar Klyne Snodgrass concludes, "The message of this parable is as antithetical to our thinking as any Jesus told. I know of no more difficult topic to apply personally or to the lives of modern Western Christians."[1]

The Bible has plenty to say on the subject of wealth and stewardship. Job declared in his defense from the ash heap, "If I have put my trust in gold or said to pure gold, 'You are my

---

1   Klyne R. Snodgrass, *Stories with Intent: A Comprehensive Guide to the Parables of Jesus* (Grand Rapids: Eerdmans, 2018), 400.

security,' if I have rejoiced over my great wealth, the fortune my hands had gained, if I have regarded the sun in its radiance or the moon moving in splendor, so that my heart was secretly enticed and my hand offered them a kiss of homage, then these also would be sins to be judged, for I would have been unfaithful to God on high" (Job 31:24–28). Job linked the worship of the stars to the worship of material possessions. He shunned the sin of idolatry, both the kind that captivates the modern Western materialist and the ancient pagan sun worshipper.

The prophet Jeremiah summed it up when he said, "'Let not the wise boast of their wisdom or the strong boast of their strength or the rich boast of their riches, but let the one who boasts boast about this: that they have the understanding to know me, that I am the Lord who exercises kindness, justice, and righteousness on earth for in these I delight,' declares the Lord" (Jer. 9:23–24).

Do We Practice What We Believe?

Namibian theologian Paul John Isaak begins his commentary on the parable of the rich fool (Luke 12:13–21) with a story about Mahatma Gandhi, when he was a lawyer in South Africa. This was long before he was a famous activist in his home country of India. In the village enclave of fellow Indians where Gandhi worked as a magistrate, there was a widow who could not get her teenage son to eat healthy food. He ate candy all the time. She hoped that Gandhi, as an authority figure, could convince her son to eat healthy foods instead of his sugar-rich diet. She asked Gandhi, "Will you talk to my son and tell him to stop eating sugar?" Gandhi was silent for a moment and then said, "Would you bring the boy back to me a week from now?" A week later, she brought the boy back to Gandhi and asked him again, "Will you now please tell my son to stop eating sugar?" But Gandhi replied, "I'm sorry. Would you please bring him back in another week?" A week passed, and the widow returned for the third time, only this time she was very upset over her son and frustrated with Gandhi. Finally, Gandhi agreed to meet with her son, and as she had hoped, Gandhi convinced her son that for his own good he must stop eating sugar and eat healthy food. The boy agreed and pledged to change his behavior. But as they were leaving, the widow took Gandhi aside and, after thanking him, asked, "When we first came to you, you asked us to come back in a week. Then, when we came back, you asked us to come back in another week. Why did you do that?" Gandhi replied, "Because I had not realized how difficult it would be for me to give up sugar."[2] The story ought to challenge us. When it comes to money and wealth, do our practices line up with our beliefs? It may be easier to preach this parable than to practice it.

A few years ago, a church I know fairly well redid their sanctuary. It was a beautiful, well-maintained worship space that was demolished down to its concrete slab. The new four-teen-million-dollar version only added two hundred seats, and

---

2   Paul John Isaak, *Africa Bible Commentary*, ed. Tokunboh Adeyemo (Grand Rapids: Zondervan, 2006), 1228.

the only major visual change was shifting the pulpit from the side to the center. It was built to be more energy efficient and wired with remote technology for video-taping. Ironically, today the worship space looks much the same as it did before the construction project. According to my friend, paying for it was not an issue. He said that there was enough wealth in his one small Sunday school class of retired businessmen and women to pay for it.

My wife, Virginia, and I have been involved in two ministries, a mainline church replant in Manhattan, Central Presbyterian Church (2010–2014), and a church-planting, humanitarian ministry in northern Ghana. The two ministries span the range from the wealthiest of the wealthy to the poorest of the poor. From the 1990s to 2016, we took periodic mission trips to Ghana to help out with pastor training, and for four years we flew up regularly to New York City to preach and lead Central Presbyterian Church. In recent years, the church has raised close to twenty million dollars to restore its landmark, Rockefeller-built church. During this same time, the ministry in Ghana has struggled to raise ten million dollars for a hospital to serve thousands in northern Ghana who have very little or no modern medical care. One wonders if the real challenge of globalization has yet to hit the Western church? There is no doubt in my mind that our money goes much further in rural Ghana than it does on Park Avenue in Manhattan. Yet both ministries are vitally important. Should there be a gospel-centered church in Manhattan? Yes, of course, even if the cost seems exorbitant. Should there be a modern hospital in northern Ghana run by a gospel-centered ministry? Undoubtedly there should be an excellent hospital in this vastly underserved region of Africa. Think of the many thousands that will benefit. The key here is tying the two regions, the two ministries, the two groups of believers together. This is the strategy that the apostle Paul commended to the church in Corinth, when he wrote, "Our desire is not that others might be relieved while you are hard pressed, but that there might be equality. At the present time your plenty will supply what they need, so that in turn their plenty will supply what you need. The goal is equality" (2 Cor. 8:13–14).

Luke's edition of Jesus's teaching on wealth leads with the story of the rich fool. Or, if you prefer another title, "the sensible materialist," or "the clever capitalist." Jesus pictures a clash of cultures in a story that upends the world's values and gets everyone's attention. In Luke, the exposition surrounding the parable is very similar to the Sermon on the Mount. Jesus calls for "a major redirection of how one thinks about and uses material resources."[3] Two more parables follow: the parable of faithful servants and an exuberant master (Luke 12:35–40) and the parable of faithless servants and a furious master (Luke 12:42–48).

THE MEANING OF LIFE

The parable of the rich fool is about the meaning of life (*psychē* = "life" or "soul" in Luke 12:19, 20, 22, 23). The parable is unique to Luke, but it fits nicely in the context of

---

3 Snodgrass, *Stories with Intent*, 389.

the Sermon on the Mount. "Someone in the crowd" asked Jesus to settle a dispute between himself and his brother. The question implies that Jesus was perceived as a rabbinic legal expert—a person called upon to settle legal conflicts. Apparently their father had died, and the older brother was unwilling to divide the inheritance. The younger brother was eager to get his share of the inheritance, and he sought Jesus out as a convenient authority figure to settle the dispute. One scholar explains, "Inheritance laws indicated that the eldest son should receive a double portion (Deut. 21:15–17). That brothers should live together without dividing the inheritance was optimal and praiseworthy."[4]

But Jesus wasn't buying it. He will not be manipulated into spending his time putting out fires. He was indifferent to this squabble between brothers over money. Jesus answered him curtly, "Man, who appointed me a judge or an arbiter between you?" (Luke 12:14). The vocative use of "man" implies displeasure. I imagine Jesus sounded frustrated or annoyed. What the man wants Jesus to do, Jesus is not interested in doing. Perhaps we can see ourselves in this man, for who hasn't come to Jesus wanting him to do something for us that Jesus had no interest in doing? The surface plea for justice covers over the rift between brothers and the grief over the loss of a father. Jesus refuses to see people as problems to be fixed. He invariably challenges people's expectations and refuses to treat the presenting symptom when there is a deeper, primary

---

4 Snodgrass, *Stories with Intent*, 394.

cause. The work of redemption is a whole-person concern. Nor does Jesus permit the inquirer to project his concerns and expectations onto him. Jesus is not a legal expert, nor your typical problem solver. His response gives the man a cool put-down, basically saying, "Your business is not my business. Skedaddle."

"ALL KINDS OF GREED"

The second part of Jesus's response is given to the anxious man obliquely. He addresses the crowd directly: "Watch out! Be on your guard against all kinds of greed; life does not consist in the abundance of possessions" (Luke 12:15). We are all in need of this truth, not just this man who wants his fair share of the family inheritance. The many facets of greed deserve our attention, because it is so easy to condemn one form of greed while embracing the legitimacy of other types of greed. Undoubtedly the man felt justified, but Jesus didn't see it that way. Jesus saw beyond the market value of real estate to the greater value of family relations and personal self-worth. It is always dangerous to measure oneself by the abundance of possessions.

The money at issue here is an inheritance. It is about money the man did not work for or earn. Someone else worked for it. Someone else accumulated this anticipated windfall that promised to inflate his ego and make him feel more important, more worthy, more significant, more secure. This is the danger of worldly wealth; in the eyes of the world it stands for status, success, and security. With it we're everything; without it we're nothing. Inherited wealth offers a powerful analogy to biblical stewardship, because everything we have and all of our possessions come from God and belong to God. We own nothing free and clear. We hold everything in trust.

The dynamic in play between the disgruntled younger brother and Jesus is fairly typical of many people's church experience. We Christians echo this man's complaint. We come to church wanting Jesus to do something for us. We want Jesus to find a job for us or make our marriage or our parenting go better. Our relationship with Jesus is transactional. We come to Jesus the way a client hires an expert or a consumer buys a product.

We come thinking to ourselves this or that needs fixing, and Jesus says curtly, "Mister, what makes you think it's any of my business to be judge or mediator for you?" (Luke 12:14, MSG). When we sell Jesus to the American consumer as the expert who fixes life's problems, we have done the kingdom of God a disservice. The Lord Jesus Christ is not a small "s" savior. He's not life's fix-it man and problem-solver. Things don't go better with Jesus, and anyone who says they do is lying to you. Jesus is not here to revamp your old life; he is here to give you a new life. We need the Savior. You and I have nothing to give in exchange for our soul. There are no transaction fees for services rendered, only a transforming faith based on God's mercy. We don't need advice; we need good news. We don't deserve affirmation; we need the atonement. Jesus isn't a life coach or an expert in what bothers us; he's the Savior and Lord of all.

To make this clear, Jesus tells the crowd a parable. "The ground of a certain rich man yielded an abundant harvest" (Luke 12:16). Farmers will immediately pick up on the compliment Jesus pays to the dirt. He gives a lot of credit here to the ground—it has rich, fertile, nutrient-laden soil.[5] Like an inheritance, the sensible capitalist can take no credit for the crop-yielding, wealth-producing ground. The rich fool cannot claim credit for the natural resources producing his wealth. The whole food chain belongs to God, because God has blessed the earth in ways that God has not blessed Mars with crop-growing dirt, along with animals and people that depend on the crops. The ground is not only responsible for agriculture, but for the industrial revolution and for smart phones. There's a lot more that comes out of the ground than wheat and soybeans. The natural resources necessary for producing wealth are creation gifts over which we are not sovereign.

But that is not what the sensible capitalist is thinking. He is thinking to himself, "What shall I do? I have no place to store my crops" (Luke 12:17). Would we really expect a rich fool, a little master of the universe, with a fixation on the bottom line, to think any other way? Probably not. He offers no thanksgiving to God for the soil and sun nor any credit to the laborers in the field for their tilling, seeding, and harvesting. Instead, he devises a plan that will drive up the price of his commodities. He'll tear down his barns and build

---

5   Psalm 65 describes the rich blessing of the land.

bigger ones to store his surplus crops. "And then I'll say to my life [*psychē*], 'Life [*psychē*], you have plenty of grain laid up for many years. Take it easy; eat, drink and be merry.'" John Chrysostom famously quipped, "Safe barns are not walls but the stomachs of the poor."[6]

The rich man's soliloquy provides a window, not only into his financial planning, but into his soul. We cannot conclude from Jesus's story that the man is trying to drive up the price of grain or that he is a self-centered loner who is only concerned with his own welfare. For all we know he may be a charitable giver—a regular deep-pocket philanthropist. All we can tell, and this is Jesus's point, is that his life consists of the abundance of his possessions. From his perspective, self-worth, self-esteem, and success are all quantifiable.

The main point of the parable is not about economics or stewardship per se. It is about life (*psychē*). Work and wealth are a testimony to what we value in life. The meaning of life for the rich fool revolves around his acquisitions—his stocks, bonds, securities, pension funds, and 401(k)s. "Life" (*psychē*) is the word that links this parable to the explanation that follows. Jesus said to the disciples, "Therefore I tell you, do not worry about your life (*psychē*), what you will eat; or about your body, what you will wear. For life is more than food, and the body more than clothes" (Luke 12:22–23). We can reduce the meaning of life to the basics, or we can live

---

6 John Chrysostom, *On Wealth and Poverty* (Crestwood, NY: St Vladimir's Seminary Press, 1984), 43.

life to the full. "Life" (*psychē*) is often translated "soul" and is used in the Psalms for direct self-address, as in "Why, my soul [*psychē*], are you downcast?" (Ps. 42:5).

"Soul" stands for our core identity. "Each person is a one-of-a-kind creature made in the 'image of God.' . . . [The word 'soul'] conveys a sense of enormous dignity and thorough-going relationality," writes Eugene Peterson. He goes on to say, "The term 'soul' is an assertion of wholeness, the totality of what it means to be a human being. 'Soul' is a barrier against reduction, against human life reduced to biology and genitals, culture and utility, race and ethnicity. It signals an interiority that permeates all exteriority, an invisibility that everywhere inhabits visibility. 'Soul' carries with it resonances of God-created, God-sustained, and God-blessed. It is our most comprehensive term for designating the core being of men and women."[7]

"But in our current culture," Peterson writes, "'soul' has given way to 'self' as the term of choice to designate who and what we are. Self is the soul minus God. Self is what is left of soul with all the transcendence and intimacy squeezed out, the self with no reference to God (transcendence) or others (intimacy)."[8] The sensible capitalist's quest for significance is self-determined. The measure of the man is found in himself and what he has achieved rather than in what he has received from God. He assumed a burden that was not his to shoulder,

---

7 Eugene H. Peterson, *Christ Plays in Ten Thousand Places: A Conversation in Spiritual Theology* (Grand Rapids: Eerdmans, 2008), 36.

8 Peterson, *Christ Plays*, 37.

a dehumanizing burden that invariably and unwittingly ends in disillusionment. By forsaking God and ignoring others, he walled himself off from the very meaning and purpose of life. He replaced soul with self. "This reduction," Peterson writes, "turns people into either problems or consumers."[9]

The inner monologue of the rich fool exudes self-confidence. He's in control. "This is what I'll do," he boasts. "I will tear down my barns and build bigger ones, and I will store my surplus grain. And I'll say to myself [I will say to my life . . . my soul], 'You have plenty of grain laid up for many years. Take life easy; eat, drink and be merry'" (Luke 12:18–19). This is the self-talk of the little trinity, me, myself, and I, that effectively destroys the soul and ruins lives. Failure is written all over this man's success. This is the easy life—the eat, drink, and be merry life—that runs counter to the easy yoke promised by Jesus (Matt. 11:28–30). Jesus's alternative route to happiness begins with a declaration of dependence, not independence. The first step under the easy yoke is an admission of overwhelming need, and the first feeling under the yoke is overwhelming sorrow. The key to happiness begins with poverty, not pride; sorrow, not fun. Beatitude-based living offers a radical new vision for life at its best. The rich fool scaled down the deep-seated spiritual longing for transcendence to a materialistic quest for success. For many people, the fear of God is nothing compared to the fear of personal failure. Job security means more than eternal security. People

---

9   Peterson, *Christ Plays*, 38.

who shrug their shoulders at the thought of divine judgment cringe at the thought of a recession.

Jesus made it clear that the value of the soul is beyond our means. Many people have told us that we don't have a soul, but only one person said that we can't afford one. Only Jesus said that even if I gained the whole world, I couldn't afford my soul. "What good will it be for someone to gain the whole world, yet forfeit their soul? Or what can anyone give in exchange for their soul?" (Matt. 16:26). Who we are and to whom we belong is more important than anything else about us including our net worth.

THE FOOL

The rich fool's inner monologue is abruptly interrupted by God's word. Even before his new building program could begin, God intervened. "You fool!" exclaimed God. "This very night your life [*psychē*] will be demanded from you. Then who will get what you have prepared for yourself?" (Luke 12:20). Jesus delivers "the Sunday punch," Robert Capon quips. "But God said to him, 'Fool! [The word is *áphrōn*, the same word Jesus used to denounce the Pharisees and scribes in Luke 11:40.] This night your life [*psychē*] is required of you; then who will own all this stuff you've spent so much time preparing?'"[10]

The Hebrew word for fool is *nābāl*, a word "which implies an aggressive perversity, epitomized in the Nabal of 1 Samuel

---

10 Robert Farrar Capon, *Kingdom, Grace, Judgment: Paradox, Outrage, and Vindication in the Parables of Jesus* (Grand Rapids: Eerdmans, 2002), 235.

25:25."[11] The Old Testament story of Nabal, a wealthy cattle owner, corresponds well to Jesus's parable. Nabal was approached by David with a simple request for hospitality (1 Sam. 25:8). But instead of responding graciously to his request, Nabal mocked and scorned David. "Who is this David?" he sneered, adding with a tone of contempt, "Many servants are breaking away from their masters these days" (1 Sam. 25:10). If it hadn't been for the courageous intervention of Abigail, Nabal's wife, David would have let lose the full fury of his wrath against Nabal and his whole household. One of Nabal's servants summed up his rich fool for a master this way: "He is such a wicked man that no one can talk with him" (1 Sam. 25:17). Nabal is an excellent illustration of Jesus's parable of the rich fool.

In a *quiet* line, Jesus adds, "This is how it is with one who lays up treasure for himself and is not rich in God's sight [*eis theōn*, literally, 'into God']."[12] The implication is clear, if you are into God, you won't be a rich fool who fails to understand the meaning of life. The rich fool is a poster boy for an empty life and an icon for material success who thrives on the blood, sweat, and toil of others. The modern outlook focuses on two outcomes, success and survival, ignoring the reality of salvation and judgment. The attitude of the rich fool is writ large "in the liberal democracies of the West," Leon Kass writes. "With science and technology pointing the way, the race for health, pleasure, and prosperity is rapidly becoming the only

---

11   Derek Kidner, *Psalms 1–73* (Downers Grove, IL: InterVarsity, 1973), 79.

12   Capon, *Kingdom, Grace, Judgment*, 235.

successful game in town."[13] The rich fool represents those who think primarily of themselves and use their resources selfishly, saying to themselves, "I've got it made. Take life [*psychē*] easy; eat, drink and be merry."

Following Matthew's interpretative strategy, Luke provides Jesus's explanation to the disciples. "Then Jesus said to his disciples: 'Therefore I tell you, do not worry about your life [*psychē*], what you will eat; or about your body, what you will wear. For life [*psychē*] is more than food, and the body more than clothes" (Luke 12:22–23). This interpretative bridge between parables spells out the great reversal of values in the kingdom of God. Instead of worrying about the basic necessities of life, like food, clothing, and shelter, we should be focused on trusting in our heavenly Father who has given us the kingdom. Jesus's message is as straightforward and uncomplicated as it could be. He used ravens, "who plainly are unencumbered by the kind of 'life-plans' we constantly make," as an example of God's care.[14] Ravens don't build barns (*apothēkē*, the same word used by the rich fool), but the Lord takes care of them. Wild flowers bloom in all their beauty without the least little effort. Jesus calls for a great reversal of values. Begin with trust and dependence upon your heavenly Father, and see how life's basic necessities are met by his gracious generosity.

---

13   Leon R. Kass, *The Beginning of Wisdom: Reading Genesis* (Chicago: University of Chicago Press, 2003), 7.
14   Capon, *Kingdom, Grace, Judgment*, 237.

JESUS'S HIERARCHY OF NEEDS

In 1943 psychologist Abraham Maslow proposed a theory of human motivation that consists of five levels. The most basic level is that of *physical needs*, like food, clothing, shelter, and health. The second level is *safety*; the third, *love and belonging*; the fourth, *self-esteem*; and the fifth, *self-actualization*. In order to progress up through the hierarchy of needs, Maslow believed, each level must be satisfied within the individual. When the needs of these various levels are met, the final goal is self-actualization.

Jesus's teaching turns Maslow's pyramid upside down. He boldly reverses Maslow's famous hierarchy of needs. Instead of setting our hearts on what we will eat or drink, we rely on our heavenly Father who knows our needs. We seek first his kingdom, "and all these things will be given to [us] as well" (Luke 12:31).

For many, worry is to living what air is to breathing. But Jesus says this is not the way it is with his disciples. "I tell you, do not worry about your life [*psychē*], what you will eat; or about your body, what you will wear. For life [*psychē*] is more than food, and the body more than clothes." Some believers are sadly convinced that the most spiritual thing to do is to worry over the future: the coming economic downturn, the collapse of the family, the educational crisis, the fear of getting cancer, the high cost of health care, and the growing violence in our cities. Jesus does not rule out responsible living. He didn't say, "Take no thought" or "Have no concerns." He said, "Do not worry," "Do not become anxious." Jesus forbid a "crippling anxiety that drives one to seek security by one's own efforts apart from the Father."[15] When we stop looking to our heavenly Father and start looking to ourselves, we are in trouble. Even the basic necessities of life are meant to become the raw material for trust in God.

Jesus made the connection between the sovereignty of God and the family budget. We can say all we want about our heart being right with God and our devotion being to him alone, but if we are consistently fretting about food or medicine or rent or car payments, our commitment to God is weak and distracted. A refusal to become anxious proves the integrity of our ambition to live a life worthy of our calling (Eph. 4:1). If Jesus was saying this to Westerners, he might phrase it differently: "How dare you rest your self-esteem on the clothes you wear or take pride in your gourmet food? Why are you so preoccupied with appearances and adventures that money can buy? How are you different from the people who don't believe in me? Where are your priorities? What really counts in life anyway, financial security or eternal security? Stop thinking about more, more, more, getting, getting, getting. Life cannot be measured in dollars and real estate."

Jesus lays out the soul-nurturing priorities for life and family. Instead of a constant preoccupation with the physical necessities of life, Jesus makes a case for focusing on first things. Stephen Covey demonstrates the importance of first things in an object lesson. He takes a large class jar and fills it

---

15   Robert A. Guelich, *The Sermon on the Mount* (Waco, TX: Word, 1982), 336.

with several big rocks. He then asks his audience if the jar is filled. They say "yes." Next, he adds pebbles to the jar, filling it to the top. "Now is the jar filled?" he asks. Again the audience agrees that it is filled. Then he adds sand, again filling the jar to the top. "Surely, the jar is filled now," he declares, and once again everyone agrees. But to the surprise of the audience he is still able to pour in a couple of pints of water. "Now that the jar is finally filled with rocks, pebbles, sand and water, what's my point?" Covey asks. Invariably the audience responds, "You can always pack more things in. Even when something is full you can squeeze more in." Covey politely disagrees. "No, the point of this object lesson is that if you don't fit the big rocks in first, you'll never get them in."[16]

Jesus requires a different set of "first things." Kingdom values turn everything upside down. Our natural disposition, which is to focus on our basic needs and look out for ourselves, runs counter to putting our trust in God. Our chief end is to glorify God and enjoy him forever.[17] It is not to make a name for ourselves, acquire worldly wealth, and insulate ourselves from the needs of the world. Jesus says, "Don't be possessed by your possessions. Get a life. Trust in your heavenly Father. If birds and flowers make out so well, how much more will you?" He wraps up this teaching with a personal word: "Don't be afraid, little flock, for your

---

16 Stephen R. Covey, *The Seven Habits of Highly Effective Families* (New York: Golden, 1997), 160–62.

17 G. I. Williamson, *The Westminster Confession of Faith*, 2nd ed. (Phillipsburg, NJ: P&R, 2003).

Father has been pleased to give you the kingdom. Sell your possessions and give to the poor. Provide purses [securities, investments] for yourselves that will not wear out, a treasure in heaven that will never fail, where no thief comes near and no moth destroys. For where your treasure is, there your heart will be also" (Luke 12:32–34).

In a parable attributed to Søren Kierkegaard, two robbers entered a jewelry store and did something strange; they switched all the price tags. They didn't steal anything. They just took the high-priced tags off the expensive jewelry and put them on the costume jewelry. Then they took the bargain price tags off the costume jewelry and put them on the very expensive jewelry. The next day the jewelry store opened for business as usual, and no one noticed the switch! Elated customers bought $10,000 rings for a few dollars, while others bought $9 necklaces for thousands of dollars. Kierkegaard summed it up this way: "My point is obvious, isn't it? The people of my day have no ability to tell the truly valuable from the virtually worthless. Not just in commerce but in the world of ideas too our age is putting on a veritable clearance sale. Everything can be had so dirt cheap that one begins to wonder whether in the end anyone will want to make a bid."[18]

---

18 Søren Kierkegaard, quoted in Gary Haller, "Surrounded! Knight of Faith: Søren Kierkegaard," First United Methodist Church, Birmingham, MI, August 30, 2015, http://fumcbirmingham.s3.amazonaws.com/wp-content/uploads/2015/01/Surrounded-Knight-of-Faith-Soren-Kierkeg-aard.pdf.

❧ 7 ❧

THE FAITHFUL
SERVANTS AND THE
EXUBERANT MASTER

LUKE 12:35–41

Pioneer missionary to China Hudson Taylor (1832–1905) wrote, "I'm an insignificant servant of the most illustrious Lord." Taylor's assertion prompts the question: Do we know who our boss is? Do we see ourselves as indentured servants to a wonderful Master? The apostles were quick to embrace the profile "slaves of Christ"—are we? My wife's aunt Katherine used to say, "You will know you have the heart of a servant when you are treated like one." Bob Dylan famously sang, "You gotta serve somebody." The question has always been, Who are you serving?

Christians know that they are living between the times as slaves of Christ awaiting the return of the Master. "The wise servant (slave) is the one who understands the significance of the end—whether soon or late—and lives accordingly. Wisdom is an eschatological virtue."[1] The parable of faithful servants and an exuberant master explores our behavior during the interval between the ascension and the second coming (1 Peter 5:8–11; 2 Peter 3:8–13). This eschatological parable is directed to the disciples for its ethical impact. The parable addresses not only the original band of disciples but all Christ's followers through time. As our striving for worldly wealth ceases, our striving for kingdom purposes increases. On this side of eternity we have not arrived, but we press on to take hold of that for which Christ Jesus took hold of us (Phil. 3:12).

THE MASTER IS COMING!

The parable of the faithful servants is a call to action. We eagerly await the coming of the Master. In Jesus's story, the master is coming from a wedding banquet, and the servants are expected to be watching and waiting, ready to jump into action at a moment's notice and "immediately open the door for him." It is not difficult to imagine John's vision of Jesus Christ standing at the door and knocking. "Here I am! I stand at the door and knock. If anyone hears my voice and opens the door, I will come in and eat with that person, and they with me" (Rev. 3:20).

The mention of the wedding banquet invokes two other notable wedding banquets: the wedding feast in Cana of Galilee, where Jesus turned the water to wine (John 2:1–11), and

---

1   Klyne R. Snodgrass, *Stories with Intent: A Comprehensive Guide to the Parables of Jesus* (Grand Rapids: Eerdmans, 2018), 503.

the marriage supper of the Lamb (Rev. 19:7–9; 21:1–22:17). The imagery emphasizes the coming of the Son of Man, first for the inauguration of our salvation, and second for the consummation of our salvation and the final judgment. As we await Christ's return, we are reminded, "It will be good for those servants whose master finds them watching when he comes" (Luke 12:37). The ESV translates "it will be good" as "blessed." The same phrase is used in verse 38: "blessed are those servants!" The word for "blessed" is *makarios*, the same Greek word used in the Beatitudes. Readiness for faithful service is described in two ways: being dressed for work (in the Greek, "let your loins stay girded," ESV note) and keeping your lamps burning bright. These two evocative images emphasize the constant readiness of the disciple.

The Israelites at the Exodus ate the Passover meal with their cloaks tucked into their belts and their sandals on their feet ready move out (Exod. 12:11; see 1 Kings 18:46; 2 Kings 4:29). The apostle Peter used this working class image when he challenged believers to "gird up the loins of your mind." He encouraged them to set their hope on the grace to be brought to them when Jesus Christ is revealed in his coming (1 Peter 1:13). If Peter were a coach, he might say to us, "Get your head in the game!" If he were a teacher or a manager he might say, "Roll up the sleeves of your mind." The mental image is of a near-Eastern laborer tucking up a long robe into his belt so that he could go about his work unhindered. Peter challenged believers to mentally and emotionally engage in the hard work of setting their hope on the grace of Christ. Dressing for kingdom work covers a full character description from putting on the full armor of God (Eph. 6:11–17) to dressing in compassion, kindness, humility, gentleness, and patience (Col. 3:12).

The second image calls for keeping their lamps trimmed and fueled so they burn bright. This image also triggers the biblical imagination. The light of gospel truth is designed to burn bright: "let your light shine before others, that they may see your good deeds and glorify your Father in heaven" (Matt. 5:16). This is the light of Christ that shines in the darkness "and the darkness has not overcome it" (John 1:5). It is the light that is put on a stand "so that those who come in can see the light" (Luke 8:16). Letting the gospel light shine brightly implies a vigilance and watchfulness. The parable challenges all believers to be ready and alert for the coming of the master, even if the coming of the master is in the middle of the night. Believers are tasked with readiness, no matter what. Prediction is not their job but staying alert and being ready to serve is. The priesthood of all believers stands ready to serve. This truth is meant to be played out practically among believers. It is the daily responsibility of the followers of Christ.

I asked a prospective seminary student at what time he became serious about following Christ. Ironically, the critical turning point in his life happened in a very ordinary way. He worked in a grocery store all through high school. He stocked shelves and bagged groceries. He said he loves working there now so much that when he comes home from college, the manager always fits him into the schedule. "But it wasn't always that way," he explained:

I used to hate the work. I found it totally demoralizing. I felt like I was everybody's servant. I literally despised it, but I needed the money. Then one day, when I was in a particularly bad mood, a customer calmly said to me, "You don't like working here, do you?" The comment really upset me. I didn't think people picked up on my bad attitude or, if they did, that it mattered much. But that little comment hit me like a ton of bricks, because I knew that a Christian shouldn't go around acting mad all the time. So, I got serious with the Lord. I confessed my terrible work ethic and prayed for strength to change my attitude. The change was remarkable. I realized that my job was not just about bagging groceries and stocking shelves but it was about serving Christ. I went from hating my job to loving it. I used to run from people, hide from my boss, and do as little work as possible. Now, whenever I'm at work, I enjoy the people, respect my boss, and do as much as I can. Back in my bad attitude days my shift seemed to last forever and I couldn't wait to get out of there, but now things are different. Somebody the other day said to me, "You like working here, don't you?"

THE MASTER SERVES

Jesus tells this parable with a surprising twist at the end. The master does something very unexpected when he comes.

"*Truly* I tell you," Jesus emphasized, "he will dress himself to serve, will have them recline at the table and will come and wait on them" (Luke 12:37, emphasis added). We were not expecting this—at least I wasn't. The scene brings to mind John 10:10 and Mark 10:45—"For even the Son of Man did not come to be served but to serve, and to give his life as a ransom for many." The master arrives home late and finds his faithful servants ready and waiting. He's in a hilarious mood.[2] The festive joy of the wedding has not worn off, and he honors and rewards his faithful servants by waiting on them. After a long night, he dresses like a servant and serves them breakfast. "The master's acts represent a stunning reversal of roles," writes Ken Bailey. "I know of no incident in contemporary life or in a story out of the past in the Middle East where such an incredible reversal of status appears."[3]

The line from Psalm 23:5, "You prepare a table before me in the presence of my enemies," impresses us as a huge understatement. God the host became God the crucified in order to give us the hospitality we need for salvation. The preparation God had in mind involved an unimaginable cost, beyond all comparison. Consider the most lavish state dinner, and it is absolutely nothing next to God's table grace.

Six months of pain-staking preparation is not uncommon for a full-course state dinner at Windsor Castle. No expense

2 Robert Farrar Capon, *Kingdom, Grace, Judgment: Paradox, Outrage, and Vindication in the Parables of Jesus* (Grand Rapids: Eerdmans, 2002), 241.

3 Kenneth E. Bailey, *Jesus through Middle Eastern Eyes: Cultural Studies in the Gospels* (Downers Grove, IL: InterVarsity, 2008), 373.

is spared. Every aspect of the royal event is planned in minute detail and orchestrated down to the minute. Hundreds of people are deployed in an event choreographed to perfection. Six different wine glasses for each of the several hundred dignitaries gives you some idea of the elaborate place setting. Customarily the Queen arrives early to walk the length of the banquet hall, inspecting the table and giving her approval. During the banquet, all attention will be focused on the Queen and everyone will follow her lead. Even though her role is largely ceremonial, to be in the presence of her Majesty the Queen is an honor few if any would take lightly.[4]

Now imagine the shock if the Queen broke with centuries of tradition and put on a servant's uniform and waited on her dinner guests. What if the Queen, the embodiment of dignity and royalty, became nothing more than one of the inconspicuous and anonymous waiters. Instead of presiding over the dinner, what if she served the dinner? And then, what if, and this would only happen in our wildest dreams, the servant-queen became subject to accusation and abuse? What if she was scourged and crucified? But as shocking as this scenario sounds, it is nothing compared to God the host becoming God the crucified. In Psalm 23, the table in the presence of our enemies is a metaphor; the cross in the life of Jesus was not.[5] The whole scene is most unusual, especially when we consider the fact that the one telling this story will

---

4 Douglas D. Webster, *Table Grace: The Role of Hospitality in the Christian Life* (Fearn, Scotland: Christian Focus, 2011), 24–25.

5 Webster, *Table Grace*, 24–25.

dress down in the upper room, wrap a towel around his waste, and wash the disciples' feet. The parable of the exuberant master foreshadows the coming of Christ and the wedding banquet of the Lord.

Peter was confused. He wondered if the challenge to readiness applied to everyone or just the disciples. He asked, "Lord, are you telling this parable to us, or to everyone?" Jesus answered his question with another parable. The parable of the faithful servants applies to all believers, but notice how Jesus shifts attention away from the servants to the hilarious master, who does what had never been done before. He strips down and puts on a servant's work clothes. Then, unexpectedly, and to the great delight of his servants, he serves them. There's a real reward for the servants who are alert and watchful. It is not difficult to find echoes and expressions of Jesus's Upper Room Discourse (John 13–17) and Paul's Christ hymn (Phil. 2:6–11) in this parable. According to Klyne Snodgrass, "The focus on faithfulness reminds us again that Christian faith is not about believing certain ideas but about living out convictions over the long haul. The church is often impressed with claims to faith. Claims and short-lived faith suffice for nothing. What counts is faithfulness to the end."[6]

Hebrews weans us away from our preoccupation with the start of the Christian life and focuses our attention on being faithful to the end—the perseverance of faith. Life is not a sprint; it's a marathon. Faithfulness to the end affirms faith

---

6 Snodgrass, *Stories with Intent*, 504–5.

from the beginning.[7] "Today we emphasize the New Birth," writes Peter Gillquist. "The ancients emphasized being faithful to the end. We moderns talk of wholeness and purposeful living; they spoke of the glories of the eternal kingdom. . . . The emphasis in our attention has shifted from the completing of the Christian life to the beginning of it."[8] James said it well: "Religion that God our Father accepts as pure and faultless is this: to look after orphans and widows in their distress and to keep oneself from being polluted by the world" (Jam. 1:27). Instead of being lazy or sluggish, the author of Hebrews says in effect, "Get a life. Mix it up. Put yourself in the company of the needy. Keep your eyes peeled for poor widows. Don't divert your eyes from the lame. Pay attention to them. Let's not make ministry into a mystery. Get in the game. Just do it!" He makes this appeal for *faithfulness to the end* personal. "We want each of you to show this same diligence to the very end," even as he leverages their personal hopes and aspirations as a motive for effort, "so that what you hope for may be fully realized" (Heb. 6:11). The parable of the faithful servants is in sync with the apostles' letters to the churches. Together they elaborate on what it means to be dressed and ready for service with lamps burning bright.

---

7 Douglas Webster, *Preaching Hebrews: The End of Religion and Faithfulness to the End* (Eugene, OR: Cascade, 2017), 1.

8 Peter Gillquist, "The Christian Life: A Marathon We Mean to Win?," *Christianity Today*, October 23, 1981, 22.

❧ 8 ❧

THE FAITHLESS SERVANT AND THE FURIOUS MASTER

LUKE 12:42–48

Jesus was intentional about the language and analogies that he used. He avoided "religious" terms. He distanced himself and his disciples from an overt connection to the temple and the priesthood. Instead of paralleling his followers with the temple, Jesus used a different analogy—the ordinary household and "secular saints." This gave rise to the New Testament's emphasis on the household of faith. The apostle Peter wrote, "As you come to him, the living Stone—rejected by humans but chosen by God and precious to him—you also, like living stones, are being built into a *spiritual house* to be a holy priesthood, offering spiritual sacrifices acceptable to God through Jesus Christ" (1 Peter 2:4–5, emphasis added). Peter's household-of-faith language underscores the relational nature of the body of Christ.[1] Matthew's version of this parable (Matt. 24:45–51) uses "servant" (*doulos*), whereas Luke uses "steward" (Luke 12:42, *oikonomos*) followed by the word "servant." The apostles go on to develop Jesus's household of faith analogy to underscore the relational nature of God's covenant community. The initiative for the apostolic development of this significant relational analogy lies in Jesus's parables. The household built by God *of people* is no less material, temporal, spatial, and concrete than if it had been built with stone and steel.

MANAGERIAL RESPONSIBILITIES

In response to Peter's question, "Lord, are you telling this parable to us, or to everyone?" Jesus tells another household parable, but this time the focus is on the manager. Jesus asks, "Who then is the faithful and wise manager, whom the master puts in charge of his servants to give them their food allowance at the proper time? It will be good for that servant whom the master finds doing so when he returns" (Luke 12:41–43). The master is looking for two qualities: faithfulness and wisdom— but not just faithfulness and wisdom, but faithfulness and wisdom *that lasts until the master returns*. Embedded in these

---

1   Klyne Snodgrass, *Ephesians: The NIV Application Commentary* (Grand Rapids: Zondervan, 1996), 136. This emphasis on the household of God can also be seen in Ephesians 2:19–22. With the literary care of a poet, the apostle Paul orchestrated a word play on the Greek word for "house" (**oικοs**). In Christ we are no longer *aliens* (πάροικοι), but members of God's *household* (**οἰκεῖοι**), *built on* (ἐποικοδομηθέντες) a sure foundation, and the *building* (οἰκοδομὴ) is *built together* (συνοικοδομεισθε) into a *dwelling place* (κατοικητήριον) of God.

two qualities is the consistency and continuance of faithfulness and wisdom over the span of the manager's tenure. Faithfulness and wisdom to the end affirms faithfulness and wisdom from the beginning. "The parable focuses on the unexpectedness of the coming, and the servant is caught unprepared," writes Klyne Snodgrass.[2] Jesus appears to be preparing the disciples for the interval between his ascension and second coming.

The particular managerial responsibility highlighted here focuses on feeding the servants. Faithful servant-managers provide good food on time for all the servants. The emphasis in the parable foreshadows Jesus's conversation with Peter following the resurrection. It is probably no accident that Luke records Peter asking the question that prompted the parable. Of all the things Jesus might have called Peter to do, "Feed my sheep" sounds the most mundane. Jesus didn't say, "Lead an army," "Launch a crusade," or "Compete with Rome." He didn't even say, "Build my kingdom." No one whose business it is to feed sheep is power-tripping. There isn't anything triumphalistic about obeying the command "Feed my sheep." Yet this little command, "Feed my sheep," sets the agenda for Peter's mission. The outspoken lead apostle was given no visions of heroic service. The only expectation he was given was of longsuffering, persevering, pastoral care. The sheep are in need of "feeding," not "herding"; "tending," not "catering." Years later, Peter expounded on the meaning of being a shepherd in the body of Christ when he wrote,

---

2 Snodgrass, *Ephesians*, 500.

To the elders among you, I appeal as a fellow elder, a witness of Christ's sufferings and one who also will share in the glory to be revealed: Be shepherds of God's flock that is under your care, serving as overseers—not because you must, but because you are willing, as God wants you to be; not greedy for money, but eager to serve; not lording it over those entrusted to you, but being examples to the flock. And when the Chief Shepherd appears, you will receive the crown of glory that will never fade away. (1 Peter 5:1–4 NIV1984)

Robert Capon develops the analogy of the dependable manager, full of common sense, feeding the staff on time:

After all the years the church has suffered under forceful preachers and winning orators, under compelling pulpiteers and clerical big mouths with egos to match, how nice to hear that Jesus expects preachers in their congregations to be nothing more than faithful household cooks. Not gourmet chefs, not banquet managers, not caterers to thousands, just Gospel pot-rattlers who can turn a decent, nourishing meal once a week. And not even a whole meal, perhaps; only the right food at the proper time. . . . The preacher has only to deliver food, not flash; Gospel, not uplift. And the preacher's congregational family doesn't even have to like it. If it's good food at the right time, they can bellyache all they want: as long as they get enough death and resurrection, some day they may even realize they've been well fed.[3]

Journalist Michael Pollan's documentary *In Defense of Food* examines the industrially driven Western diet to show how it has ruined our health. Pollan holds that all the processed "stuff" in the center aisles of the grocery store, with their flashy packaging screaming their outlandish health claims, represents the Western diet. Pollan won't dignify the merchandise in the center aisles as "food." He labels it "eatable food-like substitutes." The real food is in the produce section, without the fancy packaging. Pollan says, "The quieter the food, likely the healthier the food." His recommendation: "Eat food, not too much, mostly plants. Eat real food."[4] The household of faith needs servant managers who offer real food. These are the servant managers who are commended by the master: "Truly I tell you, he will put him in charge of all his possessions" (Luke 12:44).

Nevertheless the problem of spiritual malnourishment persists. Sermons become a recital of evangelical platitudes, privately prepared, without interaction with the thinking and

---

3   Robert Farrar Capon, *Kingdom, Grace, Judgment: Paradox, Outrage, and Vindication in the Parables of Jesus* (Grand Rapids: Eerdmans, 2002), 245.

4   Michael Pollan, *In Defense of Food*, http://www.pbs.org/food/shows/in-defense-of-food, based on his book of the same title (New York: Penguin, 2007).

praying community. They are publicly performed without lasting impact, usually in a style that does not flow from or depend upon the text. And these days it seems that most Christians are listening to sermons designed for someone else with the result that seekers are not evangelized and believers are not edified. One of my students described his early years in the faith this way:

> I am the product of the pop-evangelicalism of our current day. For most of my life I have sat in church while being inoculated with low levels of Christianity. With the IV drip-bag labeled "Self-Help Moralism" connected in one arm and "Daily-Devotionalism" in the other arm, I spent much of my life drifting on the tenuous edge of a coma. . . . Like a waking dream, I was living the "Christian life." . . . My world was one where the Bible had no power . . . and where preaching was like a giant pacifier. . . . We were deprived of true sustenance. In looking back, it is no wonder that I was depressed and contemplating suicide by the time I was twenty years old.

People gather every Sunday to hear what they have heard many times before. There is a large and appreciative market of religious consumers who want to be given a recital of familiar truths. However, a true stewardship of the gospel of grace ought to lead them into the whole counsel of God.

MANAGERS OF THE MYSTERIES OF GOD'S REVELATION

The apostle Paul described himself to the believers in Corinth with language drawn from this parable: "This, then, is how you ought to regard us: as servants of Christ and as those entrusted with the mysteries God has revealed. Now it is required that those who have been given a trust must prove faithful" (1 Cor. 4:1–2). We should want all spiritual leaders to see themselves in this way, slaves of Christ and stewards of the mysteries of God. The work of a pastor is not running around catering to people's felt needs and pumping up the admirers of Jesus. Stewards of the mystery of God's revelation are tasked with the responsibility of feeding the followers of Jesus. As the apostle declared,

> Preach the word; be prepared in season and out of season; correct, rebuke, encourage—with great patience and careful instruction. For the time will come when people will not put up with sound doctrine. Instead to suit their own desires, they will gather around them a great number of teachers to say what their itching ears want to hear. They will turn their ears away from the truth and turn aside to myths. But you, keep your head in all situations, endure hardship, do the work of an evangelist, discharge all the duties of your ministry. (2 Tim. 4:2–5)

The parable's positive thrust hones in on the common-sense responsibilities of the servant-manager, but then it suddenly and unexpectedly takes a negative turn. Jesus says, "But suppose the servant says to himself, 'My master is taking a long time in coming,' and he then begins to beat the other servants, both men and women, to eat and drink and get drunk" (Luke 12:45; see 2 Peter 3:9–10). There is no sympathy for the manager who fails to feed the servants, just as there is no sympathy for pastors who fail to feed the people of God. Excuses may abound, but there really is no excuse for dumbing down the gospel. The responsibility of being a steward of the gospel is clear and enduring.

The most surprising twist in the parable is not the manager's failure but the fury of the master's wrath when he comes home and finds out what happened. Literally, all hell breaks loose. The master of that servant orders him cut to pieces and sent to hell. "The word ('cut to pieces') is a gripping hyperbole to underscore the punishment of the unfaithful servant, the polar opposite of the blessing of the faithful servant."[5] Snodgrass observes that "weeping and gnashing of teeth" is rare. "This expression occurs only seven times in the New Testament, six of which are in Matthew (Matt. 8:12 // Luke 13:28; Matt. 13:42, 50; 22:13; 24:51; 25:30), all of them denoting end-time exclusion from the blessing of God."[6] Snodgrass believes that this expression "cut to pieces" may indicate that "Jesus's parable looks like an eschatological version of Psalm 37 applied to disciples through the use of servant imagery."[7]

---

5   Klyne R. Snodgrass, *Stories with Intent: A Comprehensive Guide to the Parables of Jesus* (Grand Rapids: Eerdmans, 2018), 503.
6   Snodgrass, *Stories with Intent*, 503.
7   Snodgrass, *Stories with Intent*, 502.

Jesus's contrasting profiles of faithful and faithless stewards may indeed echo Psalm 37. The psalmist describes the faithful and meek servant of the Lord (Ps. 37:11) as patient (37:7, 9, 34), generous (37:21, 26), and blessed by the Lord (37:9, 11, 22, 29), whereas the faithless and wicked stewards who abuse others are *cut off* (37:9, 22, 28, 34, 38) and gnash their teeth (37:12). The impatient and cruel manager fits the description of the wicked in Psalm 37, and Jesus describes a dramatic reversal of fortune. The wicked who have taken advantage of the righteous will be destroyed, literally, "cut off," but "those who hope in the LORD will inherit the land" (Ps. 37:9).

THE MASTER'S FURY

The abusive manager is like one of those false prophets Jesus warned his disciples about in the Sermon on the Mount. They say, "Lord, Lord, did we not prophesy in your name and in your name drive out demons and in your name perform many miracles?" But the Lord says, "I will tell them plainly, 'I never knew you. Away from me, you evildoers!'" (Matt. 7:15–23). Jesus's conclusion really needs no explanation. Jesus holds his servants accountable. We must not soften it or turn it into a mystery. Whether out of willful neglect or unwitting ignorance, servants who refuse to do the master's will suffer severe consequences. However, the opportunity to serve the Master is the servant's highest calling and greatest privilege. What is required is simple (Mic. 6:8). The cost of discipleship is not complicated. Too many sermons today drain the biblical text of its nutrients. Pastors serve up processed food heavy with saturated fats and preservatives, when what is needed is healthy food served on time to make the body of believers healthy. Snodgrass writes, "The focus on faithfulness reminds us again that Christian faith is not about believing certain ideas but about living out convictions over the long haul. The church is often impressed with claims to faith. Claims and short-lived faith suffice for nothing. What counts is faithfulness to the end."[8]

Luke's parable sequence begins with the rich fool, a secular, sensible capitalist, who lives for himself, and ends with a manager, a professing believer, who also lives for himself. Both the secularist and the religionist are held accountable for their actions. Jesus is not fooling around. He's deadly serious. He is requiring people to choose between kingdom values and worldly wealth. He is pressing people to choose between kingdom priorities and worldly anxieties. He is challenging people to choose between watching and waiting before God and running and striving in the rat race. Jesus knew what he was doing. He made it clear:

> I have come to bring fire on the earth, and how I wish it were already kindled! But I have a baptism to undergo, and what constraint I am under until it is completed! Do you think I came to bring peace on earth? No, I tell you, but division. From now on there will be five in one family divided against each

---

8   Snodgrass, *Stories with Intent*, 504–5.

other, three against two and two against three. They
will be divided, father against son and son against
father, mother against daughter and daughter
against mother, mother-in-law against daughter-
in-law and daughter-in-law against mother-in-law.
(Luke 12:49–53)

This prompted Oswald Chambers to write, "Jesus Christ
came to 'bring a sword' through every kind of peace that is not
based on a personal relationship with Himself."[9] Karl Barth
quotes John Calvin as saying, "Peace with God is contrasted
with every form of intoxicated security in the flesh."[10] Jesus
was under no illusion that the world would find his peace
acceptable. His followers can expect to experience trials and
tribulation in the world, but ultimately the peace of Christ will
prevail. "I have told you these things," Jesus said, "so that in
me you may have peace. In this world you will have trouble.
But take heart! I have overcome the world" (John 16:33).

---

9   Oswald Chambers, *My Utmost for His Highest* (New York: Dodd, Mead,
     1935), Dec. 19.
10   John Calvin, quoted in Karl Barth, *Dogmatics in Outline* (New York:
     Harper, 1959), 151.

❧ 9 ❧

THE BARREN FIG TREE

LUKE 13:6–9

Jesus gave the parable of the fig tree in the context of a public controversy about judgment. He was agitated with the crowd. He called them, "Hypocrites!" for their refusal to respond to the good news of the kingdom of God. He drew an analogy between weather forecasting and their inability to interpret what God was doing right now (Luke 12:54–56). He challenged the crowd's collective inability to respond to the truth (Luke 12:57–59). "Why don't you judge for yourselves what is right?" In a mini-parable Jesus pictured a legal dispute between two people. He made the case that it was better to settle matters out of court than to be subject to the judgment of the magistrate. Jesus urged people to get right with God *now* before they were subject to the coming judgment.

JUDGMENT

The theme of judgment continues in the crowd's reaction to breaking news out of Jerusalem. Pilate, the Roman governor, who would preside at Jesus's trial, killed a group of Galileans who came to Jerusalem to offer sacrifices in the temple. We are not given the details, but Pilate, whether literally or figuratively, had their blood mixed with their sacrifices. Presumably Pilate's action against the Galileans was a militant crackdown against any threat of rebellion. The religious leaders, who had a lot to gain by retaining the status quo, may have spun this as a tragic incident against Zealots whose punishment was deserved. Jesus countered, using the incident as a call to repentance. He responded, "Do you think that these Galileans were worse sinners than all the other Galileans because they suffered this way? I tell you, no! But unless you repent, you too will perish" (Luke 13:2–3). Instead of worrying about the guilt or innocence of these poor Galileans, Jesus says, in effect, "Don't worry about them; worry about yourselves!" The need of the hour is repentance. Act while you still can.

Then Jesus proceeded to make the same point with another tragedy in the news. Eighteen people died when a reservoir tower in Siloam associated with the water supply from Gihon to Jerusalem fell over. Jesus asked, "Do you think they were more guilty than all the others living in Jerusalem? I tell you, no!" (Luke 13:4–5). Instead of feeling morally superior because the accident didn't happen to them, Jesus confronted the crowd saying, "Unless you repent, you too will all perish" (Luke 13:5). He exposed the stubborn habits of fallen human nature. Other people's tragedies can be twisted to somehow make us feel better about ourselves when the danger of our own judgment remains real. Jesus refused to confuse these catastrophes with God's judgment. Instead he uses them as object lessons to lead his hearers then and now to repentance.

REPENTANCE

The parable of the barren fig tree follows a decisive call for repentance. Judgment is pending. "Within Luke's narrative," Klyne Snodgrass argues, "the warning functions as an introduction to the parable, which renders an explanation of the parable unnecessary."[1] The images of the fig tree and vineyard have deep symbolic significance for the people of God. It is a major image in the prophets (Isa. 5:1–7; 10:34; Jer. 8:10–13; Hos. 9:10, 16; Mic. 7:1–7; Hab. 3:16–17). Undoubtedly the crowd recognized the symbolic significance of the fig tree and the vineyard. Luke referenced the symbol in the preaching of John the Baptist: "The ax is already at the root of the trees, and every tree that does not produce good fruit will be cut down and thrown into the fire" (Luke 3:9; see Matt. 3:10). The fig tree and the vineyard are types rooted in salvation history. Their meaning corresponds to and finds fulfillment in the coming of Christ. Type and parable converge in an analogy that shapes our understanding of salvation. The various references to the fig tree offer various insights into the meaning of repentance, fruitfulness, and readiness, all of which have a bearing on our salvation.

---

1   Klyne R. Snodgrass, *Stories with Intent: A Comprehensive Guide to the Parables of Jesus* (Grand Rapids: Eerdmans, 2018), 262.

On another occasion, following Jesus's celebrated entrance into Jerusalem, Matthew writes,

> Early in the morning, as Jesus was on his way back to the city, he was hungry. Seeing a fig tree by the road, he went up to it but found nothing on it except leaves. Then he said to it, "May you never bear fruit again!" Immediately the tree withered.
>
> When the disciples saw this, they were amazed. "How did the fig tree wither so quickly?" they asked.
>
> Jesus replied, "Truly I tell you, if you have faith and do not doubt, not only can you do what was done to the fig tree, but also you can say to this mountain, 'Go, throw yourself into the sea,' and it will be done. If you believe, you will receive whatever you ask for in prayer." (Matt. 21:18–22; see Mark 11:12–14, 20–25)

The fruitless fig tree with its showy leaves becomes an object lesson of judgment. Jesus only needs to give the command and it is done. What is unexpected is that Jesus used this occasion to embolden the disciples, to give them confidence in the power of the gospel, and to reinforce the absolute certainty of the will of God. Nothing can stand in the way of the mission of God. The will of God withers fig trees and moves mountains, not the whims and wishes of selfish souls. Jesus used the fig tree to call his disciples to a robust faith. As Dale Bruner writes, "Jesus wants us to trust God boldly, confidently, assuredly, knowing that God is propitious to us through the fully satisfying work of Jesus."[2]

A few days later, Jesus referred to the fig tree again. He was seated on the Mount of Olives, giving his disciples his concluding Sermon on the End of the World, and this time the lesson of the fig tree was the immediacy of the harvest. He said, "Now learn this lesson from the fig tree: As soon as its twigs get tender and its leaves come out, you know that summer is near. Even so, when you see all these things, you know that it is near, right at the door. Truly I tell you, this generation will certainly not pass away until all these things have happened. Heaven and earth will pass away, but my words will never pass away" (Matt. 24:32–35; see Mark 13:28–31; Luke 21:29–33). The little leaves on the fig tree were a sign that the summer harvest was near. Once again the fig tree is a sign of pending judgment. The end is near.

There is no need to conflate all of these references to the fig tree into one.[3] Old Testament references to the fig tree serve as a *type* used by Jesus in multiple ways to encourage repentance, fruitfulness, and readiness. There are similarities between the parable of the fig tree (Luke 13:6–9) and the parable of the wheat and weeds (Matt. 13:24–30): "Both report a problem

---

2 Frederick Dale Bruner, *Matthew: A Commentary*, vol. 2, *The Churchbook*, Matthew 13–28 (Grand Rapids: Eerdmans, 2007), 368.

3 Robert Farrar Capon, *Kingdom, Grace, Judgment: Paradox, Outrage, and Vindication in the Parables of Jesus* (Grand Rapids: Eerdmans, 2002), 248. Capon writes, "The episode of the fig tree appears in all three Synoptic Gospels. Only in Luke, however, is it presented as a story told by Jesus on the way to Jerusalem; in Matthew and Mark, it appears in Holy Week as an acted parable—with Jesus himself actually cursing the fig tree and the fig tree withering away."

with plants, someone suggests immediate action, someone else urges delay, and both have reference to judgment for sin."[4]

The early church theologians allegorized the parable of the barren fig tree. Ambrose equated the vineyard to the Jewish people. The barren fig tree symbolized their failure to respond to the message of God, even though God visited them three times, first with Abraham, second with Moses, and finally with the Incarnate One. "Augustine understood the vineyard as the world," writes Snodgrass, "the fig tree as the human race, the three times as God's relation with humanity before the Law, under the Law, and under grace, the gardener as saints in the church, and cultivation and fertilization as teaching on humility/penitence and sorrow for sin."[5] The challenge for today's Christian is not to read too much into the parable and over-interpret the meaning of the barren fig tree. Snodgrass cautions, "Once again, parable interpretation is not about finding correspondences but about determining how an analogy works, yet analogies do have correspondences. We cannot begin to interpret this parable without finding metaphorical significance, but how far should we push the images? . . . Again, the important point is knowing when to stop interpreting."[6]

PRODUCTIVITY

Like the parable of the wheat and the weeds, the main point is the patience of God. God's mercy goes beyond the nature of

---

4   Snodgrass, *Stories with Intent*, 259.
5   Snodgrass, *Stories with Intent*, 260.
6   Snodgrass, *Stories with Intent*, 263.

things (Lev. 19:23–24). The only true response is repentance, for
the kingdom of God has come. Fig trees normally do not need
much care to bear fruit, but the gardener goes all out in an effort
to revive true productivity. Snodgrass draws this conclusion:

> If the privilege of being God's people does not lead
> to productivity, it leads to judgment. Especially for
> Luke, conversion involves both a break from sin and
> production of fruit, that is, life lived in obedience to
> the will of God. With this parable Israel is depicted
> as in a perilously similar position to the fruitless
> vineyard. Israel should have been like a fruitful tree,
> the very symbol of divine prosperity; instead she
> was fruitless and faced judgment. . . . The Christian
> church stands under the indictment of this parable
> as much as Israel ever did.[7]

Robert Capon allegorizes the parable in such a way as
to land the Father and the Son in a debate, if not an argument. The gardener, Capon reasons, is the Christ-figure,
who "invites the owner of the vineyard into forbearance
and forgiveness that the barren fig tree continues to live by
grace." Capon makes much of the gardener's insistence to
"leave it alone," which he interprets to mean unconditional
forgiveness is available on the basis of Christ and his cross.
Capon argues categorically that Jesus did not come to judge

---

7   Snodgrass, *Stories with Intent*, 264–65.

the world, but to save the world (John 12:47), and therefore all judgment is abandoned in the wake of the cross. Capon does not put much stock in the narrative playing a key role in interpretation. He wants to say that our repentance is unnecessary, because God's grace abounds. All is forgiven; there's no need for repentance. He writes:

> He [Jesus] does not come to see if we are sorry: he knows our repentance isn't worth the hot air we put into it. He does not come to count anything. Unlike the lord in the parable, he cares not a fig for any part of our record, good or bad. He comes only to forgive. For free. For nothing. On no basis, because like the fig tree, we are too far gone to have a basis. On no conditions, because like the dung of death he digs into our roots, he is too dead to insist on prerogatives. We are saved gratis, by grace. We do nothing and we deserve nothing; it is all, absolutely and without qualification, one huge, hilarious gift.

Surely the parable of the barren fig tree underscores God's patience (2 Peter 3:9) and the power of God's grace to invoke true, heartfelt repentance. But in a follow-up reflection on the debate between the landlord and the gardener—between the Father and the Son—Capon forces a wedge between the Father and the Son in a conflict that has absolutely no grounds, let alone a hint, in the Bible. He writes:

And all because there is indeed a Vinedresser. I can love Jesus. As I said, I don't know about his Father. The only thing I can say about God the Father is that he's lucky to have such a loveable Son. Sometimes I think that if I had to go by his track record instead of just taking Jesus's word for his good character, I wouldn't give him the time of day. And I don't know about the Holy Spirit either. So much hot air has been let off in his name that if Jesus hadn't said he was sending him, I'd write him off too. But Jesus I can love. He does everything, I do nothing; I just trust him. It is a nifty arrangement, and for a deadbeat like me, it is the only one that can possibly work. As long as I am in him, I bear fruit. As long as his death feeds my roots, I will never be cut down.[8]

This interpretation may sound exciting and dramatic, but it leaves us outside of the biblical loop. It doesn't work for several reasons. First of all the Bible never offers even the slightest hint that there is an internal conflict within the Trinity. To imply that God the Son takes a different approach to our salvation than God the Father or God the Spirit is unthinkable. Jesus was constantly reiterating that the Father and he were one (John 10:30). Besides revealing an unheard of intimacy with the Father through his prayer life, fellowship with the disciples, and his teaching, he claimed to be the only saving way to the Father

---

8   Capon, *Kingdom, Grace, and Judgment*, 251.

(John 14:6). Jesus left no doubt as to his relationship with the Father. He said, "By myself I can do nothing: I judge only as I hear, and my judgment is just, for I seek not to please myself but him who sent me" (John 5:30). To pit the Son against the Father or the Spirit is contrary to everything we know about the Holy God in three persons blessed Trinity.

Second, Luke emphasizes Jesus's concern for timely repentance and the certainty of divine judgment—two giant truths found everywhere in the Bible. Capon has uprooted the meaning of the parable of the fig tree. He pulled the truth up from its roots. He has argued that repentance is inconsequential—beneath the dignity of God to receive and impossible for humans to give. He has argued that because of Jesus's death on the cross there is no judgment for sin, and all are saved regardless of whether or not they repent and turn to God for mercy. Capon pushes the meaning of mercy to a false conclusion. If he were a medical doctor, he would be sued for malpractice. Instead, he is a physician of the soul. The potential harm is far greater. It is a perversion of grace to strip the person of a meaningful response to the love of God. Jesus calls for repentance and warns of dire consequences if we refuse. As surprising as it may seem, redemptive love, like romantic love, is willed by God to be a mutual love. It is an asymmetrical love to be sure—the love of the all-providing King for his bride—but our repentance, our turning to the Beloved in good faith, is not just hot air, it is what Christ the King expects, empowers, and enjoys.

❧ 10 ❧

THE GREAT BANQUET

LUKE 13:22–14:27

Jesus knows that truth told slant puts religious types on edge and calls into question the unbelief that masquerades as belief. He used the parable of the great banquet to expose the excuses people give for not entering the kingdom of God. The red line he drew between the excluded and the included shocked everyone, because those who thought they were excluded were included and those who thought they were included were excluded. Jesus called into question insider confidence, and he called humble outsiders into fellowship. He warned the self-righteous who justified themselves, to make every effort to enter through the narrow gate. But Jesus made it clear that their theoretical openness did not cover up their practical indifference. Rhetorical religion never substitutes for faithful obedience. Jesus's verdict was sobering: "I don't know you or where you come from. Away from me, all you evildoers!" (Luke 13:27).

The excuses Jesus exposed in his description of the narrow door and in the parable of the great banquet were the kind of excuses people gave when they were only thinking of themselves. Jesus deals here with the polite side of rejection. He challenges those who take their religion seriously, but who resist the invitation of God. He is in dialogue with decent people who pride themselves on thinking about God, but on their own terms. They are nice people. C. S. Lewis said it well: "A wholesome, integrated personality is an excellent thing. [But] a world of nice people, content in their own niceness, looking no further, turned away from God, would be just as desperately in need of salvation as a miserable world—and might even be more difficult to save."[1]

THE NARROW DOOR

Someone in the crowd asked Jesus, "Lord, are only a few people going to be saved?" Undoubtedly the questioner assumed that he was an insider in good standing. If indeed there were only a few saved, he was one of them. The inquiry has a theoretical air about it. It is the kind of religious question that is good for a theological bull session. As was his custom, Jesus deftly reframed the question. He turned an abstract debate into a personal challenge. Jesus responded, "Make every effort to enter through the narrow door, because many, I tell you, will try to enter and will not be able to" (Luke 13:24). Insiders will be outsiders and outsiders will be insiders. And by the time the truth of the matter sinks in, it will be too late. Jesus said to his listeners, "Then you will say, 'We ate and drank with you, and you taught in our streets.'" But the owner of the

---

1   C. S. Lewis, *Mere Christianity* (New York: MacMillan, 1960), 182.

house will reply, "I don't know you or where you come from. Away from me you evildoers!" (Luke 13:26–27). Familiarity should not be confused with fellowship. Those who thought they were home free are excluded. Meanwhile, those who felt like strangers were welcomed with open arms. Jesus said, "People will come from east and west and north and south, and will take their places at the feast in the kingdom of God. Indeed there are those who are last who will be first, and first who will be last" (Luke 13:29–30).

If you heard Jesus tell this story about the narrow door— insiders excluded, outsiders included—how would you feel? Jesus was talking to the very people who thought the story of salvation was all about them, but instead of bolstering their confidence he challenged their place in the story. "There will be weeping there, and gnashing of teeth, when you see Abraham, Isaac and Jacob and all the prophets in the kingdom of God, but you yourselves thrown out" (Luke 13:28). In the first instance, it appears that Jesus's teaching applies to the Jews, who thought that they were home free whether they responded to the Messiah or not. But in the second instance, it applies to anyone who places their confidence in themselves or in their religious tradition, rather than in the mercy of God. Familiarity with Christianity is no substitute for the faith and faithfulness of Christ. Attending religious services is not the same as worshiping Jesus as Lord. Decency and respectability are a far cry from taking up your cross and following Jesus. Listening to sermons may be a good habit to cultivate, but listening alone, without a personal response and practical obedience to the word of God, is not helpful and over time may harden the heart and stiffen the will.

JESUS WILL NOT BE MANAGED

The Pharisees tried to manage Jesus. They wanted to contain and control him. Their party loyalty and religiosity apparently made it impossible for them to recognize that Jesus was the Messiah. They really had no idea who they were dealing with. They thought they could defuse the political situation and the religious controversy by getting Jesus to go away. "Leave this place and go somewhere else. Herod wants to kill you" (Luke 13:31). But Jesus was determined to fulfill the mission. He had already set his face toward Jerusalem, which was ground zero in salvation history (Luke 9:51). It was in the region of Jerusalem that Abraham almost sacrificed his son Isaac, and it was just outside of Jerusalem that God was about to give up his one and only Son for our salvation. Jesus stated his purpose bluntly, "I must press on today and tomorrow and the next day—for surely no prophet can die outside Jerusalem!" (Luke 13:33).

Jesus knew he was heading for the climax of his ministry in Jerusalem. It was there that the will of God and the will of humans would meet at the cross in a life-and-death struggle. "O Jerusalem, Jerusalem, you who kill the prophets and stone those sent to you, how often I have longed to gather your children together, as a hen gathers her chicks under her wings, but you were not willing!" (Luke 13:34 NIV1984). This is the high-stakes setting for Jesus's parable of the great banquet.

Those who thought they had an inside track on their quest to satisfy the righteousness of God have boldly positioned themselves against the yet-to-be-recognized Messiah. They stand proudly as his enemies. Ironically, those who assumed they were favored by God were in reality bound for hell. Jesus tried to impress upon them the seriousness of their rejection of the Lord's Anointed One, but they didn't get it. They were adamant in their refusal to believe. In one instance, suspicion and curiosity prompted a prominent Pharisee to host dinner with Jesus as the dubious guest of honor.

TENSION AROUND THE TABLE

Luke reports that Jesus was carefully watched. From the moment he walked through the door, his words and actions were scrutinized. There never has been anything attractive about this kind of hospitality. Yet, as we all know, this kind of socializing is fairly typical and readily apparent at many social gatherings. Human nature, with its propensity for pettiness and peevishness, takes a prominent seat at the table. Subtle innuendos, carefully phrased put-downs, and games of one-upmanship are standard fare even among friends. On this special occasion, Jesus was not among friends but among critics and rivals who were ready to pounce. He was in the company of bloated egos with inflated notions of self-righteousness. He wasn't invited to a celebration; he was invited to an interrogation. You can imagine the Pharisees saying, "If we can't get rid of him once and for all, we can at least make his life miserable."

Jesus was not to blame for the tension at the table, yet it could not be avoided. From the beginning, it was a setup, a trap set by the Pharisees ready to spring. And right there in front of him was a man suffering from dropsy (edema). His body retained large amounts of fluid. Congestive heart failure was a likely cause. We don't know if the Pharisees had concluded that this man was suffering because of his own sin, but they were using him to test Jesus. He may have been a strategically placed guest, or maybe he just showed up because he heard Jesus was there. Either way, he provided the kind of challenge the Pharisees were looking for. It was the Sabbath, and Jesus would have to either reject the man or reject the Sabbath. Luke frames the tension perfectly: "There in front of him was a man suffering from dropsy" (Luke 14:2 NIV 1984)

Turning to the Pharisees, Jesus asked, "Is it lawful to heal on the Sabbath or not?" (Luke 14:3). His question was met with silence. It was undoubtedly a long, protracted, embarrassing silence. This is the kind of silence that revealed the chasm between the Pharisees and Jesus. The Pharisees met human need with silent judgment and unspoken condemnation. Jesus met human suffering with compassion and healing. Luke described the healing in three quick phrases: "So taking hold of the man, he healed him and sent him away" (Luke 14:4). Instead of ignoring the man, Jesus embraced him. Then, he followed up the healing miracle with another question for the Pharisees. "If one of you has a son or an ox that falls into a well on the Sabbath day, will you not immediately pull him out?" (Luke 14:5). His question exposed their hard-heartedness and their self-serving application of the law. These self-designated insiders were really outsiders to the mercy and grace of God.

Luke's account gives us a sense of the contrast between the Pharisee's tension-filled dinner and Jesus's description of the great banquet. We were meant to view the two descriptions side by side. The suspicion and silent disapproval of the Pharisee's dinner is set in contrast to the grace and joy of the great banquet. These two radically different forms of hospitality have nothing in common. Jesus noticed how the guests vied for places of honor at the table, prompting him to tell a mini-parable about a wedding feast. "When someone invites you to a wedding feast, do not take the place of honor," Jesus warned, "for a person more distinguished than you may have been invited. If so, the host who invited both of you will come and say to you, 'Give this person your seat.' Then, humiliated, you will have to take the least important place. But when you are invited, take the lowest place, so that when your host comes, he will say to you, 'Friend, move up to a better place.' Then you will be honored in the presence of all the other guests. For all those who exalt themselves will be humbled, and those who humble themselves will be exalted" (Luke 14:8–11).

Undoubtedly everyone at the table got the surface meaning of Jesus's moralistic point. If you want to save yourself from embarrassment, don't presume to be more important than you are. Be humble. But Jesus had a deeper meaning in mind, one in keeping with his reoccurring theme: "the last will be first and the first will be last" (Luke 13:30). Jesus chided the prominent Pharisee on his guest list: "When you give a luncheon or dinner, do not invite your friends, your brothers or sisters, your relatives, or your rich neighbors; if you do, they may invite you back and so you will be repaid. But when you give a banquet, invite the poor, the crippled, the lame, the blind, and you will be blessed. Although they cannot repay you, you will be repaid at the resurrection of the righteous" (Luke 14:12–14). With that said, I don't imagine the so-called prominent Pharisee was planning on inviting Jesus to dinner ever again. Unexpectedly, at least for the host, Jesus assumed a prophetic stature, spoke in an authoritative voice, and dominated the table discussion.

Our hospitality is a demonstration of the grace of God and a foreshadowing of the kingdom of God. Luke does not tell us how the senior Pharisee responded to Jesus, but someone tried to rescue this tense and awkward moment with an enthusiastic comment: "Blessed is the person who will eat at the feast in the kingdom of God" (Luke 14:15). The "benediction" implies that those at the dinner party felt that they were the chosen ones—the elect. If anyone was going to be feasting in the kingdom of God, they were. This unfounded confidence in their own righteousness and pride of race was matched by their skepticism and suspicion of Jesus. The relationship between self-righteous superiority and hard-hearted blindness is important to note.

In the message that follows, Jesus says in effect, "Wait a minute! Watch out! Those who assume they are *in* are really *out*!" Jesus confronted their suspicions, rebuked their silence, and challenged their pride, but there was no evidence that his message was penetrating their hard hearts. The well-intentioned attempt to lighten the mood and send everyone home feeling good about themselves was countered by Jesus's friendly, subversive speech. He began the parable of the great banquet, "A certain man was preparing a great banquet and invited many guests."[2] The invitations were sent out, and the preparations were made ready. Jesus captures the movement of God on our behalf in this single line. The subtext is clear: the kingdom of God has come. The trajectory of the parable points to the cross and the resurrection. The long-standing invitation is on everyone's calendar; today is the day. The servants are sent out to inform the guests, "Come, for everything is now ready" (Luke 14:7). But instead of receiving an enthusiastic response, the servants get lame excuses from everyone. Unbelievable. Maybe we can imagine this in the West, where the imperial self reigns, but in the Middle East—no way! The great banquet

---

2 Snodgrass, *Stories with Intent*, 305–6. Snodgrass argues that Luke's great banquet (Luke 14) and Matthew's royal wedding banquet (Matt. 22) are similar but distinct parables: (1) There is very little verbal correspondence between the two accounts (of the 223 words in Matthew 22:1–14, only twelve are identical in Luke 14:15–24). (2) Both parables are framed differently in the narrative. Luke's parable is closely related to his three dialogues on discipleship (9:57–62), the three requirements of discipleship (14:26–33), and the comparison of the days of the Son of Man to the activities and judgment in the days of Noah and Lot (17:26–31). Matthew's parable of the wedding feast is close to and apparently shaped by the parable of the wicked tenants. (3) Snodgrass asks, "Is it not likely that Jesus spoke a given parable on a number of occasions and in different contexts, adapting it each time, perhaps to the circumstances? A parable like that of the banquet, especially if it was a challenge to Jesus's contemporaries, may have been told numerous times in various places and forms" (310).

represents the joy of community, the fulfillment of expectations, and the reality of shalom. It was hardly something to
be easily dismissed with mundane excuses. When Jesus said,
"They all alike began to make excuses," the crowd must have
gasped in disbelief. Who would do such a thing?

MUNDANE EXCUSES

Jesus tells the story with three excuses, which recalls the
parable of the seed and soils, with its three negative soil types:
the hard-packed, seed-resistant ground; the rocky ground that
permits only shallow growth; and the ground overgrown with
thorns. We need not over analyze these three ordinary, everyday excuses.[3] The first person bought a field and decided that
now was the opportune time to see it. The second person wanted to test-drive his new oxen. And the third person begged
off because he was recently married. Today we might not be
so shocked. Compared to first-century Middle Easterners, I
imagine we are more moody and fickle. We make excuses all

---

3 Snodgrass (*Stories with Intent*, 315) writes, "How does one know to assign
   representational significance to some features of the parable and not to
   others? No reasonable person would identify specifically the three people
   who reject the invitation or the elements in the excuses. No one assigns
   significance to the poor, lame, blind, and crippled; they are treated literally or at least understood as summarized social outcasts. Why then do
   interpreters feel the various times the servant went out must have representational significance? . . . The expectation of an eschatological banquet
   . . . [means] that the host of that meal is either God or the Messiah. The
   servant points to emissaries from God who bring the invitation, but only
   in general terms. All that is needed in the analogy is people who reject and
   others to whom the invitation is extended. The parable does not invite
   speculation to identify any other feature."

the time. We live in the moment. Individual whim trumps loyalty to community. In the story, Jesus means for us to see these lame excuses as thinly veiled insults. With good reason, the master was provoked. His invited guests knew for some time that this day was coming. Mundane matters of business and family could wait for another day. Everyone knew that the master had gone to considerable expense preparing for the banquet. Everything was ready.

The angry homeowner told his servant, "Go out quickly into the streets and alleys of the town and bring in the poor, the crippled, the blind and the lame." The servant reported to the master that what he requested had already been done, adding, "Sir . . . there is still room." One way or another the master was set on having a full house. "Go out to the roads and country lanes," he ordered the servant, "and make them come in, so that my house will be full. I tell you, not one of those men who were invited will get a taste of my banquet" (Luke 14:21–24). The master implies that even if the original invitees changed their mind and wanted to come to the great banquet, they no longer could. The opportunity was gone; the invitation was officially withdrawn. Joseph Fitzmyer writes, "Those who are excluded from the banquet have only themselves to thank; God will not drag the unwilling into it against their will."[4] "The focus of the parable is on the invitations spurned by one group and extended to others unexpectedly,"

---

4 Joseph A. Fitzmyer, *The Gospel according to Luke: The Anchor Bible*, 28a (New York: Doubleday, 1985), 2:1053.

writes Snodgrass. "This is what is given prominence by the structure. The question the parable addresses is not 'What counts as shame and honor?' or 'What should be one's attitude to the poor?' but 'Who will be present at the banquet?'"[5]

THE HOST

The master's final word is a word of judgment against those who were called but refused to come. The verb "to call" (*kaleō*), translated "invite," is used twelve times in this passage (Luke 14:8, 9, 10, 12, 13). The master's angry verdict against such people pledged that they would not even get "a taste" of the banquet. The parable of the great banquet implies a great reversal. Those who thought they were the elect, those self-justifying religious wonks who were judging his every move, face exclusion because of their refusal to respond to the call of God through the one sent by God—Jesus, the Christ. God's call opens up the fullness of the gospel to all people Jew and Gentile alike. The invitation goes out to the ends of the earth. To receive this call is to be blessed, chosen, predestined, redeemed, saved by grace, and rooted and established in love (Eph. 1:3–14).

The Lord Jesus chose the great banquet as a metaphor for the joy and fellowship of his Presence. Like the prodigal son who was welcomed home with a feast and celebration (Luke 15:23), we anticipate that glorious day of unspeakable joy. The lover's words in the Song of Songs can become our words: "He

---

5   Snodgrass, *Stories with Intent*, 313.

has taken me to the banquet hall, and his banner over me is love" (Song 2:4 NIV1984). What a day of rejoicing that will be! The Lord is not only our Shepherd but our Host: "You prepare a table before me in the presence of my enemies. You anoint my head with oil; my cup overflows. Surely goodness and love will follow me all the days of my life, and I will dwell in the house of the LORD forever" (Ps. 23:5–6).

The voice of the host and the voice of Jesus merge when he says, "I tell you, not one of those who were invited will get a taste of my banquet" (Luke 14:24). We are meant to hear this parable as a warning against thinking that we have a privileged place in the kingdom of God regardless of our responsiveness to the coming of God (Luke 19:41). The sin of presumption is the danger to be avoided. The people who glibly excused themselves from the celebration of salvation because of their mundane affairs hits too close to home for comfort. Are we eager to respond to the presence of God? Do we share the Lord's desire for a full house? Are we ready and willing to bring in "the poor, the crippled, the blind and the lame" (Luke 14:21)? Jesus used this parable to process his own experience of being rejected as well as to promote a faithful resilience in spite of opposition, and so should we.[6]

Jesus spoke the parables of the narrow door and the great banquet in an atmosphere of suspicion, skepticism, silent disapproval, and elitism. He was not received well. His target audience didn't respond with joyful anticipation, but with

---

6 Snodgrass, *Stories with Intent*, 316–17.

evident disdain and disapproval. They thought they had an inside track on salvation, but Jesus showed them otherwise. The Jews thought they were *in* because of their heritage and their religion. Many today, Jews and Gentiles alike, think they are *in* because God would never, ever exclude them from salvation. But Jesus shows us otherwise. We can choose to make excuses or we can choose to receive Christ's invitation. If we choose excuses, we have no one to thank for exclusion but ourselves.

In the letter to the church of Laodicea, the apostle John receives an unforgettable vision of Jesus entreating professing believers to open up their lives to him. "Here I am! I stand at the door and knock. If anyone hears my voice and opens the door, I will go in and eat with him, and he with me. To him who overcomes, I will give the right to sit with me on my throne, just as I overcame and sat down with my Father on his throne. He who has an ear, let him hear what the Spirit says to the churches" (Rev. 3:20–22). We either offer excuses, or we receive the embrace of the risen Lord Jesus Christ.

❧ 11 ❧

THE TOWER BUILDER
AND THE KING AT WAR

LUKE 14:25–35

T he inclusiveness of the kingdom of God is pictured in the parable of the great banquet. Privileged religious insiders are excluded because of their excuses, and underprivileged outsiders are included because of their responsiveness to the king's gracious and compelling invitation. Luke follows up this description of radical inclusiveness with teaching on the radical cost of discipleship. Jesus intended the church to live in the dynamic synergy of gospel invitation and costly discipleship. By divine design we are meant to struggle in the *positive* tension between an inclusive invitation and a radical commitment.

Between the parable of the great banquet and the parables of the lost sheep, lost coin, and lost sons, Luke underscores Jesus's emphasis on the cost of discipleship. He juxtaposes the joy of the great banquet with the demands of cross-bearing discipleship. Jesus is quick to insist on the transformation of admirers into followers. The cost of discipleship is a significant theme throughout Luke's travel narrative (Luke 9:51–19:44). The whole section is bracketed with the demands of discipleship and the warning to calculate the cost.

> No one who puts a hand to the plow and looks back is fit for service in the kingdom of God. (Luke 9:62)

> I tell you that to everyone who has, more will be given, but as for the one who has nothing, even what they have will be taken away. (Luke 19:26)

CHRIST-LESS CHRISTIANITY

In 1850, the Danish Christian thinker Søren Kierkegaard argued that when the church no longer distinguishes between people who admire Jesus and those who follow Jesus, we have a situation best described as Christianity without Christ. This Christ-less Christianity preaches individual empowerment and redefines faith as a private, hidden inwardness instead of a genuine life commitment to Jesus Christ. Evangelism entertains rather than convicts, and ethics is guided by the spirit of the times and cultural respectability. Christianity without Christ substitutes a moralistic rich young ruler for a cross-bearing disciple.

Kierkegaard acknowledged that it was easy to blur the distinction between admiration and obedience and mistake an admirer for a follower. Jesus may be celebrated as the answer for every question, the slogan for every praise, and the solution for every problem. Everything is in the name of

Jesus, but no one is willing to become like Jesus. Admiration replaces discipleship. Jesus is a symbol for success, an icon for living, but no one imitates his life. The church that entertains the admirers of Jesus and caters to their felt needs inevitably attracts a host of self-absorbed weaklings who have no intention of changing their egocentric ways. They use their many weaknesses to lobby the church into paying attention to them. They tend to be narcissistic, hungry for attention, eager to have their opinion heard and absorbed in their own story.

Kierkegaard boldly opposed Christ-less Christianity and insisted that the life of Jesus "from beginning to end, was calculated only to procure *followers*, and calculated to make *admirers* impossible."[1]

> His life was *the Truth*, which constitutes precisely the relationship in which admiration is untruth. . . . But when *the truth*, true to itself in being the truth, little by little, more and more definitely, unfolds itself as the truth, the moment comes when no admirer can hold out with it, a moment when it shakes admirers from it as the storm shakes the worm-eaten fruit from the tree.[2]

For Kierkegaard the difference between Christianity without Christ, and Christianity with Christ, is the difference

---

1 Søren Kierkegaard, *Training in Christianity*, trans. Walter Lowrie (Princeton, NJ: Princeton University Press, 1957), 232.

2 Kierkegaard, *Training in Christianity*, 239 (emphasis original).

between admiring Jesus and following Jesus. Disciples are called to become like Jesus. They understand that following Jesus is not optional. It is a prerequisite for living the normal Christian life. We are not talking about an advanced level of spirituality or a higher order of commitment, but basic New Testament Christianity. As Jesus said, "A student is not above his teacher, nor a servant above his master. It is enough for the student to be like his teacher, and the servant like his master" (Matt. 10:24–25 NIV1984).

Søren Kierkegaard held that the desire to admire instead of imitate was not the invention of bad people: "No, it is the flabby invention of what one may call the better sort of people, but weak people for all that, in their effort to hold themselves aloof."[3] Instead of working out their salvation with fear and trembling, admirers choose the features of Christianity that they like best, such as inspirational services and programs that will meet their needs. Some churches seem to cater to the spirit of admiration. They attract large numbers of admirers and make little effort to preach the cost of discipleship. Admirers follow an iconic, heroic Jesus, but he is not the crucified and risen Lord.

Helmut Thielicke describes admirers this way: "For many people this Jesus of Nazareth is a figure which, to be sure, does not really sustain their lives, but nevertheless gives some comfort because of the fact that someone like him ever existed." Thielicke goes on to say that such a Jesus is not the

---

3 Kierkegaard, *Training in Christianity*, 237.

real Jesus at all, but a figment of the admirer's imagination. The real Jesus "is constantly wrenching us out of this self-made dreamworld. . . .We need repeatedly to be astonished, oftentimes even chilled, by this Figure, who is completely different from what we make in our dreams and fantasies."[4] This is exactly what Jesus does by teaching us to calculate the cost of discipleship over against love of family. He makes it a matter of common-sense wisdom. Have we counted the cost?

COUNTING THE COST

"Large crowds" kill discipleship. Jesus wastes no time placating admirers. He goes for the jugular. "If anyone comes to me and does not hate father and mother, wife and children, brothers and sisters—yes, even their own life—such a person cannot be my disciple" (Luke 14:26). Why does Jesus tell us to love our enemy and hate our family when the world expects us to hate our enemy and love our family? For one reason only: he is Lord. "Love" and "hate" are words used for their shock value to underscore absolute devotion to the Lord Jesus Christ in any and all situations. There is no relationship outside the sphere of his sovereignty and our devotion. Because of Christ, the enemy deserves our love and the family member our "hate," which is to say, family ranks below the Lord. The difference between my loyalty and love for the Lord and my loyalty and love for my family is as great as the difference between love and hate.

---

4 Helmut Thielicke, *The Waiting Father: Sermons on the Parables of Jesus* (New York: Harper & Row, 1959), 148.

Love for the Lord and love for family need not be rival loves when they are ranked relative to the Lordship of Jesus Christ.

Helmut Thielicke asks, "Would it ever occur to me that the devil could use the love I have for my child in order to separate me from God?"[5] If God has given us children, are we not bound to love them and care for them? Yes. For sure. But the question, and it's a complicated one, is how do I really love my children? Most parents admit that at times their well-intentioned love has been unloving. We struggle over the difference between loving and spoiling, encouraging and condoning, disciplining and enabling. How do I really love my child? How do I rank my child's involvement in sports with his or her growth in the grace and admonition of the Lord? Do we dote on our children instead of showing them the affection of Christ Jesus?

David Goetz raises a similar concern in *Death by Suburb: How to Keep the Suburbs from Killing Your Soul*. He discusses the dangers of turning children into immortality symbols, objects of parental self-glorification who bear the burden of having to prove parental significance. Goetz writes, "You know you're on the right course when your children are less immortality symbols and more living stories of God's grace."[6] For Goetz, "Life, then, is found not in immortality symbols but in mortality symbols." He writes, "A father in early midlife recently commented about his special needs son who was approaching his teenage years: 'God has been

---

5   Thielicke, *Waiting Father*, 152.
6   David L. Goetz, *Death by Suburb: How to Keep the Suburbs from Killing Your Soul* (San Francisco: Harper, 2006), 58.

merciful, patient, and steady through our experience with Jacob. I loathe the thought of who I might be had God not brought him into my life.'"[7]

Good parents don't just attend to their children's needs, they carry them in their heart. Parents who are disciples of Jesus learn what Jerry Sittser experienced: "I once *performed* as a parent; now I *am* a parent."[8] Parenting is the most highly integrative calling that we can possibly fulfill. "The parent's main task," writes Eugene Peterson, "is to be vulnerable in a living demonstration that adulthood is full, alive and Christian."[9]

Let's be clear. The love of family is an integral part of costly discipleship. What Jesus meant by his radical comparison was that family must never become an excuse that distances us from following him. Loving our family provides the opportunity for loving the Lord our God with all our heart, mind, strength, and soul, and our neighbor as ourselves. Jesus was in the habit of driving his truth home in radical ways, in ways much bolder than we often acknowledge. One way to hear this message differently is to imagine the Tuscaloosa pastor on Sunday morning saying from the pulpit, "If you are truly serious about following Lord Jesus Christ you will hate Alabama football." I am afraid some people would not wait for an explanation before bolting for the door.

---

7 Goetz, *Death by Suburb*, 190–91.
8 Gerald L. Sittser, *A Grace Disguised: How the Soul Grows through Loss* (Grand Rapids: Zondervan, 1996), 90 (emphasis original).
9 Eugene H. Peterson, *Growing Up with Your Teenager* (Old Tappan, NJ: Revell, 1976), 18.

Can sports be an integral part of cross-bearing discipleship? Yes, indeed. What Jesus rejects is the temptation to make too much of sports, to turn sports into a god placed alongside Christ. When sports becomes a competitor against the Lord for our devotion and worship, we need to hear Jesus's radical word and repent. Sports can provide a significant opportunity to serve the Lord Jesus with our whole being and our neighbor as ourselves. Sports was never meant to be the excuse that distances us from following Christ.

WHO AMONG YOU?

The parable of the tower builder appeals to everyday common sense to warn the prospective disciple to weigh the cost of discipleship. Who would start to build a tower without calculating the cost of the project? No one. No self-respecting person would intentionally subject themselves to such an unnecessary embarrassment, especially in an honor/shame culture. Once again, no king would ever pick a fight with a king whose army was twice the size of his army. It would be equally foolish for anyone to decide to follow Jesus without weighing the cost of discipleship.

Some scholars suggest that these two similar parables warn in two different directions.[10] The tower builder must count the cost of discipleship, but the king must count the cost of non-discipleship. "In the first parable Jesus says, 'Sit down and reckon whether you can afford to follow me.' In the second parable he says: 'Sit down and reckon whether you can afford

---

10   Snodgrass, *Stories with Intent*, 386.

to refuse my demands.'"[11] There is a price to be paid either way. Regarding this theme, two passages from well-known Christian thinkers deserve to be placed side by side. The first is from Dietrich Bonhoeffer's classic attack against "easy believism" in *The Cost of Discipleship*, and it is followed by Dallas Willard's cogent description of the cost of non-discipleship. Bonhoeffer writes,

> Cheap grace is grace without discipleship, grace without the cross, grace without Jesus Christ, living and incarnate. . . . It is costly because it cost a person his life, and it is grace because it gives a person the only true life. It is costly because it condemns sin, and grace because it justifies the sinner. Above all, it is costly because it cost God the life of his Son: "You were bought at a price," and what has cost God much cannot be cheap for us. Above all, it is grace because God did not reckon his Son too dear a price to pay for our life, but delivered him up for us. Costly grace is the Incarnation of God.[12]

Dallas Willard writes:

> Non-discipleship costs abiding peace, a life penetrated throughout by love, faith that sees everything in the

---

11 A. M. Hunter, *Interpreting the Parables* (Philadelphia: Westminster, 1960), 65.

12 Dietrich Bonhoeffer, *The Cost of Discipleship* (New York: Macmillan, 1963), 47–48.

light of God's overriding governance for good, hopefulness that stands firm in the most discouraging of circumstances, power to do what is right and withstand the forces of evil. In short, it costs exactly that abundance of life Jesus said he came to bring (John 10:10). The cross-shaped yoke of Christ is after all an instrument of liberation and power to those who live in it with him and learn the meekness and lowliness of heart that brings rest to the soul. . . . The correct perspective is to see following Christ not only as the necessity it is, but as the fulfillment of the highest human possibilities and as life on the highest plane.[13]

Luke closes this section with a final word picture used by Jesus to describe true discipleship: it is salty. "Salt is good," Jesus said, "but if it loses its saltiness, how can it be made salty again? It is fit neither for the soil nor for the manure pile; it is thrown out" (Luke 14:34–35). Jesus reiterates three times "you cannot be my disciple": if you don't hate your life, if you don't carry your cross, and if you don't give up everything, "you cannot be my disciple." The clarity is penetratingly absolute. It is impossible to miss the message.

---

13   Dallas Willard, *The Spirit of the Disciplines: Understanding How God Changes Lives* (New York: Harper Collins, 1999), 263

❧ 12 ❧

THE LOST SHEEP,
THE LOST COIN,
AND THE LOST SONS

LUKE 15:1–32

Klyne Snodgrass entitles what traditionally has been called the parable of the prodigal son as the parable of the compassionate father and his two lost sons. "For some it is the gospel within the gospel, or even the most beautiful short story ever told. . . . This is a two-stage, double indirect narrative parable. In its two stages are two 'discourses.' It is the longest of Jesus's parables and has more discourse than any other parable."[1] A double indirect parable is one in which the subject matter and the people in question are both changed to enable insight from a new perspective.

---

1 Klyne R. Snodgrass, *Stories with Intent: A Comprehensive Guide to the Parables of Jesus* (Grand Rapids: Eerdmans, 2018), 117, 118. Snodgrass links this parable to Gen. 33; Deut. 21:17–21; Pss. 103, 133; Prov. 24:30–34; 27:10; 28:7, 19; Jer. 31:18–20; and Mal. 3:7.

There are straightforward associations in the parable with God, sinners, and the "righteous." Snodgrass argues that the details of the parable have purpose, "but they are not allegorical representations." Thus, the details of the prodigal's flight have a purpose—to convey the prodigal's degradation, especially to the Jews hearing the story, but they don't stand for theological realities. Again, the father's extravagant actions picture the father's love, but they do not stand for theological ideas. The robe, the ring, the shoes, and the fatted calf do not represent something other than full restoration.[2] N. T. Wright believes the parable portrays the exile and restoration of Israel. It is the story of Israel in miniature (Jer. 31:18–20).[3] Snodgrass writes, "No parable provides as much material for theological reflection as this one."[4]

THE COMPASSIONATE FATHER

Since this parable is very familiar to many, I aim to come at it slant and build on the parental analogy. At first glance, the Bible has little to say about parenting, especially if we are looking for a "how-to" parenting guide. There appears to be a real lack of explicit prescriptive material on parenting in the Bible. We don't find a biblical list of the ten easy steps for effective parenting, but what we do find is God's wisdom in

---

2 Snodgrass, *Stories with Intent*, 136.
3 See N. T. Wright, *Jesus and the Victory of God: Christian Origins and the Question of God*, vol. 2 (Philadelphia: Fortress, 1996), 125–31, 242, 254–55.
4 Snodgrass, *Stories with Intent*, 141.

how to be a person who knows the Father. Instead of being given a set of parenting do's and don'ts, we learn what it means to be like our heavenly Father. We discover the relationship between being in Christ and becoming a good parent.

The parable of the lost sons, along with the parables of the lost sheep and the lost coin, are all about God's persistent, passionate grace for the lost. The Lord is like the waiting father who longs for his lost son. The Lord is like the shepherd who leaves his flock in the open country and searches for that one lost sheep until he finds it. The Lord is like the woman who will not rest until she finds her missing coin. The audience for these three parables is divided into two groups: "tax collectors and sinners," who gather around Jesus "to hear him," and the Pharisees and the teachers of the law, who stand on the edge of the crowd muttering among themselves, "This man welcomes sinners and eats with them" (Luke 15:2). Luke encourages us to see the difference between those who listen and those who mutter.

All three parables focus on God's saving grace for the lost. The first two prepare us for the parable of the lost sons. It is interesting to explore the parable from the angle of parenting. For parents who follow Jesus, the core issue is *not* educating children for a successful career. It is *not* about raising them so that they are decent, law-abiding, drug-free, nice people. It is about parenting in such a way that our sons and daughters respond to the grace of God. It is about disciple making. The Father's love is offered to lost sinners for the sake of their salvation. A fresh approach to this familiar parable calls for the parent to be like the heavenly Father.

The parable invites us to identify with all three characters. If we are in the "far country," alienated and estranged from God, we are invited to come home and experience the love of God. If we are like the older son—dutiful, religious, meritorious, but unaware of God's grace and mercy—we are invited to celebrate the Father's love and enter into the joy of the Lord. However, we often miss the invitation to model ourselves after the main character in the parable, the loving father.

When my uncle Paul died, we traveled to Wisconsin for his funeral. Paul was a committed Christian, who was known for his love and friendship. He lived into his eighties, not as an admirer of Jesus, but as a follower. He was gifted in relating to people, especially young people. He made all kinds of people feel comfortable in his presence. He demonstrated genuine interest and real concern for others. He had a way of showing compassion and bringing Christ into people's lives that was authentic and meaningful. Many, including scores of young people, came to his memorial service. Several grandchildren spoke, eulogizing their grandfather and giving credit to the power of the gospel in his life. They thanked the Lord for his wisdom, friendship, and love. I was impressed with how attentive everyone was to the testimony of the young people.

Then the pastor came to pulpit, and with an air of self-importance, he announced that it was now his responsibility to preach the gospel. He said it just that way, even though the young people had already been testifying to the gospel in the life of Uncle Paul for half an hour. The pastor's sermon text was Luke 15, the parable of the prodigal son. Without commenting on what had already been said, he launched into his sermon. He began by stressing the lostness of Uncle Paul. "We all know that at some point Paul Haumersen was lost. He had to be lost, so he must have been like the prodigal son."

The only person in the story the pastor thought he could identify my uncle with was the prodigal, the lost son who needed to come to his senses in the far country and return home to receive his father's love. It never occurred to the preacher that the life we were remembering and celebrating was a beautiful testimony to the father's love. The pastor might have explored how the gospel-shaped life of Paul Haumersen reflected the love of the father. Instead, it seemed like the elder brother in the parable, the one who represented the religious leaders, was delivering the sermon, and he had to emphasize the lostness of Uncle Paul in order to make Jesus look good.

We may hesitate to make the waiting father a model for our love, even though it is natural for a loving parent to contemplate this parable and see themselves in the longsuffering father. There are three people we can identify with in the parable. There are two lost sons, not just one. One lost son is a secularist; the other is dutifully religious. One is a hedonist; the other, a legalist. One is self-centered; the other is self-righteous. We are reserved about identifying with the father's love. Perhaps our reticence has more to do with our aversion to responsibility than our reverence for God. To see the heavenly Father's love as the model for our love sets the bar far too high for those who think humanistically. But for those in Christ, the model of the father's love is compelling.

The love of the father sets the standard against which the prodigal rebels, but the father's love eagerly waits for the return of his child.

In the Sermon on the Mount, Jesus said, "Be perfect, therefore, as your heavenly Father is perfect" (Matt. 5:48). He expected his followers to surpass the righteousness of the Pharisees and the teachers of the law with a heart-righteousness (Matt. 5:20). It is fitting for a true child of God to take after the heavenly Father. Instead of reacting against others with resentment, revenge, and retaliation, Jesus called for an alternative model based on the Father's love. Our family likeness comes through "when we love with an all-embracing love like his."[5] As Jesus said, "Whoever does the will of my Father in heaven is my brother and sister and mother" (Matt. 12:50). Thus, the power of this parable is found not only in receiving the heavenly Father's embrace, but in modeling the heavenly Father's love. Whether we identify with the younger son or the older brother, we have to realize that we are called to be like the Father, full of compassion, waiting to extend mercy, longing for the homecoming.

PRODIGAL FATHERS

When lost sons fail to come to their senses before having their own children, they become prodigal fathers. There is no age limit on running away from God or resenting the Father's

---

5 John R. W. Stott, *Christian Counter-Culture: The Message of the Sermon on the Mount* (Downers Grove, IL: InterVarsity, 1978), 122.

love. Sons can easily reach their forties or fifties and still refuse to come home. They can starve to death emotionally and spiritually in the far country, having cut themselves off from their Lord and their family.

A pastor friend of mine heard from a stranger that his father had died. Twenty-eight years ago his father had abandoned his wife and his two sons for another woman. For almost three decades his father moved around the country, rarely spending more than a year in one place. When he died, he was living in a trailer park in Florida. He told some of his friends that he thought his son was a pastor in Colorado. In an attempt to let his family know that he died, one of his trailer-park friends contacted a pastor he knew in Colorado who recognized the name and was able put him in touch with his sons. The two sons flew to Florida for his funeral. The service was attended by several friends from the trailer park. At the graveside, the funeral-home pastor asked if the sons wanted to speak. The oldest son said a few words, followed by his brother who spoke until he broke down in sobs. After the service, they went through their father's belongings. They discovered a prayer journal in which their father had listed his daily prayer concerns. At the top of the list were the names of his two sons. In that very difficult experience, there was a note of God's grace.

Some people cannot read the parable of the prodigal son without feeling the pain and loss of their prodigal father, who is radically different from the father pictured in the parable. When the bonds of love between parent and child are broken by abandonment, abuse, disinterest, or selfishness, we may find it especially difficult to relate to God as our heavenly Father. Some people say they cannot imagine God's love because their families are too dysfunctional and broken. They feel they are living in the far country but to no fault of their own. They identify with the pain of the lost son in the far country, but they have no home to go back to. For those who suffer this estrangement, it is important to say how much our heavenly Father loves and longs for them. In spite of prodigal fathers, God's love redeems, forgives, restores, and reconciles. Like the father in the story, their heavenly Father stands ready to embrace them. The parable affirms the psalmist's hope, "Though my father and mother forsake me, the LORD will receive me" (Ps. 27:10).

There is no hint in the parable of a father out of touch with his children or emotionally distant. The father pictured here is fully present, emotionally engaged, and responsive to both sons. He is neither passive nor aggressive, but considerate and respectful of his sons. He freely uses the language of love. Traditionally, the focus has been on the first son, but the Father relates to both sons. When the father goes out to plead with the older son and reassure him of his love, he refers to him affectionately as his child (*teknon*).

Biblical scholars emphasize that the father in Jesus's parable does not fit the Middle Eastern stereotype of a father. What father would divide up his property and give his son a share of his inheritance before he died? The younger son's request is tantamount to wishing his father dead so he can get his inheritance. No self-respecting Middle Eastern father would humiliate himself by running to his estranged son, throw his arms around him, and kiss him. Scholars have difficulty imaging a father pleading with the older son to accept his decision to kill the fattened calf. Not only does the father suffer the shame of a rebellious son, but he then shames himself by lowering himself to plead with his self-righteous son. He gives up his inheritance, then he lavishes affection on his wayward son when he returns home, and finally, he begs his hardhearted older son to accept his loving ways. This highly unusual father contradicts cultural expectations. He appears to have little concern for Middle Eastern dignity. His affection for his sons transcends tradition. Yet as Snodgrass maintains, "The father's actions are not so exaggerated and unexpected that they fall outside the range of human behavior. While some fathers may reject prodigals or require conditions for acceptance, others express tenderness and love."[6]

Jesus's description of the father is not tethered to culture but to biblical revelation. The precedent for the father lies not in cultural customs but in the Bible. Jesus has in mind the heavenly Father, not your typical Middle Eastern father. It may be dramatically inconsistent for a Middle Eastern father to divide up the inheritance before he dies, but God the Father does it all the time. "He causes his sun to rise on the evil and the good, and sends rain on the righteous and the unrighteous" (Matt. 5:45). God blesses rebellious prodigals

---

6 Snodgrass, *Stories with Intent*, 133.

with good health and great talents every day. A Middle Eastern father may find it humiliating to run after his son and display such compassion, but such love belongs to the heavenly Father.

> As a father has compassion on his children, so the LORD has compassion on those who fear him; for he knows how we are formed, he remembers that we are dust. (Ps. 103:13–14)

Like God the Father, the father in the parable is not willing that any should be lost (Matt. 18:14) but that "everyone [should] come to repentance" (2 Peter 3:9). A Middle Eastern father might have disowned his son and cut him off, but not the Father known to Jesus. A Middle Eastern father might never have pleaded with his older son, but our heavenly Father is entreating us all the time. Undoubtedly we were meant to see in this parable the love of the Father in the love of the Son. The titles given by the prophet are shared by Father and Son: "Wonderful Counselor, Mighty God, Everlasting Father, Prince of Peace" (Isa. 9:6). The parable reflects the apostle's doxology, "Praise be to the God and Father of our Lord Jesus Christ, the Father of compassion and the God of all comfort" (2 Cor. 1:3).

THE LOVING FATHER

Parents who are concerned about their children coming to God can learn a great deal from how Jesus shows us the heavenly Father's love. This parable encourages us to put ourselves in the place of the father and model in our families

God's gracious love for us. Several important truths are worth noting. First, the failure of the two sons is no reflection on the father. Jesus tells the story of a rebellious son and a resentful son in order to reveal the heavenly Father's love. The sins of the sons are not because of the father. The sons do not fail because of some deficiency or inadequacy on the part of the father, but because of their own willful reaction against the father. Unlike our heavenly Father, we make mistakes. No parent is perfect, and many of us have a keen sense of our inadequacy, but faithful parents can have rebellious, resentful children. Sometimes we stop showing the love we should because we feel like failures. We blame ourselves for our children's rebellion, and we experience deep feelings of failure. The father in the parable is able to continue loving his sons because he does not absorb their failure as his own. We should learn from this model. Blaming ourselves for sons or daughters who insist on going into the far country and living as they please will interfere with loving them and praying for them.

Second, it is significant that the rebellious son had to leave his father's presence to live as he pleased. As long as he lived at home, he was not free to engage in his wild living. Grace is the outstanding characteristic of the father's response to his prodigal son, but such grace is only evident against the clear teaching of the law of God. If the father had been a permissive father instead of a loving father, the son could have done just as he pleased in the presence of the father. The fact that he could not points to the God-honoring will of the father. In fact, the law of the father undoubtedly contributed to the younger son's radical and rebellious request for his inheritance. The father's love placed limits on the freedom of the younger son, who found it necessary to distance himself from the presence of the father's righteousness and love.

In the parable, there is a profound sense of the distance between the presence of the father and the far country, but this is often not the case today. Prodigal sons and daughters do as they please and still live at home. Christian parents often tolerate children who show little respect for parental authority or obedience to the will of God. I believe the parable is instructive at this point. A Christian way of life and a pagan way of life cannot coexist in the same household, under the same roof, at least not for an extended period of time. Perhaps prodigals should move out, even if it means that they receive a portion of their inheritance!

The Christian community has at times unwittingly contributed to prodigal rebellion. We have naively instituted a rite of passage for prodigals by sending them off to university to "sow their wild oats." Campus life becomes the occasion for some young people raised in Christian homes to squander their lives and their wealth in cultural conformity and moral depravity. They are not defined as prodigals, and there is no clear break with their Christian home. Yet their rejection of God's will is evident and costly. They become victims of their choices, just like the prodigal son. We need to do a better job teaching our sons and daughters what it means to be resident aliens and chosen outsiders in a culture that does not practice Jesus's kingdom ethic. The apostle Peter writes,

> Do not live the rest of your earthly lives for evil human desires, but rather for the will of God. For you have spent enough time in the past doing what pagans choose to do—living in debauchery, lust, drunkenness, orgies, carousing and detestable idolatry. They are surprised that you do not join them in their reckless, wild living, and they heap abuse on you. (1 Peter 4:2–4)

With that said, we must understand that the grace and compassion of the father for his son is completely consistent with the son's inability to live any way he pleased in the presence of his father. Law and grace go together in the will of God and in faithful parenting.

Third, the son's experience in the far country confirms what we know of the world. The world affords the freedom to live as we please, but this freedom is often accompanied by cruelty. For a while, a selfish world may be a fun and exciting place to be, but inevitably a selfish world turns against its own, and they become victims. Whether they fall through addiction or success, poverty or luxury, loneliness or fame, a selfish world exacts its "pound of flesh." The pursuit of selfishness always proves painful. When the prodigal "came to his senses," he couldn't stop thinking about his father. He knew he didn't merit the father's love, but he needed the father's love. "So he got up and went to his father." Sadly, the goodness of God is often not perceived until we see the evil of the world. The grace of God is not grasped until we see our own wickedness. Henri Nouwen meditates on this state of lostness:

> As long as I keep looking for my true self in the world of conditional love, I will remain "hooked" to the world—trying, failing, and trying again. It is a world that fosters addictions because what it offers cannot satisfy the deepest craving of my heart. . . . "Addiction" might be the best word to explain the lostness that so deeply permeates contemporary society. Our addictions make us cling to what the world proclaims as the keys to self-fulfillment: accumulation of wealth and power; attainment of status and admiration; lavish consumption of food and drink, and sexual gratification without distinguishing between lust and love. These addictions create expectations that cannot but fail to satisfy our deepest needs. As long as we live within the world's delusions, our addictions condemn us to futile quests in "the distant country," leaving us to face an endless series of disillusionments while our sense of self remains unfulfilled. In these days of increasing addictions, we have wandered far away from our Father's home. . . .
>
> I am the prodigal son every time I search for unconditional love where it cannot be found. . . . I am constantly surprised at how I keep taking the gifts

God has given me—my health, my intellectual and emotional gifts—and keep using them to impress people, receive affirmation and praise, and compete for rewards, instead of developing them for the glory of God. . . . The prodigal son's "No" reflects Adam's original rebellion.[7]

The heavenly Father waits for grace to bring about repentance and confession: "Father, I have sinned against heaven and against you. I am no longer worthy to be called your son" (Luke 15:21). Professor Snodgrass draws out the power of this parable: "If Scripture seeks to give us an identity, which it does, this parable is a prime identity-shaping text. It says, in effect, that humans are not legitimately inhabitants of the far country, that they are not prodigals or slaves. Rather, they are children of their father and belong to their father. . . . Grace lets you be who you are supposed to be even though you do not deserve to or may not want to. The elder son is suspicious of joy and sees himself as equivalent to a servant, but the father insists that he is a son as well."[8] The prodigal son is seen here as a type for Israel. If the people in Malachi's day had simply said what the prodigal said, "Father, I have sinned," God's case against the people would have been dropped.

Fourth, we can learn from the unconditional love of our heavenly Father how to love our children. If our children have

<hr>

7   Henri J. M. Nouwen, *The Return of the Prodigal Son: A Story of Homecoming* (New York: Image Books, 1994), 42–43.

8   Snodgrass, *Stories with Intent*, 141.

rejected the grace of God, we can love them by longing for their return and being prepared to welcome them with open arms. Love is demonstrated not only in the embrace that comes at the end of the journey home, but in the waiting and praying that parents do as they hold their children in their heart. Parents who have experienced the embrace of the Father see themselves in the love of the waiting father. We are not only the recipients of this love but the embodiment of this love. The description of the father's love helps us to visualize what our love should be like: "But while he was still a long way off, his father saw him and was filled with compassion for him; he ran to his son, threw his arms around him and kissed him" (Luke 15:20). Even as God's love for us is immediate, costly, and unrestrained, so our love should be. Love holds nothing back. "Quick! Bring the best robe and put it on him. Put a ring on his finger and sandals on his feet. Bring the fattened calf and kill it. Let's have a feast and celebrate. For this son of mine was dead and is alive again; he was lost and is found" (Luke 15:22).

Fifth, not only do prodigal sons sometimes become prodigal fathers, but resentful sons can become resentful fathers. They may be decent, hardworking fathers, but they measure life by what they achieve, not by what they receive by grace. They selfishly resist becoming loving fathers out of pride and anger. In the parable, the oldest son lives in the presence of his father's love without ever paying attention to his father's heart or entering into his father's passion. He has all the privileges of sonship, but feels like a hired hand. He is bound by duty—slaving away. Is the father to blame for his oldest son's resentment? He accuses his father of favoritism and ingratitude. He whines, "You never gave me even a young goat so I could celebrate with my friends" (Luke 15:29). But the charges are groundless. Far from being indifferent, the loving father has left the celebration to plead with his oldest son. The resentful son refers to his brother as "this son of yours" and insists on defining him by his sinful past, but the loving father pleads with his oldest son, "My son, you are always with me, and everything I have is yours. But we had to celebrate and be glad, because this brother of yours was dead and is alive again; he was lost and is found" (Luke 15:31–32). The oldest son could write off his younger brother with a derogatory reference to "*this son of yours*," but the loving father insists on celebrating, "because *this brother of yours* . . . was lost and is found."

In the parable of the prodigal son, it is the example of the father's love that catches the attention of mothers and fathers. If our heavenly Father "did not spare his own Son, but gave him up for us all" (Rom. 8:32), how then shall we love our daughters and sons? If our heavenly Father has embraced us by his grace through the forgiveness of our sin, how much more should we be willing to love our children and do whatever it takes to show them the love of God in Christ. The embrace of the Father's love is a picture of salvation, but many today are not looking for salvation. They are looking for significance. Lost sons and daughters today long for meaning and purpose. It is more likely that they frame the challenge of life as a quest for survival than a search for salvation. For many, *redemption* is reduced to getting a lucky break or a moment of affirmation. Life is a struggle for survival fueled by the human spirit and the existential self. But in the parable of the lost sons, life is a struggle in our soul between self-rule and God's will, and it can only come to resolution by the grace and mercy of God. Apart from the saving grace of the Lord Jesus Christ, there is no hope, but with Christ we can experience an abundant life even in affliction and suffering.[9]

---

9 Douglas D. Webster, *The Christ Letter: A Christological Approach to Preaching and Practicing Ephesians* (Eugene, OR: Cascade Books, 2012), 31–33.

❧ 13 ❧

THE SHREWD MANAGER

If parables are truth told slant, the parable of the shrewd manager may be the most slanted.[1] Jesus juxtaposes the self-serving strategy of the world with the self-sacrificing strategy of the kingdom of God. If we distance the parable from its gospel context, all bets are off and the interpretation is up for grabs.[2] But if we respect Luke's placement of the

---

1 Klyne R. Snodgrass (*Stories with Intent: A Comprehensive Guide to the Parables of Jesus* [Grand Rapids: Eerdmans, 2018], 406–10) lists a number of possible interpretations, such as the following: 1) The steward's radical action in the world serves as an analogy for radical action in another sphere. 2) The parable teaches the right use of resources and the validity of God's standards. The steward made the master look like a righteous man in the eyes of the community. 3) The steward has foregone his own usurious commission to win favor. 4) The parable is an eschatological warning to sinners to entrust everything to God's mercy. 5) The parable is about the master's conversion from greed to honor. 6) It is an eschatological warning to Israel. "The parable is an analogical argument, not an allegorical interpretation" (410).

2 Robert Farrar Capon (*Kingdom, Grace, and Judgment*, 307) argues that the parable (Luke 16:1–9) is independent of the extraneous material to follow (Luke 16:10–15). The unjust steward is a Christ-figure showing

parable in its textual context and pay attention to the tension in the text, we will see Jesus's straightforward interpretation of the parable.

The way we handle worldly wealth proves which operating system we are running on, the world's software package or the kingdom of God's. If money is our master, we are operating like the devious, self-serving manager in Jesus's parable. Whatever it takes to get ahead is our goal. The name of the game is survival. We are operating according to a self-serving rationale. But if the Lord is our master, we see money ("unrighteous wealth," Luke 16:11 ESV), as a strategic way to reflect the priorities of the kingdom of God. The way of the world, with its "me-first" mentality and its self-serving strategies, is modeled by the shrewd manager.

THE PRODIGAL MANAGER

The shrewd manager has something in common with the prodigal son in the previous parable (Luke 15:11–32). They are both wasting someone else's possessions. But if the point of the parable of the lost son is that wherever sin is,

---

"that grace cannot come to the world through respectability. Respectability regards only life, success, winning; it will have no truck with the grace that works by death and losing—which is the only kind of grace there is." This interpretation makes the shrewd steward a countercultural hero who is willing to buck the system. Kenneth E. Bailey (*Jesus through Middle Eastern Eyes: Cultural Studies in the Gospels*, 332–342) agrees and contends that Luke 16:9–13 is best interpreted independent from the parable. Bailey holds that the parable is about grace. The manager is condemned for his actions "but praised for his confidence in his master's gracious nature" (340). The steward is a rascal but a clever rascal who depends on the mercy of the master.

grace abounds, the point of the unjust steward is that the world knows how to handle money according to worldly principles better than Christians know how to handle money according to kingdom principles. Given the context, the point is clear. "The real theme of the story is money: the leading role is played by 'unrighteous mammon.'"[3] There is no dichotomy between spirituality and material concerns. There is a monetary side to true spirituality that ought to reflect the Master's will. Worldly wealth plays a role. The first principle of biblical stewardship is that everything we have belongs to God who is the true Master of the universe. We hold nothing free and clear. As Abraham Kuyper famously said, "There is not a square inch in the whole domain of our human existence over which Christ, who is Sovereign over all, does not cry, Mine!" This is not the peevish complaint of the spoiled child but the reverent testimony of the voice of creation (Psalm 19).

Martin Luther drew attention to the Lord's "special term for wealth"—"'the mammon of unrighteousness' because of the dishonest use to which it is put." But later in his sermon he adds a further reason. "The Lord does not call Mammon unrighteous solely because some use it dishonestly; he calls it also something alien, because it is a temporal treasure and does not endure forever, as does the spiritual. Eternal life is our (that is, the Christians') treasure. It is the real treasure that

---

3   Helmut Thielicke, *The Waiting Father: Sermons on the Parables of Jesus* (New York: Harper & Row, 1959), 95.

remains for eternity. But, Mammon is an earthly treasure; it is not ours but the worldling's. It is a perishable treasure and does not endure forever. It is distributed in this world, most of all among the heathen and the unbelieving, although believers also make use of it."[4]

The simplicity of the story focuses our attention. An un-ethical manager swindles his master and then shrewdly defends himself when he is caught. We need not burden the account with extraneous speculation and Middle Eastern customs.[5] We need not argue about legal due process and customary financial negotiations. It is a distraction to ask why the master did not launch an investigation. Nor are we expected to inquire into commission fees and interest rates for olive oil and wheat. The point of the story is simple: a manager ripped off his master, and a lot of money was involved.[6] He got caught, and he

---

4   Martin Luther, *The Complete Sermons of Martin Luther* (Grand Rapids: Baker, 2000), 6:351, 356.

5   John Calvin, Commentary on a *Harmony of the Evangelists*, vol. 2 (Grand Rapids: Baker, 1981), 176. Calvin writes, "Though the parable appears to be harsh and far-fetched, yet the conclusion makes it evident, that the design of Christ was nothing else than what I have stated ['to deal kindly and generously with our neighbors']. And hence we see, that to inquire with great exactness into every minute part of a parable is an absurd mode of philosophizing."

6   Snodgrass, *Stories with Intent*, 413. Snodgrass writes, "It is true to say that Luke is not sympathetic with the rich, to say the least. A glance at the parable of the Rich Man and Lazarus (16:19–31) shows what Luke wants to say to the rich—to say nothing of the woes to the rich in 6:24–26. Still, to argue that the parable is about the rich man, his insensitivity, and his resulting conversion or graciousness is to contort the parable in directions it was not intended to go. Not all rich people in Luke are condemned merely for being rich. One has only to think of the women who supported Jesus (8:3); the returning master (12:36–46); the banquet giver (14:16);

determined that he had three options: first, get a new job—a ditch-digging job; second, beg for money; and third, endear himself to his clients in order to win their favor and land a new job. Not surprisingly, he chose the third option. He was too weak to work and too proud to beg, but he knew how to play the game. He called in his deep-pocket clients one at a time and privately negotiated fantastic deals before anyone knew that he had lost his job. It was all very clever, deceptive, illegal, and self-serving, but he was pretty sure he could pull it off, and he did. The *materialist* master had to hand it to the *dishonest* manager for taking advantage of the situation. The shrewd manager knew how to look out for himself.

KINGDOM STRATEGY

Jesus told this parable to set up a stunning contrast between the ways of the world and the Jesus way. There is a right way and a wrong way to look out for yourself. You can lie, cheat, steal, and swindle to gain the upper hand in a transactional world, or you can use worldly wealth to befriend, support, and show compassion in a hurting world framed by transcendent meaning. Calvin wrote, "The leading object of this parable is, to show that we ought to deal kindly and generously with our neighbors; that when we come to the

---

the father of the prodigal (15:11–32); Zacchaeus, who is specifically called rich (19:1–10); and the nobleman who gives money to invest (19:11–27). Nothing in the story suggests that the rich man should be viewed negatively or that he is the focus or that he is concerned with regaining honor. . . . The focus of the story must be seen in the steward, his actions, and the master's response to those actions."

judgment-seat of God, we reap the fruit of our liberality."[7] The contrast is between selfishness motivated by self-preservation, as exemplified by the shrewd manager, and self-sacrifice for the sake of others, as exemplified by the disciple of Christ. It is either life motivated by greed or life motivated by the grace of the Lord Jesus Christ who, "though he was rich, yet for [our] sake became poor, so that through his poverty [we] might become rich" (2 Cor. 8:9).

The world is good at doing things in a worldly way, but Christians are not so good at doing things in a Christian way. Martin Luther emphasized this when he said in a sermon:

> We see every day, all too often, how the world pursues its own ends so devotedly, because it has its interests at heart and spares no pain or effort to get them. . . . On the other hand, we see how the children of light, that is, confessed Christians, are unproductive, listless, negligent, and indolent in divine matters, even though they know that God delights in their efforts and that they will enjoy his pleasure in eternity. For them it is a great struggle to do what is good. . . . Draw a profitable lesson from the awful conduct [of the world] and look at it this way: If a peasant, burgher, merchant, blacksmith, wife, maid, and so on, can serve the devil with such diligence, sparing no pains, why shouldn't I want

---

7 Calvin, *Harmony of Matthew, Mark, and Luke,* 2:176.

to serve my Lord in the same manner, with whom one day I hope to share eternity.[8]

We are called to sanctify worldly wealth by using it in an unworldly way. Instead of idolizing it and making it into a god, we are meant to make it a servant. By God's grace we make it holy. On this side of eternity, money is meant to serve kingdom purposes. This is not a moralistic parable about curbing materialism. It is about setting kingdom priorities in the use of worldly wealth, precisely because we have been bought with a price, the precious blood of Christ (1 Cor. 6:9; 1 Peter 1:19).

Luke reminds us at the end of this narrative section that the Pharisees have been in earshot all this time, and they have been muttering among themselves, saying, "This man welcomes sinners and eats with them" (Luke 15:2). They were not shy about showing their collective disdain and disrespect for Jesus. Luke attributes their disdainful attitude toward Jesus to their love of money. Literally, the Pharisees "lifted up their noses to him."[9] The materialist master, the shrewd ex-manager, and the Pharisees were all in the same boat. The characters in the parable were foils for the real lovers of money, the religious leaders, the Pharisees. But Jesus has the last word, and it is directed at them like a laser beam. The non-materialist Master, who is Lord of all, says, "You are the

---

8 Luther, *Complete Sermons*, 6:353.
9 Bailey, *Jesus through Middle Eastern Eyes*, 380.

ones who justify yourselves in the eyes of others, but God knows your hearts. What people value highly is detestable in God's sight." Worldly wealth attracts the attention of religious professionals. You could have the wisdom of Solomon, but without his wealth, you are nothing in the eyes of Pharisees and like-minded Christian fundraisers.

Malcolm Gladwell, in *David and Goliath,* explores the ability of "outsiders" to turn difficult situations to their advantage. He illustrates his thesis with the biblical story of David and Goliath. On the surface, it looks like Goliath, standing nine feet tall, has a great advantage over the much smaller David in this winner-take-all "single combat" challenge. Goliath wore a bronze helmet and one hundred pounds of body armor. He was armed with a javelin, spear, and sword. But apparently he hadn't heard the old adage "You don't bring a knife to a gun fight." David the shepherd boy had no intention of honoring the prescribed rituals of hand-to-hand combat. He was armed with a slingshot and five smooth stones. But it only took one small stone to fell the big Philistine. Gladwell quotes historian Robert Dohrenwend's assessment: "Goliath has as much chance against David as a Bronze Age warrior with a sword would have against an [opponent] armed with a .45 automatic pistol."[10]

Gladwell writes of many outliers who are clever strategists like the shrewd manager in Jesus's parable. Underdogs and

---

10   Malcolm Gladwell, *David and Goliath: Underdogs, Misfits, and the Art of Battling Giants* (New York: Little, Brown, 2013), 12.

misfits find a way to beat the system and rise above their disadvantages. They are risk-takers and rule-benders. They do whatever it takes to get ahead. They compensate for their weaknesses by being borderline disagreeable and pragmatically deceptive. They may bluff and bully, but they don't surrender easily to failure. Instead of adapting to the world, they find ways to make the world adapt to them. Gladwell offers a compelling description of the underdog getting the job done by hook or by crook.

The shrewd manager was accused of wasting his master's funds, so he cleverly made some quick deals with his master's debtors. By slicing their debts in half, he made a few fast friends, and when the master heard about it, he was impressed. He commended the dishonest manager because he acted shrewdly. Then Jesus made this telling observation: "For the people of this world are more shrewd in dealing with their own kind than are the people of the light" (Luke 16:8). In other words, what underdogs do out of self-love to get ahead, Christ's followers ought to do out of Christ's love for the sake of others. What if living in the world with Christ's kingdom strategy was not a disadvantage but an advantage? Instead of envying the way the world works, what if Christians embraced integrity, compassion, social justice, and holy living? If we apply Gladwell's thesis, we may begin to realize that Christ's kingdom strategy competes more effectively in the world than a worldly strategy. If the shrewd manager can outsmart the world through his worldliness, can Christians thrive in the world by not being of the world? Jesus doesn't want his disciples to outwit the world with the shrewd manager's strategies (duplicity and deception), but he does want us to outwit the world with truth and goodness.

The 2019 college admissions scandal in America is analogous to the parable of the shrewd manager. A government investigation known as "Operation Varsity Blues" led to more than fifty people being charged with fraud in a nationwide scheme to circumvent admissions standards and get students into prestigious universities. The defendants in the case include wealthy parents, Hollywood actresses, coaches, and college prep executives. The scheme involved fixing SAT/ACT test scores and bribing coaches to recruit students regardless of their athletic ability. U.S. attorney for Massachusetts Andrew Lelling said, "This case is about the widening corruption of elite college admissions through the steady application of wealth combined with fraud."[11] The 6.5-million-dollar fraud case shows to what extent parents will go to get their children into Yale or Stanford or Georgetown.

If we leverage this case the way Jesus leveraged the story of the shrewd manager, we ask ourselves to what extent are we willing to go to see our sons and daughters grow in the grace and knowledge of the Lord Jesus Christ. How do clever fraud strategies match up with costly strategies of faithfulness? How does the world's duplicity and deceptiveness compare to the

---

11 Eric Levenson and Mark Morales, "Wealthy Parents, Actresses, Coaches, among Those Charged in Massive College Cheating Admission Scandal, Federal Prosecutors Say," *CNN*, March 13, 2019, https://www.cnn.com/2019/03/12/us/college-admission-cheating-scheme/index.html.

Christian's dedication and devotion? As Jesus said, "For the people of this world are more shrewd in dealing with their own kind than are the people of the light" (Luke 16:8).

THE JESUS WAY

Humanly speaking, we are wired to play the cultural game. But the Jesus way is radically different. The principle of the world is "your life for mine." The principle of the cross is "my life for yours." The world is better at duplicity than Christians are at integrity. The world knows how to leverage hate better than Christians know how to leverage love. The world follows self-rule better than Christians follow the wisdom of the Savior.[12]

My Beeson colleague Dr. Robert Smith Jr. tells a story that relates to this parable.[13] On Christmas Day 1960, eleven-year-old Robert and his seven-year-old brother Willie received the gifts they wanted. Robert received a ten-speed English Racer and his brother a single-speed Huffy bike. "There was only

---

12 Snodgrass (*Stories with Intent*, 417–18) writes, "The accusation is still painfully true that the people of this age are wiser in their arena than the 'children of light' are in theirs. Is it because with one eye on this age and one eye on the kingdom—a necessary split vision—we allow ourselves to be determined more by our age than Christ's kingdom? Christians are dominated by the same concerns as the rest of society, but Jesus's teaching is intended to give us a different set of concerns. . . . Once again the subject of works-righteousness may suggest itself, but only because we have distorted the subjects of faith and obedience. In Jesus's teaching obedience to the will of the Father determines eternal destiny and earns approval. The idea of faith without such obedience is nonsense."

13 Robert Smith Jr., *The Oasis of God* (Mountain Home, AR: BorderStone, 2014), 235–36.

one problem," says Robert; "my brother made the mistake of getting on my bike and riding it before I could ride it." An argument ensued, and a fight broke out between the brothers right there in the front yard. When their mother came out, they stopped fighting, but then their mother made a move that reminds me of Jesus's move in this parable. She looked at her boys and said, "Hit him, Little Robert." "Hit him, Jimbo" (Willie's nickname). "If you don't keep fighting I am going to tear both of you up." Their mother had never said anything like that before. They punched and kicked each other until their noses bled and they exhausted themselves. They took out all their meanness on each other.

Only then did their mother say, "You have broken my heart today. I went through the valley of the shadow of death to give birth to you. When I didn't have money for lunch, I made sure you had lunch money. When I had to wear tattered clothes, I made sure that there were no holes in your clothes because I didn't want your friends to make fun of you." Robert remembers thinking that he wanted her to stop and say, "OK, I am going to whip you now." But she didn't. She kept remembering how she provided for her boys and loved them until both boys stood there crying. Their mean streaks were exposed by the love of their Mama. Robert said they never fought again because they didn't want to break their mother's heart. Robert's mother, Ozella Smith, as she stood and watched, pushed the world's strategy to the breaking point (brothers fighting brothers) and then juxtaposed it with her mother's love. Jesus commended the shrewd manager for doing what the world does best, serving the self at the expense of others, and then he juxtaposed the cruciform strategy of the kingdom to show how his followers should live. The way of the world versus the way of Christ was presented in bold relief.

The equation of worldly success with the Jesus way is so common that Christian statesman Vernon Grounds feared that theological seminaries were "unwittingly inoculating students with the virus of worldly success." He warned, "Maybe we are subtly communicating the message that success in God's service is to be noticeably superior. Maybe we have been failing to communicate a clear-cut biblical understanding of success. And maybe, therefore, we fail to prepare our graduates for an experience of failure which from God's standpoint is praiseworthy success." Are we teaching the strategies of the world or the strategies of the kingdom? "God's standards of success differ radically from those of the world," Grounds argued. "So in Luke 16:15 our Lord Jesus flatly affirms, 'What people value highly is detestable in God's sight.'" He continues:

> The Bible turns values topsy-turvy, puts on top things fallen man puts on the bottom, and ranks last things fallen man puts first. It praises the weakness which is strength and denounces the strength which is weakness. It praises the poverty which is wealth and denounces the wealth which is poverty. It praises the dying which is living and denounces the living which is dying. No wonder, then, that it

praises the failure which is success and denounces the success which is failure.[14]

---

14 Vernon Grounds, "Faith for Failure: A Meditation on Motivation for Ministry," *TSF Bulletin*, March–April 1986, 4.

✧14✧

THE RICH MAN AND LAZARUS

LUKE 16:19–31

In his four-part sermon series on the parable of the rich man and Lazarus (Luke 16:19–31), John Chrysostom, a leading fourth-century preacher and theologian, began his third sermon with an extended pastoral encouragement to his congregation urging them to study God's Word for themselves. He invited them to read and study the biblical passage for the Sunday sermon through the week so as "to make your understanding more ready to learn when you hear what I will say afterwards." John made a strong case for the ordinary believer at work in the world to study and understand God's Word:

> I also entreat you, and do not cease entreating you, not only to pay attention here to what I say, but also when you are at home, to persevere continually in reading the divine Scriptures. When I have been with each of you in private, I have not stopped giving

you the same advice. Do not let anyone say to me those vain words, worthy of a heavy condemnation, "I cannot leave the courthouse, I administer the business of the city, I practice a craft, I have a wife, I am raising children, I am in charge of a household, I am a man of the world; reading the Scriptures is not for me, but for those who have been set apart, who have settled on the mountaintops, who keep this way of life continuously [monastic life]."

What are you saying? That attending to the Scriptures is not for you, since you are surrounded by a multitude of cares? Rather it is for you more than for them. They do not need the help of the divine Scriptures as much as those who are involved in occupations. The monks, who are released from the clamor of the marketplace and have fixed huts in the wilderness, who own nothing in common with anyone, but practice wisdom without fear in the calm of that quiet life, as if resting in a harbor, enjoy great security; but we, as if tossing in the midst of the sea, driven by a multitude of sins, always need the continuous and ceaseless aid of the Scriptures. They rest far from the battle, and so they do not receive many wounds; but you stand continuously in the front rank, and you receive continual blows. So you need more remedies.[1]

---

1   John Chrysostom, *On Wealth and Poverty* (Crestwood, NY: St Vladimir's Seminary Press, 1984), 58–59.

I wonder if there was something special about this particular parable that inspired John Chrysostom to encourage his church members to study the Bible on their own so that they would be more receptive to his preaching. Perhaps he thought that if the congregation conscientiously studied the Bible their understanding and use of worldly wealth would be transformed. He makes a strong case for believers to engage God's Word on their own, and on the issue of worldly wealth, wise pastors entrust their people to the Holy Spirit for genuine transformation.

WORLDLY WEALTH

The context in Luke's gospel is important for interpreting this parable. The narrative description of money-loving Pharisees who sneer at Jesus sets the scene not only for the parable of the shrewd manager (Luke 16:1–12) but also for the parable of the rich man and Lazarus. Jesus's bottom line—"What people value highly is detestable in God's sight" (Luke 16:15)—is well-illustrated in Luke's parables. The parable of the rich man exposes the wealthy person's volition and motive and proves that a rich person's self-justifying rationale is no match for reality. Jesus uses this rich man's lifestyle as empirical proof against him. The fact that he is dressed in purple and fine linen, the most expensive and ostentatious clothing available, is not a neutral fact. His eating habits advertise his greed. If he feasted sumptuously seven days a week, he must have ignored the Sabbath.[2]

---

2 Klyne R. Snodgrass, *Stories with Intent: A Comprehensive Guide to the Parables of Jesus* (Grand Rapids: Eerdmans, 2018), 419. "This is a single

We need not dwell on all the worldly ways he was rich. We may be tempted to expand the notion of riches to include intellectual riches or relational capital or creative gifts, but Jesus leaves the definition of riches in dollars, and so should we.[3] Jesus was not shy about drawing a conclusion from the material evidence of this rich person's self-centered lifestyle. Too many people today want everything money can buy plus the respect and esteem of a grateful public. But they can't have it both ways. Money is a jealous god, rendering altruistic charity a marginal sideline for the rich. The charade is played out with the false mantra that too much generosity enables poverty. If real, personal sacrifice on behalf of others is not in our lives, then we should take a good look in the mirror and see the rich man from the parable staring back at us.

Hopefully Christians are becoming more aware of the idolatrous power of money and wealth to seriously distort their values and disrupt their lives. There is a beautiful side to evil represented by the rich man in the parable that is seductive and damaging. Everything may be legal and acceptable in consumer capitalism but the moral and spiritual impact is devastating. When twentysomethings sign five-hundred-million dollar contracts to play in the NFL while their peers earn sixty thousand a year to teach elementary school, we are witnessing the demise of a decadent culture. "Current levels of

---

indirect, two-stage narrative parable that serves as a warning. No transfer of the subject is required."

3   Helmut Thielicke, *The Waiting Father: Sermons on the Parables of Jesus* (New York: Harper & Row, 1959), 44.

inequality arc almost beyond belief," writes environmentalist Bill McKibben. "The world's eight richest men possess more wealth than the bottom half of humanity [combined]." In the Unites States the three richest men have more wealth than the bottom 150 million people taken together. One of the richest men in the world, Amazon founder Jeff Bezos, "would have to spend $28 million every day just to keep his wealth from growing."[4] These concerns may be beyond us— and we may joke that they are above our pay grade—but I imagine the apostle John drawing a direct line from Jesus's parable of the Rich Man and Lazarus to his description of the Great City in the Book of Revelation (Rev. 17–18).

Martin Luther, in his sermon on this parable, felt that the warning of the rich man's judgment was directed at the Pharisees (Luke 16:14–15) because of their love of money and their self-justifying ways. "Unfortunately, as we know," Luther wrote, "such people most often think of themselves pious and without greed. Vice has been turned to virtue. Greed nowadays has come to be viewed as talented, smart, careful stewardship. And as with greed, so sin in general is dressed up to look like virtue and not vice. . . . Neither prince nor peasant, nobleman nor average citizen is any longer considered greedy, but only upstanding, the common consensus being that the man who prudently provides for himself is a resourceful person who knows how to take care of himself."

---

4 Bill McKibben, *Falter: Has the Human Game Begun to Play Itself Out?* (New York: Henry Holt, 2019), 86.

Luther's excursus on sin is helpful:

> The same holds true for other sins: Pride is no longer
> pride, or sin, but honor. The proud man is no longer
> deemed arrogant but honorable, a commanding
> person, worthy of respect, a credit to his genera-
> tion. Anger and envy are no longer that, or sin, but
> righteousness, zealousness, and virtue. The man
> who storms [rages], or is envious, or who loses his
> cool is now considered industrious, with a passion
> for what is fair, and justly angry when high-handed
> injustice is done to him. Thus there are no sinners
> in the world, but—God have mercy!—the world
> is full of holy people. In Seneca's words, when this
> happens, that vice is turned into virtue and honor,
> there no longer is hope or a way out; everything is
> lost. . . . When greed is denominated productiveness;
> arrogance; honor; anger; zeal; then we have to leave
> it unrebuked, even as now.[5]

Luther's point is simply this: when everybody is greedy, no
one thinks of themselves as greedy. When everyone is corrupt,
no one's conscience is troubled.

Luther commented further on the rich man:

---

5 Martin Luther, *The Complete Sermons of Martin Luther* (Grand Rapids:
   Baker, 2000), 6:224–25.

It was not a sin for this rich man to clothe himself, to eat and drink; for God created clothing, food, and drink, and says that it is a blessing from him. The one [who] receives it may use it in accord with his needs. But to be greedy is wrong and a sin. Christ clearly says, "There was a rich man." Now the word "rich" is a very problematical word in many places of Holy Scripture. Abraham also is rich, but Scripture does not for this reason call him a rich man; but "rich" in Scripture means almost as much as an unscrupulous shyster or wicked man, as spoken in Isaiah 53:9: "He made his grave with the wicked and with the rich in his death." There the prophet takes "rich" and "wicked" as parallel realities meaning the same thing. His point is that Christ died and was buried as an evildoer, a rogue, and a scoundrel, even though he had done wrong to no one.

Luther has the rich man saying to himself, "If a man's poor, then he's cursed; if rich, he's blessed; I am rich, and, therefore, I am blessed and have kept God's commandment; Lazarus, on the other hand, is poor, and that's because he is a sinner and God has punished him."[6]

Every fall, preachers preach on stewardship. *Religiously* understood, "stewardship" is when a greedy church makes greedy Christians feel guilty, so the church can profit from their greed

---

6 Luther, *Complete Sermons*, 6:229.

and guilt. If the line sounds cynical, it is because it occurred to me while sitting in a beautiful three-thousand-seat, hi-tech sanctuary, equipped with huge video screens and a state-of-the art sound system, situated on a multimillion-dollar church campus. The pastor was preaching from the prophet Haggai (see Hag. 1:4, 9). In his sermon, he avoided leveling any indictment against the materialism of the congregation. He was quick to reassure the audience that the Lord wanted them to prosper and enjoy the good life. "Success," he assured them, "can be a sign of God's blessing." However, he felt compelled to inform them that their church was *in ruins*—yes, that's right, *in ruins*—just like the house of God in Haggai's day, because they were three hundred thousand dollars behind in the general operating budget. "In a manner of speaking," he said, "you could say we too are *in ruins!*" No one gasped at this description. But they should have.

Søren Kierkegaard lamented that Christianity without Christ sought "to accomplish a great deal in the world, and to win great multitudes who desire also to be Christians only up to a certain point." The possibility of offense was to be avoided at all cost. The purpose of this type of Christianity, Kierkegaard contended, was not to become like Jesus but to gain the approval and esteem of others. Self-respect rather than self-denial was the motivation for Christianity without Christ. Kierkegaard claimed that avoiding the offense of the gospel was "out of hypocrisy or out of whimpering human sympathy for yourself or others." He concluded that the preaching of the day perpetually emphasized success and triumph—"in short, one hears only sermons, which might properly end with Hurrah! rather than with Amen."[7] Becoming a Christian, complained Kierkegaard, meant joining a parade, not taking up a cross.

Sometime ago I was leading a Bible study for a group of businessmen in the book of James. The discussion on James 2:5, "Has not God chosen those who are poor in the eyes of the world to be rich in faith . . . ?" proved provocative, because one wealthy CEO insisted that all poor people were immoral. He argued that to be poor in American meant that a person was lazy and irresponsible. He had no regard for systemic poverty, no appreciation for economic and educational disparity. If you were poor, it was your own fault, and you only had yourself to blame. Apparently the rich man's perspectives are alive and well even among professing believers.

THE INVISIBLE PERSON

The class-conscious rich man was blind to Lazarus's desperate need, but God in his mercy was fully aware of Lazarus's painful plight. The rich man practiced persistent indifference and disregard for the man who suffered just outside his gate, but God in his justice saw everything. The rich man's blindness contrasts with Jesus's constant concern for the poor throughout his ministry. When Jesus was invited to the home of Simon the Pharisee, Jesus asked him, "Do you see this woman?" (Luke 7:44). Yes, of course he saw the woman. She was weeping

---

7 Søren Kierkegaard, *Training in Christianity* (Princeton, NJ: Princeton University Press, 1957), 108–9.

and wiping Jesus's feet with her tears, and she was pouring expensive perfume on him. But Simon pretended not to see her—he ignored her. When Jesus was leaving the temple for the last time, Jesus noticed the poor widow, but the disciples were enamored with the beautiful stones (Luke 21:1–4; Matthew 24:1–2). The disciples chose not to see the poor widow.

"What the parable attacks," Klyne Snodgrass concludes, "is a particular kind of wealth, wealth that does not see poverty and suffering. . . . As in the parables of the Good Samaritan, the Two Debtors, and the Sheep and the Goats, even though it is not explicit, the issue here is the willingness and ability to see a person in need and respond. The rich man's wealth and self-centeredness do not allow him to see Lazarus. . . . The ability to see is a mark of Christian discipleship."[8]

Jesus did not share this parable in order to justify God in the wake of injustice. Nor did he give this parable to inspire political action and bring about structural social change. The point of the parable lies behind these necessary justice issues and dwells on the meaning of the person in relationship to God and one another. Lazarus is dignified with a name, which means "one whom God helps." In the story, Lazarus is an emaciated beggar propped up at a nameless rich man's gate ("Lazarus" is a shortened form of Eliezer or Eleazar, Abraham's servant in Genesis 15:2). He is covered with sores and so weak he is unable to keep the dogs at bay that lick his sores, rendering him ceremonially unclean. The sharp

---

8 Snodgrass, *Stories with Intent*, 433–34.

contrast between ostentatious wealth and desperate poverty is extreme.[9] A certain rich man, dressed in purple, living in luxury, is paired with a beggar named Lazarus, covered with sores, longing to eat the rich man's crumbs.

If we saw this rich man in our typical cultural setting, rather than in Jesus's parable, we probably would see him differently. Instead of seeing him as a despicable fat cat, we might celebrate him as a highly respected pillar of society, "of whom all may have spoken well; of whom none could say worse than he was willing to dwell at ease."[10] Throughout history, conspicuous consumption and moral indifference have remained respectable sins. The parable presents the disparity between rich and poor as a harsh reality, but economic inequality and poverty have long been the default social condition of our human depravity. This is the social reality Jesus envisions as he tells this parable.

I doubt whether Jesus expected scholars to debate whether the dogs licking Lazarus's sores were a good thing or a bad thing.[11] Luther sees the dogs positively, "They do what they are

---

9   Kenneth E. Bailey, *Jesus through Middle Eastern Eyes: Cultural Studies in the Gospels* (Downers Grove, IL: InterVarsity, 2008), 380. Bailey writes, "This parable is the third of a trilogy. In the first a *prodigal* wastes his *father's* possessions (Lk 15:11–32). In the second a *dishonest steward* wastes his *master's* possessions (Lk 16:1–8). And in the third, a *rich man* wastes his *own* possessions."

10   Richard C. Trench, *Notes on the Parables of Our Lord* (Trenton, NJ: Revell, 1953), 453.

11   Bailey, *Jesus through Middle Eastern Eyes*, 385. Bailey acknowledges that dogs are seen in a negative light in the Bible (Isa. 56:10; 66:3; Phil. 3:2; Rev. 22:15), but he argues the rich man's guard dogs licked Lazarus's wounds as a sign of affection and that the dogs' saliva facilitated healing (385–86).

capable of doing; they use the best member they have, namely their helpful tongues, and lick his sores and lap up his pus. How easily the rich man could have taken care of this."[12] It is not fair that Lazarus should be so weak that others have to carry him to the gate and leave him there to beg. "But where sin increased, grace increased all the more" (Rom. 5:20). God's unmerited saving grace lifts Lazarus from his hell on earth and places him in heaven in the company of Abraham. One person had everything but God and the other person had nothing but God. Luther comments:

> We must make the proper distinction: the poor man doesn't come into heaven because he is poor, nor the rich man into hell because he is rich; rather it was a case that the poor man accommodated himself well to the fact that he was poor, while the rich man failed to handle his riches properly. A distinction easily made, but not easily kept! Our "old Adam" remains an evil rascal. Once he knows that wealth in itself is not bad and poverty not good and that everything revolves around how a man handles them, he straightaway turns the distinction into a cover-up.

Luther argues that the proof that the rich man did not handle his wealth righteously was Lazarus at his gate. "Each person has to be on guard against the kind of self-deception

---

12 Luther, *Complete Sermons*, 6:230.

that happened to this 'fat-cat.'"[13] As an aside, Luther laments in his sermon that people gave "under the papacy" charitably and willingly, but now "under the gospel no one gives any more. . . . And the longer one preaches the gospel, the deeper people are submerged in greed, arrogance, and sensuality. . . . So completely has the devil taken hold of people."[14]

John Chrysostom meditates on Lazarus's condition in his first sermon on this parable.[15] He expounds on nine "chastisements" imposed on Lazarus "not to punish him, but to make him more glorious."[16] Chrysostom dissected Lazarus's suffering into nine specific features. I don't think any contemporary pastor would do it the way he did it in Antioch in 388. But John Chrysostom felt the need to dwell on this description of suffering. It was his way of identifying with Lazarus. Abject poverty, plus painful sores, along with their *combination* add up to three strikes against Lazarus. John asked his congregation, "Do you see both poverty and disease besieging his body to the extreme degree?" Fourth, Lazarus was destitute and lonely, without family and friends. Fifth, there was no one console him with a word of comfort or a gift of kindness "since the rich man's whole household was corrupt."[17] Sixth, Lazarus observed daily the disparity between his poverty and pain and the rich man's wealth and pleasure.

---

13 Luther, *Complete Sermons*, 6:232.
14 Luther, *Complete Sermons*, 6:233.
15 Chrysostom, *On Wealth and Poverty*, 10–11. Roth dates Chrysostom's sermon series on Lazarus and the rich man in early January 388 or 389.
16 Chrysostom, *On Wealth and Poverty*, 29.
17 Chrysostom, *On Wealth and Poverty*, 30.

Seventh, there were no fellow sufferers, no companions, lying next to him and sharing in his struggle. Eighth, he was unable to console himself with the hope of the resurrection, because the Christian teaching on the resurrection had not yet come. Ninth, Lazarus suffered the constant slander of his reputation. Chrysostom writes, "For most people, when they see someone in hunger, chronic illness, and extremes of misfortune, do not allow him a good reputation, but judge his life by his troubles, and think he is surely in such misery because of wickedness."[18]

THE CHASM BETWEEN HEAVEN AND HELL

The parable has the feel of a dream; a good dream for Lazarus who awakes in heaven as Abraham's guest of honor and an awful nightmare for the rich man who wakes up in the torment of hell. In the dialogue that follows, Lazarus never says a word. He feels no anger, expresses no revenge. He is at peace, totally at rest, a picture of *shalom*, basking in the presence of Abraham. True to form, the rich man ignores him now as he always has. He cannot bring himself to see Lazarus as anything other than a low-class lackey. Hell itself doesn't appear to put a dent in his pride. He calls out, "Father Abraham, have pity on me and send Lazarus to dip the tip of his finger in water and cool my tongue, because I am in agony in this fire." The rich man is unable to grasp that Abraham and Lazarus are brothers in the Lord and on equal footing!

---

18 Chrysostom, *On Wealth and Poverty*, 31–32.

In spite of the rich man's ingrained pride and class consciousness, Abraham responds gently, affectionately, "My dear boy." He
uses the same word that the Father in the parable of the prodigal
son used with the offended elder son (*teknon*, instead of *huios*,
see Luke 15:31). Abraham describes the new reality. First, there
is the great reversal, the difference between how it was and how
it should be. The tables of justice have turned. Lazarus receives
good things and the rich man bad things; Lazarus is comforted
and the rich man is in agony. Second, a great chasm has been set
in place (by God), preventing anyone to go from heaven to hell
or from hell to heaven. This boundary is fixed in time and place
and imposes limits on any sense of responsibility and compassion.
What's done is done. There is a finality about the life we live on
this side of eternity. The warning has been given over and over.

The rich man established his significance on his own terms.
In his mind he dismantled the connection between heaven
and earth, and in doing so, he was a very modern man—the
secular, self-made man. A society of restless nomads looking
for a little heaven on earth, defining identity on their own
terms, insisting on transactional relationships to meet their
needs, and then wondering why they suffer from insignificance
and loneliness. Absorbed in their own life stories, they miss
the opportunity of becoming involved in the greater drama of
God's salvation history. In a lame attempt to give themselves
purpose, they reject the purpose God intended for them.[19]

---

19 Psalm 49 on the denial of death and Psalm 73 on moral pain draw out the
    meaning of the parable.

The self grows accustomed to an endless search for meaning and purpose without ever expecting to find salvation, let alone significance. Life is wrapped around small pursuits, like shopping or sports, to avoid having to deal with life in any serious way. In our effort to make a little heaven on earth, the secular self forgets about heaven altogether. Social analyst Daniel Yankelovich describes the rich man and those who follow his example:

> By concentrating day and night on your feelings, potentials, needs, wants and desires, and by learning to assert them more freely, you do not become a freer, more spontaneous, more creative self; you become a narrower, more self-centered, more isolated one. You do not grow, you shrink.[20]

The rich man in this parabolic dream is not used to taking "no" for an answer. He begs father Abraham to send Lazarus to his family in order to warn his five brothers. There are six brothers in all, which as Ken Bailey points out, is the number of evil. Undoubtedly all five brothers knew Lazarus *but not by name*, having met the beggar at the gate many times on their way to their brother's sumptuous feasts. "Had they accepted Lazarus as a brother, there would have been seven of them (the number of perfection)."[21]

---

20   Daniel Yankelovich, *New Rules: Searching for Self-Fulfillment in a World Turned Upside Down* (New York: Bantam Books, 1982), 239.
21   Bailey, *Jesus through Middle Eastern Eyes*, 392.

The rich man's plea is met with a simple truth. Abraham replied, "They have Moses and the Prophets; let them listen to them" (Luke 16:29; see 24:27). The implication is easily understood. There is no mystery as to how to live life. It is found right there in the revelation of God. Meaning and purpose is not human made nor measured by the accumulation of things. Life is best measured, not by what we achieve, but by what we receive. The Law and the Prophets lay out our responsibility to one another. Provision for foreigners, orphans, and widows proves the Lord's blessing (Deut. 14:28–29). Generosity and debt forgiveness are built into the economy of the people of God ("there need be no poor people among you, for in the land the LORD your God is giving you to possess as your inheritance, he will richly bless you, if only you fully obey the LORD your God and are careful to follow all these commands," Deut. 15:4–5).[22]

The rich man's response, "No, father Abraham, but if someone from the dead goes to them, they will repent," implies that something more than the revelation of God is needed. The Bible alone fails to convince those who are engrossed in the things of the world. The rich man's request for someone from the dead to return, someone like Lazarus, to warn his brothers of judgment is ironic because Luke wrote his gospel

---

22 Darrell L. Bock, *Luke: The NIV Application Commentary* (Grand Rapids: Zondervan, 2009), 433–34. Bock lists the following texts to prove the point: Deut. 7:12; 22:1–2; 23:19; 24:7; 25:13–14; Isa. 3:14–15; 5:7–8; 10:1–3; 32:6–7; 58:3, 6–7, 10; Jer. 5:26–28; 7:5–6; Ezek. 18:12–18; 33:15; Amos 2:6–8; 5:11–12; 8:4–6; Mic. 2:1–2; 3:1–3; 6:10–11; Zech. 7:9–10; Mal. 3:5.

after Jesus raised the real Lazarus from the dead, and after Jesus was crucified, resurrected, and ascended. Abraham's response proves true: "If they do not listen to Moses and the Prophets, they will not be convinced even if someone rises from the dead" (Luke 16:31). After Lazarus was raised from the dead, the Pharisees and Sanhedrin doubled down in their plot to put Jesus to death.

The rich man knows his destiny is fixed. He is stuck in hell forever. He hopes Lazarus can bridge the great chasm to bring him a little comfort, but failing that, at least he could warn his brothers. His final plea is for Lazarus to return and warn his brothers of their pending doom, "so that they will not also come to this place of torment" (Luke 16:28). But the parable is all about grace, not works. Jesus never implied that the rich man could buy his way into heaven through philanthropy. It is not a matter of working for righteousness the way he worked for wealth. Even if the rich man's five brothers were warned and scared into trying harder and doing better, they were still lost and destined for the judgment. It was never about works and always about acting justly, loving mercy, and walking humbly before God (Mic. 6:8). Lazarus's salvation was all about grace. He is the picture of utter weakness and need. He embodies the first beatitude of Jesus's Sermon on the Mount. As Mahalia Jackson sang, "Just as I am without one plea, but that thy blood was shed for me." Lazarus is the one whom God helps, not because he merits God's favor but because God extends his mercy to the needy.

The parable is a penetrating reminder of God's justice and our shared humanity. The rich man lived a self-satisfied, self-centered existence, independent of God. Behind his walled compound and in his position of power and privilege, he closed himself off from suffering humanity. He claimed ethnic and religious pride ("Father Abraham"), but refused to live as a child of Abraham and a son of the law. He stood for the Law and the Prophets in theory, but not in practice. Like Job's counselors, he equated material wealth with God's blessing and poverty as God's judgment. The rich man had a twisted theology that exonerated himself and condemned Lazarus. He had no sense of destiny other than his present-moment happiness. His only sense of accountability was his accountant's bottom line. He personified a transactional world turned away from God and turned in upon itself.

The Christ figure in the parable is Lazarus. It is reasonable to assume that Jesus envisioned himself suffering on the cross as he told this parable. He was heading to Jerusalem to be crucified by the sons of Abraham who were steeped in racial pride, who championed themselves as the guardians of the Law and Prophets, and yet who refused to obey the law or live into its promise. In telling this parable, Jesus looked beyond the cross to the resurrection and to the judgment.[23]

---

23 There is a tendency to use a parable as a platform for much more than the parable was intended to convey. In his third sermon on the parable, Chrysostom describes "a vast great sea of ideas" opening up before him and his congregation. He sees in the parable a comprehensive description of salvation. "Therefore when you see anyone living in wickedness but suffering no misfortunes in this life, do not call him lucky, but weep and

Lazarus is not only a Christ figure but also a disciple figure. He represents all who have taken up their cross to follow Jesus. On this side of eternity, the world may pity them, persecute them, or ignore them. Their state of grace may also be like Lazarus—a state of suffering with no hope of improvement on this side of eternity. This is why the apostle Paul said, "I consider that our present sufferings are not worth comparing with the glory that will be revealed in us" (Rom. 8:18). Luther concludes:

---

mourn for him, because he will endure all the misfortunes in the next life, just like this rich man. Again, when you see anyone cultivating virtue, but enduring a multitude of trials call him lucky, envy him, because all his sins are being dissolved in this life, and a great reward for his endurance is being prepared in the next life; just as it happened for this man Lazarus" (Chrysostom, *On Wealth and Poverty*, 62, 77–78). This suggests that the person who receives divine reward has merited salvation by patiently enduring misfortunes. The lucky person is the one who receives punishment on this side of eternity. Steeped in his ideas of a sacerdotal priesthood, sacramentalism, and works righteousness, Chrysostom envisions the virtuous person "paying the penalty for sins" here and now. The good person's suffering is redemptive for the sins they have committed, and the rich person's good life is an indictment for the sins that will be punished in the next life. We rightly wince when we hear Chrysostom say, "It is a great good to have your hope of salvation in your own righteous acts" because we know that our salvation does not rest in our good works. Chrysostom offers a moralistic interpretation of the parable: "If we live in prosperity, let us make ourselves secure; brought to our senses by other's punishment, let us give thanks with repentance and compunction and continual confession. If we have transgressed at all in the present life, let us put the sin away, and with great zeal washing away all the stain of our life, let us call upon God to count us all worthy when we are released from this life to go there, where not with the rich man but with Lazarus we may enjoy the bosom of the patriarch and feast on immortal good things." The fact that Chrysostom adds, "May all of us attain to these, by the grace and love of our Lord Jesus Christ" does not remove the moralistic emphasis on works righteousness that pervades his treatment of the parable.

In this example of the rich man and poor Lazarus, we have a terrifying and earnest lesson against covetousness. It is a particularly shameful evil at work among greedy, loveless people, full of great injustice, thwarting all the fruits of the gospel. The Lord rebukes this evil, therefore, for good reason, especially since it adorns itself as a virtue, refusing to be viewed as sin. If we find ourselves in it, may God help us, so that we come free of it. Amen.[24]

---

24 Luther, *Complete Sermons*, 6:240.

❧15❧

THE HARDWORKING SERVANT

LUKE 17:1–10

Throughout Luke's travel narrative, we are aware that Jesus is heading to the cross. Along the way, Jesus challenged the religious leaders and instructed his disciples. In the parable of the hard working servant, Jesus's attention shifts from the crowd and the religious leaders to the small band of disciples. Three linked sayings set the stage. Each saying has an unexpected verbal twist, and the use of hyperbolic images gets our attention. First, the consequence for causing a little one to stumble is worse than if you were thrown into the sea with a millstone around your neck. Second, forgiveness is required when a person sins against you and repents, even if it's seven times in the day. Third, faith as small as a tiny mustard seed is able to uproot a mulberry tree and plant it in the sea. These three crisp attention-getting one-liners on acute sensitivity for the well-being of the young; unwavering forgiveness for a sin-prone friend; and a bold, genuine faith in God, all focus on what it means to follow the Lord Jesus and thereby set up the next parable, Jesus's no-big-deal-work-ethic parable.

EARTHY DISCIPLESHIP

Disciples who respond to the call of God, who embrace the call to salvation, service, sacrifice, and simplicity, never put God in their debt. Disciples are not accruing credit through their faithful service. They are simply doing what is expected of them—what God's grace has equipped and empowered them to do. Jesus told the story this way:

> Suppose one of you has a servant plowing or looking after his sheep. Will he say to the servant when he comes in from the field, "Come along now and sit down to eat"? Won't he rather say, "Prepare my supper, get yourself ready and wait on me while I eat and drink; after that you may eat and drink"? Will he thank the servant because he did what he was told to do? So you also, when you have done everything you were told to do, should say, "We are unworthy servants; we have only done our duty." (Luke 17:7–10)

Jesus couples a sensitivity to sin, a readiness to forgive, and a willingness to trust in God with an attitude of humble service. This no-big-deal-work-ethic parable is not about labor relations. It is certainly not a resource for an executive to use to pressure subordinates into submission and diligence. If the crowd had heard this parable, they might have misconstrued its purpose. And if the religious leaders had heard it, they might have felt the story defended their authority. Only the disciples were in a position to understand this parable. Jesus was addressing the work ethic of the kingdom of God. Simon Kistemaker explains, "The context of the parable is the cold, impersonal relationship of the ancient world in which a slave was expected to obey whatever his master told him to do. If the owner instructed the servant to plow the field during the day and to prepare supper upon returning home, he merely obeyed because he knew that this was his task. It was as simple as that. And for doing his task the slave did not receive a 'thank you,' for it was not customary to thank slaves."[1] The hyperbole in this case is found in imagining the unimaginable: the master treating the servant after a long day's work as if he were a dinner guest, "Come along now and sit down to eat." That's just not how servants were treated.

LABOR OF LOVE

The parable is about serving God with gratitude because of God's grace rather than serving with an attitude of entitlement because of our effort.[2] God is never in our debt. God

---

1   Simon J. Kistemaker, *The Parables: Understanding the Stories Jesus Told* (Grand Rapids: Baker, 2002), 247.

2   Robert Capon insists that this parable is not about work at all. Jesus is not instilling a kingdom work ethic of sensitivity, forgiveness, faith, and faithfulness. Capon quotes the Lord's perspective: "You've got only one job to do and that's to drop dead for me. That's all I need from you, because everything else that needs doing, I do. And I'm not going to thank you for what you do, or reward you for what you achieve, because no matter

never owes us a favor, no matter how hard we may labor. "A life of the most blameless holiness and love is no more than God requires. It is no ground on which a special reward can be demanded. It is not reason for expecting promotion or praise."[3] The point is not that the Lord treats us like servants or refuses to reward us. In an earlier parable, Jesus told the story of a master who rewarded his diligent, faithful servants by inviting them to dinner and humbly serving them (Luke 12:37). And in the upper room, Jesus washed the disciples' feet as an example of how they should serve one another (John 13:5). On that occasion, Jesus said, "I no longer call you servants, because servants do not know their master's business. Instead, I have called you friends, for everything that I learned from my Father I have made known to you" (John 15:15). However, the fact that the disciple's relationship with the Lord goes beyond the status of a servant does not mean that disciples bargain with God. His grace and favor are always more than we deserve and fill us with joy and gratitude.

Yet if we're honest, to embrace the role of the servant does not come naturally. What comes naturally is a sense of entitlement. We act as if God owes us. We feel overworked and unappreciated, more concerned with how people honor and respect us than how we honor and respect the Lord. Our

---

how nifty any of it may be, it's all useless for my purposes—all tainted, like even your faith, with your boring commitment to winning" (Robert Farrar Capon, *Kingdom, Grace, Judgment: Paradox, Outrage, and Vindication in the Parables of Jesus* [Grand Rapids: Eerdmans, 2002], 322).

3   Charles R. Eerdman, *The Gospel of Luke* (Philadelphia: Westminster, 1966), 174.

worldly priorities leave very little room for God in our lives. But what if we reverse this mindset, put our excuses aside, and acknowledge our privilege to serve at the pleasure of the Lord? Jesus lays out the daily, ordinary work of the disciple: accountability, forgiveness, and faithfulness. This is the real work: nurturing the young in the faith; forgiving those who sin against us, even when they sin against us repeatedly; and exercising our faith, no matter how small, for the sake of Christ's kingdom. Instead of complaining when we have done everything expected of us, we simply say, "The work is done. What we were told to do, we did" (Luke 17:10 MSG). The apostle Paul summarized the believer's work ethic beautifully when he said, "We proclaim [Christ], admonishing and teaching everyone with all wisdom, so that we may present everyone fully mature in Christ. To this end I strenuously contend with all the energy Christ so powerfully works in me" (Col. 1:28–29).

❧16❧

THE PERSISTENT WIDOW

LUKE 18:1–8

There is a difference between truth told slant and clever opinions ricocheting off the wall. Robert Capon insists that the judge "who neither feared God nor cared what people thought" is a perfect "stand-in for God" because the *bad-judge-God-type* flies in the face of conformity to respectable religion. The bad judge fits with Jesus breaking the mold and doing the unexpected. God is willing "to be perceived as a bad God" in order to save the likes of you and me. Capon quotes Romans 5:8, "While we were yet sinners, Christ died for us."[1]

There is no greater truth than the grace of Christ, but it is a bewildering interpretative leap to identify the bad judge, who cares for neither God nor man, as a Christ figure—the antihero, the countercultural God who goes rogue so that

---

1 Robert Farrar Capon, *Kingdom, Grace, Judgment: Paradox, Outrage, and Vindication in the Parables of Jesus* (Grand Rapids: Eerdmans, 2002), 332.

his disruptive badness will illustrate the goodness of God. Capon sums it up this way: "Here is a jurist, a practitioner of the law, whom Jesus will portray as a barefaced agent of grace—and whom he will portray that way precisely because he breaks the rules of his profession and puts himself out of the judging business."[2]

Capon is right. The gospel flies in the face of respectable religion; in fact the gospel of Jesus Christ ends all religions. But the interpreter of the parable need not pretend he is playing with a Rubik's Cube to understand the parable of the persistent widow. The meaning of the parable is straightforward. The unjust judge is not a Christ figure. He is a crooked judge who is denying justice to the weak and powerless. If anyone is a Christ figure in the parable, it is the widow who suffers rejection and refusal. Remember, the one who is telling the story is Jesus. He is headed to Jerusalem to suffer the greatest injustice of all at the hands of the recognized political, judicial, and religious authorities.

Capon's creative imagination has little to do with the meaning of the parable and explains why he wishes to cut out Luke's introduction, which gives us the key to interpreting the parable: "Then Jesus told his disciples a parable to show them that they should always pray and not give up" (Luke 18:1). For Capon this interpretation is too boring. The parable could not possibly mean something as prosaic as persevering in prayer and worship until Christ comes again. Ken Bailey's remark is

---

2 Capon, *Kingdom, Grace, and Judgment*, 330–31.

both ironic and reassuring when he writes, "Surely Luke's understanding of the focus of the parable is superior to the views of any modern commentator (including me)."[3] Klyne Snodgrass sees the parable as addressed by Jesus to his disciples. It is a *how much more* parable. He writes, "If even an unjust judge will vindicate a widow who keeps coming to him, how much more will God answer the cries for vindication from his people. With this picture of the elect crying to God for vindication, one should compare Revelation 6:10."[4] In the apostle John's vision, persecuted and martyred saints cry out in a loud voice, "How long, Sovereign Lord, holy and true, until you judge the inhabitants of the earth and avenge our blood?" (Rev. 6:10).

THE UNJUST JUDGE

The first figure in the parable is a certain unscrupulous judge "who neither feared God nor cared what people thought" (Luke 18:1). The way Jesus frames this judge sets him up as a modern character who cares for nothing and no one other than himself. From the parable we know that the modern age did not invent such characters. There have always been people around who have sought positions of power for selfish gain. The judge is not unique. It is not hard to imagine a person who does not fear God nor care about people in

---

3 Kenneth E. Bailey, *Jesus through Middle Eastern Eyes: Cultural Studies in the Gospels* (Downers Grove, IL: InterVarsity, 2008), 263–64. Bailey writes, "The parable is not a balloon to be carried with the wind of the interpreter's experience or perceptions. Rather, the text itself provides the author/editor's understanding of what the parable is about."
4 Snodgrass, *Stories with Intent*, 455.

any profession. They are standard fare and stock characters in politics and business. Every profession has them. They are part and parcel of the human condition. Self-interest rules the day. The judge is an archetypal portrait of heartless indifference and injustice. He is the picture of pride.

C. S. Lewis, in *Mere Christianity,* calls pride "the great sin." Pride is "the essential vice, the utmost evil." Pride is essentially competitive—the wish to be richer, smarter, more powerful, more attractive, more celebrated than others. "In God you come up against something which is in every respect immeasurably superior to yourself. Unless you know God as that— and, therefore, know yourself as nothing in comparison—you do not know God at all. As long as you are proud you cannot know God. A proud man is always looking down on things and people: and, of course, as long as you are looking down, you cannot see something that is above you."[5]

The second figure in the parable is a widow who keeps coming to the judge to plead her case for justice against her adversary.[6] The Bible pays attention to the plight of widows with concern for widows being a mark of faithfulness (Exod. 22:22; Deut. 24:17; 27:19; Jer. 22:3; Zech. 7:10; see also Exod. 34:6; Prov. 24:15; Lam. 1:1–2; James 1:27).[7] We are

---

5   C. S. Lewis, *Mere Christianity* (New York: MacMillan, 1960), 124.

6   Capon (*Kingdom, Grace, and Judgment,* 331) paints the picture of the widow as a loser who has not come to grips with her poverty. She is not a picture of humility and persistence. The widow represents the lost who are unable to face the facts of their overwhelming need.

7   Snodgrass (*Stories with Intent,* 453) writes, "Widows were often left with no means of support. If her husband left an estate, she did not inherit it, although provision for her upkeep would be made. If she remained in

not told anything about the specifics of her case, only that she perseveres in her pursuit of justice. But the widow has no leverage with the judge, because he doesn't fear God and he doesn't care for people. He doesn't care what people think of him. He doesn't value the law for maintaining justice, nor does he see the widow as an image bearer of God who deserves to be defended by the law. The old Puritan saying applies: "When you ungod God, you unman Man." The judge has an office designed to safeguard the rights of others and preserve justice for the weak. But sadly he reneged on that responsibility long ago, if he ever committed to it in the first place. Calling him a "judge" is a misnomer. He stands for the polite and cultured yet unjust person whose only real thought is for him- or herself. Self-interest displaces the rule of law and the moral order. Not to care what people think of you is the worst possible form of pride. C. S. Lewis explains,

> The real black, diabolical Pride, comes when you look down on others so much that you do not care what they think of you. Of course, it is very right, and often our duty, not to care what people think of us, if we do so for the right reason; namely, because we care so incomparably more what God thinks. But the Proud man has a different reason

---

her husband's family, she had an inferior, almost servile, position. If she returned to her family, the money exchanged at the wedding had to be given back. Widows were so victimized that they were often sold as slaves for debt."

for not caring. He says, "Why should I care for the applause of that rabble as if their opinion were worth anything?"[8]

THE JUSTICE-SEEKING WIDOW

But in spite of the judge, who could not care less about God or people, the widow continued to make her case and plead for justice, saying, "Grant me justice against my adversary." Ken Bailey observes that "the chivalry that surrounds women in Middle Eastern culture is striking." If the widow was a man, he "would be thrown out at once if he tried to pester the judge with his shouting. But the widow can manage if she has courage and persistence."[9] Apparently, for this particular judge, Middle Eastern social mores outlasted moral imperatives.

The widow became such a nuisance and aggravation to the judge that he finally gave in. Self-interest, rather than justice, caused the judge to relent and change his mind. Snodgrass comments, "The judge fears not that the woman will strike him, but that she will annoy him to death."[10] Jesus tells the story in such a way that we hear the judge's inner monologue within his "little trinity" of "me, myself, and I," saying, "Even though I don't fear God or care what people think, yet because this widow keeps bothering me, I will see that she gets justice, so that she won't eventually come and attack me!"

---

8   C. S. Lewis, *Mere Christianity* (New York: MacMillan, 1960), 126.
9   Bailey, *Jesus through Middle Eastern Eyes*, 264.
10 Snodgrass, *Stories with Intent*, 458.

(Luke 18:4–5). The judge's pride was no match for the widow's humility. She wore him down. Both characters could not care less what people thought of them, but for completely different reasons. The judge, because his ego was above it all; and the widow, because her cause was just. She captures the meaning of the third beatitude: "Blessed are the meek, for they shall inherit the earth" (Matt. 5:5; Ps. 37:1–11).

Jesus frames the parable in the context of the coming kingdom of God. The widow's persevering, persistent prayer is the model for all disciples as they await the coming kingdom of God. "The injunction to pray and not give up derives its significance from the context of the whole eschatological discourse, which began in Luke 17:20. The disciples will long to see one of the days of the Son of Man, but will not (Luke 17:22), and people will go about their lives and be caught unprepared as in former instances of judgment. The opposite of becoming weary is steadfastness, faithfulness, and readiness."[11] Meanwhile, we continue to pray, "May your kingdom come." The persistent widow is our model of perseverance.

THE JUST GOD

Jesus sets up a contrast between the begrudging response of an unjust judge and the eager, loving response of the God of justice. If there is any delay in bringing about a just judgment, it is because the Lord is not wanting anyone to perish but everyone to come to repentance (2 Peter 3:9). But there

---

11   Snodgrass, *Stories with Intent*, 457.

should be no doubt that the Lord will bring about justice for his chosen ones and respond to their cry. The answer to Jesus's rhetorical question "Will he keep putting them off?" is a resounding *No*. As we have said, if there is a Christ figure in this parable, it is the widow, who is humble and persistent before an evil judge, a judge who doesn't care about God and who doesn't care about people.

Jesus is heading to Jerusalem where he will encounter the Sanhedrin, a body of unjust judges. Then he will be paraded in front of Herod and Pilate, a Jewish puppet king and a Roman commander on a regrettable assignment to Palestine. Neither official cared about God or justice. Jesus takes this small picture of a widow pursuing justice and uses it to intentionally frame the ultimate issue of mercy and justice for the entire human race. He is like this widow, only in his case, he will go to the cross to secure our salvation. The whole eschatological issue of cosmic justice is pictured here in miniature. The Lord longs to bring about this justice and judgment, and when he does, it will be just and quick. The parable is not about "badgering God until we get our desires."[12] But it is about persistent prayer, and it is about God honoring our perseverance in a hostile world that God is intent on saving. Snodgrass writes, "Vindication has begun with the kingdom and the resurrection of Jesus, but it awaits God's future eschatological action. The evidence of faithfulness and a primary path to alertness and faithfulness

---

12   Snodgrass, *Stories with Intent*, 462.

is prayer, constant involvement with God as we interpret and deal with the world in which we live."[13]

Jesus's final word is sobering, "However, when the Son of Man comes, will he find faith on the earth?" (Luke 18:8). His eschatological vision of the coming of the Son of Man implies that believers will experience a serious challenge to their faith and faithfulness. Vindication is assured, but to remain faithful to the end will not prove easy. The parable of the persistent widow echoes the concern of the parable of the faithful servants (Luke 12:35–40): "You also must be ready, because the Son of Man will come at an hour when you do not expect him" (Luke 12:40).

---

13 Snodgrass, *Stories with Intent*, 462.

❦ 17 ❦

THE PHARISEE AND
THE TAX COLLECTOR

LUKE 18:9–14

The themes of mercy over merit and humility over pride continue with the story of the Pharisee and the tax collector. In a series of pictures, Luke contrasts the recipients of salvation with those who reject the way of salvation: the persistent widow versus the proud judge, the self-mortifying tax collector versus the self-righteous Pharisee. Luke's account of Jesus's reception of the little children drives the message home. Jesus said, "Let the little children come to me, and do not hinder them, for the kingdom of God belongs to such as these. Truly I tell you, anyone who will not receive the kingdom of God like a little child will never enter it" (Luke 18:16–17).

LUKE SETS THE STAGE

Luke's narrative places little children and the rich young ruler side by side. In one frame we see little children being brought to Jesus, and in the next frame we see an eager young man running up to Jesus. Children are contrasted with a self-confident, self-sufficient young man who possesses wealth and power. The children make no claim to righteousness, but the rich young ruler claims to have kept the law since he was a boy. Luke sets up a contrast, the clash of two kingdoms: the kingdom of the world represented by the young man and the kingdom of God represented by little children.

For too many Christians, the rich young ruler is the epitome of what we want our children to become—a self-confident young man with a healthy self-image, a well-rounded education, and a solid sense of morality. He has it all—health, wealth, power, and morality. His parents must have been very proud. If they were anything like parents today, they might be tempted to turn him into an "immortality symbol."[1] "How profoundly ironic is the kingdom of God," writes James Edwards. "The children in the former story who possess nothing are not told that they lack anything, but rather that the kingdom of God is theirs; yet this man who possesses everything still lacks something! Only when he sells all he has—only when he becomes like a vulnerable child—will he possess everything."[2] Jesus addressed the disciples as children: "Children, how hard it is to enter the kingdom of God!" (Mark 10:24). Suddenly we realize that we all must become like children,

---

1 See my earlier comments in chapter 11 (page 166) regarding "immortality symbols" discussed in David L. Goetz, *Death by Suburb: How to Keep the Suburbs from Killing Your Soul* (San Francisco: Harper, 2006).

2 James R. Edwards, *The Gospel according to Mark: The Pillar New Testament Commentary* (Grand Rapids: Eerdmans, 2001), 312.

that "unless [we] change and become like little children, [we] will never enter the kingdom of heaven" (Matt. 18:3).

The Lord turns everything upside down. The people who deserve our attention are on the bottom, not the top. Normal adult issues, sensitivities, problems, and priorities pale in comparison to welcoming and nurturing these little ones for Christ and his kingdom. Children embody the perquisites for discipleship, because they are needy and dependent. Jesus teaches us to care for his children first in the order of service, to attend to their growth as our greatest concern, to see in them our best example of grace at work, and to follow their lead in humble dependence upon our Lord and Savior. Our children serve as redemptive analogies within the household of faith reminding us of the Father's love, the Son's sacrifice, and the Spirit's filling. Paul writes, "In love he predestined us for adoption to sonship through Jesus Christ, in accordance with his pleasure and will—to the praise of his glorious grace, which he has freely given us in the One he loves" (Eph. 1:4–6).

The flow of the narrative, along with Luke's thesis-like introduction, guides our interpretation of the parable of the Pharisee and the tax collector. Luke writes, "To some who were confident of their own righteousness and looked down on everyone else, Jesus told this parable" (Luke 18:9). Luke takes the mystery out of the meaning of the parable, but leaves all the drama to Jesus. For anyone sitting in a church worship service and hearing a sermon, this picture of two individuals, the Pharisee and the tax collector, hits home. Maybe those who have been raised in church can more readily identify with the

Pharisee. We feel good about ourselves when we compare ourselves to others. We are so used to boosting our egos by making these comparisons that we hardly notice what we are doing. People, like myself, who are tasked with the responsibility of serving a church are particularly inclined to this self-serving, self-justifying habit—an undoubtedly pernicious habit.

CONTRASTING PROFILES

Luke compares two polar opposite characters, and as Snodgrass insists, "we are not to see through the two characters to some other reality; rather we are to see them."[3] He writes, "Much of Luke's material emphasizes the acceptance of inferior and excluded people into the kingdom."[4] The parable of the Pharisee and the tax collector relates to the humility of the prodigal son and the pride of the older brother (Luke 15:11–32). It compares the attitudes of Simon the Pharisee with the woman who washed Jesus's feet (Luke 7:36–50), and it contrasts the polite scorn of the privileged guests with the joyous reception of the outcasts (Luke 14:15–24). Zacchaeus is a model for the forgiveness of the tax collector (Luke 19:1–10). Snodgrass describes this parable as a verbal slap in the face. He writes, "Jesus called a man righteous who was known to be unrighteous and refused this description for a man whom everyone would recognize as a righteous person. . . . Modern readers must

---

3 Klyne R. Snodgrass, *Stories with Intent: A Comprehensive Guide to the Parables of Jesus* (Grand Rapids: Eerdmans, 2018), 469.
4 Snodgrass, *Stories with Intent*, 466.

make the effort to realize the shock of Jesus's statement to his first-century Jewish hearers."[5]

The parable of the Pharisee and tax collector causes well-intentioned Christians to question their sinful tendency to self-righteous self-justification. The insidious nature of pride raises its ugly head in the middle of all our good work. We Christian leaders especially can become "passive agents of process"—religious professionals, running a religious organization, priding ourselves on our "on interpersonal skills, administrative talents, and ability to organize community."[6] Instead of thinking of ourselves with sober judgment (Rom. 12:3), we think of ourselves as essential to God's operation. Instead of being humble stewards of the mysteries of God (1 Cor. 4:1), we become managers of a religious institution. Earl Palmer, retired pastor of University Presbyterian Church in Seattle, frames the danger this way: "I begin to imagine that the most important task for me as a Christian is to manage this institution and to make it succeed for God's purposes. . . . I am organizing the organization and when my own expectations for that organization become too important to me, I have lost the vision of the mystery of God's presence in my own life and among these people who are God's people."[7]

---

5 Snodgrass, *Stories with Intent*, 473–74.

6 David F. Wells, *No Place for Truth; Or, Whatever Happened to Evangelical Theology?* (Grand Rapids: Eerdmans, 1994), 234.

7 Earl F. Palmer, *Integrity in a World of Pretense: Insights from the Book of Philippians* (Downers Grove, IL: InterVarsity, 1992), 41.

Most of the people hearing Jesus tell this story revered and respected the Pharisees. The crowd of regular folk would not have dared to compare themselves to these strict guardians of the law. The Pharisees were honored as earnest believers who obeyed the law at the highest level. This is why Robert Capon says, "Forget the prejudice that Jesus's frequently stinging remarks about Pharisees have formed in your mind. Give this particular Pharisee all the credit you can."[8] We should do this, according to Capon, because Jesus meant for us to identify with the Pharisee. It makes no difference whether you identify this religious man as a Baptist or an Episcopalian. He is a good man, a religious man, respected in the community and honored in the church. This Pharisee went well beyond the norm. He fasted twice a week, probably on Tuesday and Thursday, and not for himself alone but for all of Israel. He was committed to prayer and fasting.

The problem, however, is that this good, decent, and highly respected religious man is really worse off than the crooked tax collector he spies out of the corner of his eye. The Pharisee sees himself as a scrupulous observer of the Old Testament law, but God sees him as an arrogant, self-justifying hypocrite who looks down on the tax collector—and, as shocking as it may seem, we are meant to see ourselves in him. Like the Pharisee, we are tempted to base our self-worth and our relationship to God on our comparative analysis of others. The Pharisee

---

8   Robert Farrar Capon, *Kingdom, Grace, Judgment: Paradox, Outrage, and Vindication in the Parables of Jesus* (Grand Rapids: Eerdmans, 2002), 338.

believed he merited God's favor because of his good deeds and his religious practices. And if that wasn't bad enough, his self-justifying pride is on full display in his prayer as he stands in the temple before the great high altar as atonement offerings are being made. The blood of a lamb is sprinkled on the altar for the sins of Israel, even as the Pharisee prays, "God, I thank you that I am not like other people—robbers, evildoers, adulterers—or even like this tax collector. I fast twice a week and give a tenth of all I get" (Luke 18:11–12).

Worship doesn't always bring out the best in people. Sometimes, as in this case, it accentuates the worst. Self-evaluation and self-justification based on looking down on others produces ugly pride. Helmut Thielicke writes, "Anybody who looks downward and measures himself by the weaknesses of his fellow men immediately becomes proud; or, better, what he is concerned about is not primarily to run down others but rather by running down others to make himself look good and feel good."[9]

C. S. Lewis asks,

> How is it that people who are quite obviously eaten up with Pride can say they believe in God and appear to themselves very religious? I am afraid it means they are worshiping an imaginary God. They theoretically admit themselves to be nothing in the

---

9   Helmut Thielicke, *The Waiting Father: Sermons on the Parables of Jesus* (New York: Harper & Row, 1959), 132.

presence of this phantom God, but are really all
the time imagining how He approves of them and
thinks them far better than ordinary people: that
is, they pay a pennyworth of imaginary humility
to Him and get out of it a pound's worth of Pride
towards their fellow-men. . . . Whenever we find
that our religious life is making us feel that we are
good—above all, that we are better than someone
else—I think we may be sure that we are being acted on, not by God, but by the devil. The real test
of being in the presence of God is, that you either
forget about yourself altogether or see yourself as
a small, dirty object. It is better to forget about
yourself altogether.[10]

MERCY OVER MERIT

Paradoxically, the person we should want to identify with
in this parable is the tax collector. He is above all else mindful that he is in the presence of God. Whereas the Pharisee
stood apart and above, the tax collector stood at a distance
and below. He cannot even bring himself to look up to heav-
en. He is distraught over his sins. His body language speaks
volumes. We picture him trembling, his sad face wincing in
pain, buried in his hands. His voice pleads, "God, have mercy
on me, a sinner." Ken Bailey remarks that the text does not
use the common word for mercy, *eleeō*, but instead uses the

---

10   Lewis, *Mere Christianity*, 124–25.

theological term *hilaskomai*, which means to "make atonement." When the tax collector used this word for mercy, he expanded on the meaning of mercy by crying out, "O God, make an atonement for me, a sinner!"

Jesus commends the tax collector for his humility before God. Pride pushes for merit; humility pleads for mercy. In his humility, the tax collector represents the kind of follower the Father is looking for. "For all those who exalt themselves will be humbled, and those who humble themselves will be exalted" (Luke 18:14; see Luke 14:11; Matt. 18:4; 23:12; 1 Peter 5:6). He embodies Jesus's beatitudes in his humble dependence upon the mercy of God and in his mourning for his sins. Jesus draws a sharp distinction between this humble man and the proud religious man. The tax collector went home justified before God; the Pharisee did not. Bailey writes, "The tax collector yearns to accept the gift of God's justification, while the Pharisee feels he has already earned it."[11] The tax collector is a recipient of God's mercy. He cannot save himself. He returns home "justified," "humbled," and "exalted," because God has done for him what he could never do for himself.[12]

Jesus leaves us with a positive picture of the tax collector returning home justified before God. But Helmut Thielicke finishes his sermon on this parable giving an unexpectedly sour note. He reflects on the danger of people turning their conversion story into a source of pride and vainglory. They hit the road

---

11   Kenneth E. Bailey, *Jesus through Middle Eastern Eyes: Cultural Studies in the Gospels* (Downers Grove, IL: InterVarsity, 2008), 350.
12   Snodgrass, *Stories with Intent*, 474.

with their story of grace, and before you know it, "the devil has turned the whole thing into a pious and vain autobiography." Thielicke is agitated over this possibility, even though Jesus gives us no hint of such a problem. Thielicke warns,

> When a man has had an experience of God let him beware of telling it to men and making comparisons. The sulphurous stench of hell is nothing compared with the evil odor emitted by divine grace gone putrid. The grace of God actually can be corrupted by spiritual vanity. And the so-called children of the world are quick to note this and are repelled by it. How many a non-Christian, for whom Christ died just as he died for you and for me, has learned to know the grace of God only in this fetid form that reeks of pride and has turned away in disgust, preferring to stick with his honest nihilism?[13]

Robert Capon develops a more complicated scenario. He doesn't quite accept Jesus's commendation of the tax collector's humility. Capon wants to say that both men are guilty, but only the tax collector really grasps the truth of his guilt. But in the end, both men will be saved by grace. Neither one can "win the game of justification." They're both losers; they're both dead in their sins. And yet both will be saved no matter what happens in the end. The advantage the tax collector has

---

13 Thielicke, *Waiting Father*, 133.

is that he's able to receive the gift of justification right now, but the Pharisee is "so busy doing the bookkeeping on a life he cannot hold that he will never be able to enjoy himself." Capon's premise implies a universal salvation that justifies all, tax collector and Pharisee alike, regardless of their response to God. For Capon, the real danger is turning the tax collector into a Pharisee, *by expecting his life to change*. Even a little reform, Capon reasons, destroys the story "by sending the publican back for his second visit with the Pharisee's speech in his pocket?"[14] Capon seems dissatisfied with how Jesus and Luke handle the story. He can't quite believe that Jesus made a new man out of the tax collector. He suspects that the publican will flip and become a hypocrite. In response to Capon's interpretation, you might ask yourself what the tax collector's week was like after he left the temple. Was he a changed man—changed from the inside-out? Was his conversion genuine, or did life go on as it always had?

Ken Bailey points out the significant parallel between this parable and Isaiah 66:1–6 as another instance in which a parable follows closely an Old Testament theme.[15] When Jesus tells this story, he is essentially preaching Isaiah 66:1–6. The prophet opens and closes with a reference to the temple first to reiterate that no temple can contain the Lord. "Heaven is my

---

14 Capon, *Kingdom, Grace, and Judgment*, 342–43.
15 Bailey, *Jesus through Middle Eastern Eyes*, 350. Bailey links the parable of the good shepherd (Luke 15:4–7) to Psalm 23; the parable of the prodigal son contains fifty-one points of similarity and contrasts to the story of Jacob in Genesis 27:1–36:8; and the parable of the two builders in Luke 6:46–49 to Isaiah 28:14–18.

throne, and earth is my footstool," says the Lord. Second, the temple is described as a place of judgment. The commotion Isaiah heard throughout the city is coming from the temple where the Lord is "repaying his enemies all they deserve" (Isa. 66:6). The text zeroes in on self-justifying religion that has gone bad: a sacrificial system that has become a desecration, offerings that mock God and defile the giver, and prayers that dishonor God by paying homage to idols. The temple worshipers "have chosen their own ways," says the Lord. They delight in what they call "worship," but the Lord calls it an abomination. Temple-sanctioned self-justification requires swift judgment. The only glimmer of anything positive comes from the Lord's brief statement: "These are the ones I look on with favor: those who are humble and contrite in spirit, and who tremble at my word" (Isa. 66:2).

In the parable of the Pharisee and the tax collector, Jesus is working the angles between empty religion and beatitude-based humility. Snodgrass agrees; he writes, on the one hand, "God is not a God impressed with pious acts and feelings of superiority. He is, rather, a God of mercy who responds to the needs and honest prayers of people. On the other hand, God is not a God whose mercy can be taken for granted. Within the parable the tax collector does not even know the outcome of his prayer. The verdict of acquittal stands outside the parable. . . . The parable raises the question of how our assessment of people squares with God's assessment."[16]

---

16 Snodgrass, *Stories with Intent*, 474–75.

❧18❧

THE WORKERS IN THE VINEYARD

MATTHEW 20:1–6

The parable of the workers in the vineyard is a warning to spiritual pride and a testimony to God's grace. To everyone who has worked long and hard for Christ, this parable is for you. And for those who have had little to do with Christ and wondered if there was still time to become involved in the Lord's kingdom work, this parable is for you, too. Only Jesus was able to design his teaching to reach the full spectrum of people, and he did it all the time. His teaching covered the human condition from top to bottom and all points in between. The word of God evangelizes and edifies. For those of us who are preachers, we want to reach seekers with the gospel, and we want to grow Christians in the gospel. One sermon can do both. The evangelistic power of the gospel and the theologically rich meaning of the gospel can be held together in a positive tension. We are not trying to strike a balance between evangelism and edification. We are seeking to weave together invitation and instruction in such a way that seekers from week to week are "seeing how faith in Christ actually works and brings about life change. . . . They are being evangelized very effectively, not superficially, even as Christians are being built up."[1] Tim Keller writes, "We need evangelistic sermons that edify, as well as edifying sermons that evangelize."[2]

This parable reminds us of the parable of the lost sons. We tend to see ourselves either in the repentant son who returns home to the loving embrace of the father or in the elder brother who resented his father's compassion. The prodigal son is a picture of God's unlimited grace, and the elder brother is a picture of religious resentment and self-righteous pride. Jesus was constantly working all the angles of human need in his parables. He did this even from the cross when he invited the repentant thief into his kingdom ("Today you will be with me in paradise," Luke 23:43), cared for his mother ("Woman, behold your son; son, behold your mother," John 19:26–27), and honored his Father ("Father, into your hands I commit my spirit," Luke 23:46). The Spirit of God speaks to the person who knows nothing of the grace of God, as well as to the person who, after many years of familiarity with God's grace, may have begun to take it for granted. The parable of the workers in the vineyard may be summed up in a line: *Mercy's minimum wage is always greater than merit's maximum compensation.*

---

1 Timothy Keller, *Preaching: Communicating Faith in an Age of Skepticism* (New York: Viking, 2005), 120.

2 Timothy Keller, *Center Church: Doing Balanced, Gospel-Centered Ministry in Your City* (Grand Rapids: Zondervan, 2012), 317.

BY THE NUMBERS

The shock value of this parable is in the numbers. Those who worked for just one hour at the end of the day, from 5:00 p.m. to 6:00 p.m., received the same daily wage as those who worked a full twelve-hour shift. This is beyond unfair; it is insulting. Who wouldn't react? It doesn't make sense. However, it should be noted that the landowner was faithful to his agreement with the early morning crew. He paid them what he had promised—a fair day's wage. Why then didn't he dismiss them first with a denarius and send them on their way? Why make them wait around to the end to see "the sweatless upstarts who put in barely an hour get the exact same pay? Anyone who has worked manually for a full day can easily identify with their outrage. The boss's decision defies economics."[3]

Jesus had a way with numbers that was calculated to get people's attention. When the poor widow put in two mites, an amount worth a mere fraction of a penny, Jesus said, "I tell you, this poor widow has put more into the treasury than all the others" (Mark 12:43). On another occasion, Jesus told a story of a shepherd who left ninety-nine sheep in the open country to look for one lost sheep. For the sake of the one lost lamb he risked the entire flock (Luke 15:1–7). When Mary poured out a pint of expensive perfume on Jesus's feet, worth three hundred denarii, a year's worth of wages, Jesus defended her alleged wastefulness as a beautiful act of worship. When

---

3 Philip Yancey, "The Atrocious Mathematics of the Gospel," *Christianity Today* 28, no. 8 (May 18, 1984), 38.

Jesus played the numbers, he arrived at a very different bottom line than the conventional wisdom. The gospel upends all of our assumptions about worth and value and turns everything upside down. Jesus told the truth slant to get people to think. Even so, it's easy to overthink a parable, especially when we ignore the context of the parable.[4] We ignore Luke's inspired context at our interpretative peril, resulting in interpretations that Jesus never intended. This parable is not about employment practices or immigration policies. As R. T. France exclaims, "There is no need to explain the hiring of additional workers at various stages in the day as normal practice—this is a parable, not a sociological study!"[5] The parable is not about wealthy landowners in any century, ancient or modern, showing compassion for day laborers. Nor is it about the landowner in need of extra workers to make sure he gathered

---

4   Klyne R. Snodgrass writes: "Parables are analogies, and analogies have correspondences or they cannot work. The symbolic world of the parable points to God and those seeking to serve him, as already indicated. However, correspondences that make analogies work are a far cry from turning a story that is not allegory into allegory, which both the church and biblical scholars have often done. The attempt to see Jews represented in the first hired and the Gentiles in the last hired—even in the mind of Matthew— requires a divining rod that the text does not give. . . . No parable should be expected to present a detailed theological picture about the eternal state of all its characters. Parable interpretation is about how the analogy works, not deciding how each element fits with theology or Jesus's relation to his contemporaries" (*Stories with Intent: A Comprehensive Guide to the Parables of Jesus* [Grand Rapids: Eerdmans, 2018], 373, 375). Gentile acceptance of the crucified and risen Messiah is a theme running through the New Testament. Snodgrass warns of overinterpreting the parables and reading into them certain specifics that may or may not be there.

5   R. T. France, *Matthew: New International Commentary* (Grand Rapids: Eerdmans, 2007), 290.

his vintage harvest before it spoiled. It is not about supply-side economics. It is not about labor shortages. The motive for the master paying the same wage to the latecomers as he did to the early workers has nothing to do with the special merit of the latecomers or their pressing economic need.

WHAT'S IN IT FOR US?

Jesus's parable appears to have been prompted by Peter's question: "What's in it for us?" Its interpretive key is found in Jesus's statement, which is repeated twice, "The last will be first, and the first will be last" (Matt. 19:30; 20:16). Once again, the context is critical for interpretation. Jesus was approached by a rich young ruler who wanted to know what he had to do to receive eternal life. Jesus told this wealthy man, who was confident of his own righteousness, to sell his possessions and give to the poor and come follow him. Unable to part with his money, the young man went away sad. Jesus said to his disciples, "Truly I tell you, it is hard for someone who is rich to enter the kingdom of heaven. Again I tell you, it is easier for a camel to go through the eye of a needle than for someone who is rich to enter the kingdom of God." This radical statement shocked the disciples. They blurted out, "Who then can be saved?" Jesus replied, "With [human beings] this is impossible, but with God all things are possible" (Matt. 19:23–26).

Apparently, without even pausing to reflect on what Jesus said about God doing the impossible, Peter chimed in, saying in effect, "We have left everything to follow you! What's in it for us?" Did Peter successfully avoid the idol of money and wealth only to lay hold of the idol of self-justification?[6] Peter was not hindered from following Jesus because of his material possessions, but he appears to be wrestling with his pride. Surely there must be some reward for signing up early. Does Peter believe that he is a better person than the rich young ruler because he left everything to follow Jesus? Apparently so. Does he give God the credit for leaving everything behind and following Jesus? Not likely. Peter is tempted here to turn the mercy of God into a merit badge he earned on his own.

Jesus answered Peter's question, What's in it for us? with a *promise* and a *warning*. He began with an extraordinary *promise*. The future holds exciting possibilities for those who have left all to follow him. They can expect royal responsibilities in a new world order, along with this-world rewards and relational fulfillment beyond their imagination. Everything given up to follow Jesus will pale in significance compared to the reward received when the Son of Man comes to sit on his throne (Matt. 19:28). "But" says Jesus, and here comes the *warning*, "many who are first will be last, and many who are last will be first." Spiritual pride prompts a warning that takes the pedagogical form of a parable. Jesus leads with the positive, but he pointedly addresses the underlying motive that lies behind Peter's question. Dale Bruner writes, "Faithful teaching will give equal time to both promise and warning,

---

6   Frederick Dale Bruner, *Matthew: A Commentary*, vol. 2, *The Churchbook*, Matthew 13–28 (Grand Rapids: Eerdmans, 2007), 311.

ministering both gospel and law, to lead the people of God on the hard, narrow road to their rich inheritance."[7]

The parable's singular meaning is best understood from three different points of view, those of the landowner, the early workers, and the latecomers. Each party gives us an angle on the singular meaning of the parable: spiritual pride has no place in God's vineyard. Klyne Snodgrass sets the parable in its context. He writes, "The context is carefully framed by Matthew at least in 19:13–20:34 to deal with issues of status, wealth, greed, and discipleship. The underlying message in this section is the reversal of the world's values." Here is how Snodgrass contextualizes these themes in Matthew's gospel. In places I have paraphrased and abbreviated his description:

19:13–15: "The disciples are corrected for trying to keep children away; of such are the kingdom."

19:16–22: "The rich man is instructed about his failure to keep the law by loving his neighbors, the poor, with his wealth and is called to deny himself, take up his cross, and follow Jesus."

19:23–26: "The disciples are instructed on the deceit of money, perhaps the most obvious reversal of values."

---

7   Bruner, *Matthew*, 2:315.

19:27–30: Peter asks his question, and Jesus responds with a promise in verse 30 and a summary proverb.

20:1–16: Jesus tells the parable.

20:17–19: Jesus explains that he has to die to bring about this reversal of values.

20:20–28: The mother of sons of Zebedee makes her request, which sets up Jesus's instruction on the reversal of values.

20:29–34: Jesus heals the two blind men who have the right attitude. Their eyes are opened and they follow Jesus.[8]

Jesus's prediction of his death for the third time (Matthew 20:17–19) in the context of his teaching on the reversal of values underscores the truth that Jesus had to die to bring about this transformation of values. This key theological orientation is necessary to the interpretation of the parable.

LANDLORD

The subject of the entire parable is the sovereign landlord. He owns the vineyard, hires the workers himself, sets the terms

---

8 Snodgrass, *Stories with Intent*, 368–69. I have modified and abbreviated Snodgrass's description.

of the contract, oversees payroll, and explains the rationale for his actions. He agrees to a denarius, which was considered a generous day's pay. Bruner explains, "Thus by computing what the day wage is in any culture now we can roughly compute the value of the denarius then."[9] The landlord is a picture of the Lord who takes all the initiative in establishing the kingdom of God and calling people to himself. And just as the landlord called people out of idleness into work, the Lord calls people out of frustration and futility into kingdom work.

Like the landlord, "the church that follows the Lord goes out again and again with the call of the gospel."[10] We never stop calling people out of their idleness and emptiness into a life of meaningful work. We are challenged to be the salt of the earth and light of the world as Jesus described in the Sermon on the Mount (Matt. 5:13–16). This is the work that seeks first his kingdom and his righteousness (Matt. 6:33). The landlord asks the last group of laborers, "Why have you been standing here all day long doing nothing?" The question implies that there is more to life than doing nothing, and everything apart from kingdom work is nothing. We have all seen day laborers standing around a building supply store waiting to be hired. Now picture that scene with all types of professionals instead of migrant day-laborers. Think of teachers, doctors, nurses, lawyers, judges, and parents milling around a street corner waiting to be employed. It doesn't matter who you are, or what your

---

9 Bruner, *Matthew*, 2:319.
10 Bruner, *Matthew*, 2:319.

training and education is, if you are not employed in kingdom work, you're really not working. You may be pulling down a big salary and putting in long hours, but you're still unemployed in God's kingdom work. Uselessness is not only a problem for the unemployed but also for the well-employed who have not responded to the call of God. Futility is the systemic problem of those uninvolved in God's kingdom work. All Christians are called to kingdom work and holy vocations regardless of their educational and professional training. All Christians are called to salvation, service, sacrifice, and simplicity. Christopher Wright raises the question we should be asking:

> Is *the church as a whole* reflecting the wholeness of God's redemption? Is the church (thinking here of the local church as the organism effectively and strategically placed for God's mission in any given community) aware of all that God's mission summons them to participate in? Is the church through the combined engagement of *all* its members, applying the redemptive power of the cross of Christ to *all* the effects of sin and evil in the surrounding lives, society and environment?[11]

We need the whole church to manifest the manifold wisdom of God (Eph. 3:10). We need mothers, dentists,

---

11   Christopher J. H. Wright, *The Mission of God: Unlocking the Bible's Grand Narrative* (Downers Grove, IL: InterVaristy, 2006), 322 (emphasis is his).

homebuilders, politicians, educators, engineers, evangelists—
you name it; we need the whole vocational range of *real* mis-
sionaries who bear witness to Christ and his cross in their daily
lives and work. This is why we emphasized the priesthood of
all believers and every-member ministry and the shared gifts
of the Spirit. This is why we have said that all believers are
called to salvation, service, sacrifice and simplicity.[12]

Bruner writes, "Discipling or evangelism is, among other
things, the engaging of other men and women in the world's
most important and exciting work. 'Follow me, and I will
make you fishers of people!' (Matt. 4:19)."[13] The harvest is
great and there is always a need for more workers. The Lord
of the harvest is always calling more workers into his kingdom
work. To be a Christian is to be a disciple, and to be a disciple is
to be a worker. If you are not related to this particular landlord,
you are unemployed, no matter how hard you're working.[14]

Jesus's kingdom work does not envision "button-hole"
evangelism. We aren't grabbing people by their lapels and
getting in their faces, saying, "Come to Jesus!" But Jesus did

---

12 Webster, *Living in Tension*, 187.
13 Bruner, *Matthew*, 2:319.
14 Snodgrass (*Stories with Intent*, 372) writes: "The view that the parable con-
    fronts exploitation of workers and that the owner is a negative figure has
    no basis. . . . [William] Herzog thinks the frequent trips of the owner
    originally underscored his unilateral power; the owner presents a 'take it
    or leave it' proposition. . . . The reversal of the order of payment is viewed
    as an affront to the first hired workers, a deliberate attempt to keep them
    subjugated. . . . If this were the meaning of the parable, then most people
    would have to give up any hope of understanding Jesus's parables, for
    nothing provides a bridge from the text to any of the conclusions Herzog
    draws."

envision living life in such a way that everything about us is shaped by his gospel. We are called to a life that has "salt and light" impact. Jesus had in mind followers like Gantumur Badrakh, a Mongolian believer. In 2001, he taught English at the Defense University of Mongolia. He was abruptly removed from his teaching position without explanation. Sometime later the principal of the school told him that he was ordered by the commanding officer to fire Gantumur because he was a Christian. The principal told Gantumur that he defended him to the commander. Besides being an excellent English instructor, Gantumur never spoke of Christ in the classroom or used his position to proselytize. The commander replied, "I don't care. He is teaching who he is, even without saying it."[15]

LEADERS

The second perspective comes from the early laborers who arrived for work at 6 a.m. They worked about twelve times longer than the latecomers who arrived at 5 p.m. These early workers worked all day long, from sunrise to sunset. They are like Peter, and other Christian leaders, who joined Jesus early and gave up everything to follow him. The "firsts" are tempted to ask, "What's in it for us?" At the end of the day, the owner of the vineyard said to the supervisor, "Call the workers and pay them their wages, beginning with the last ones hired and going on to the first." No landowner in his right mind would

---

15 Gantumur Badrakh is a graduate of Beeson Divinity School. His story is used with permission.

do it this way. If he wanted to be fair and generous, wouldn't he pay the early workers first and, after they were dismissed, proceed to pay the latecomers a denarius? By reversing the order, Jesus builds suspense and adds an unexpected twist in the story. We are reminded once again, right in the middle of the story, that the first will be last and the last first. Naturally, the tired workers, who had worked all day, expected to be paid more than the agreed upon wage. When they saw the latecomers receive a denarius, they must have been excited about their generous bonus. But when each received *only* a denarius, they were upset. Imagine yourself in their situation. How would you feel? First they grumbled, and then they spoke up: "These men who were hired last worked only one hour . . . and you have made them equal to us who have borne the burden of the work and the heat of the day" (Matt. 20:12).

The parable causes us to wrestle with our disappointment with God. We, too, can feel like these grumblers who have worked all day in the Lord's vineyard. We compare ourselves to others and complain that God has not met our expectations. We have done more and worked harder than the next guy, or so we feel, and yet he or she seems to get all the blessings. Where is our reward? We grumble and complain that God is unfair, even if it is only to ourselves.

Such comparisons are discouraged in God's kingdom work. They expose our underlying self-importance. Peter compared himself to the rich young ruler and said to the Lord, "What's in it for us?" His self-conscious sacrifice, "we left everything," thinly conceals his spiritual pride. Instead of boasting of God's

grace, he boasted of *his* sacrifice. He was like the elder brother
in the parable of the prodigal son (Luke 15:25–32) who could
not grasp the generosity of the father's love. This was a hard
lesson for Peter to learn, and it is a hard lesson for us to learn.
Like Peter, we naturally compare ourselves to others to see if we
are getting a good deal and receiving the recognition we think
we deserve. Following Peter's restoration on the beach, the
risen Jesus said to him, "I tell you, when you were younger you
dressed yourself and went where you wanted; but when you are
old you will stretch out your hands, and someone else will dress
you and lead you where you do not want to go." Peter's almost
instinctive reaction was to ask about John's future ("Lord, what
about him?"). "What is that to you?" Jesus responded. "You
must follow me" (John 21:18, 21–22). Making these kinds of
comparisons doesn't work when it comes to God's kingdom
work. Each of us is different, and we are all called to follow
the Lord Jesus. We share a common calling and commission,
within which we have unique responsibilities and challenges.
We entrust ourselves to the providence of God, and we submit
to his will. Some believers labor under extreme conditions while
others seem to have it very easy, but we all need to support one
another and serve the Lord and his church.

Helmut Thielicke warned, "You will never be able to see
the goodness of God with a jealous eye. . . . When envy seizes
hold upon me I must stop this nerve-racking calculation as
to whether God is giving more to somebody else than to me.
Instead, I should thank him for what he has given to me and
pray that he may also support and comfort that other person

in those secret trials and troubles of which I have no knowledge at all."[16] Luther said, "God cannot stand it that we boast . . . of anything other than his grace."[17] The apostle Paul wrote, "We do not dare to classify or compare ourselves with some who commend themselves. When they measure themselves by themselves and compare themselves with themselves, they are not wise." He goes on to say, "'Let the one who boasts boast in the Lord.' For it is not the one who commends himself who is approved, but the one whom the Lord commends" (2 Cor. 10:12, 17–18).

The gospel of Matthew is the most law-oriented of the four gospel accounts, and yet we see how close Matthew's theology of salvation is to the theology of the apostle Paul. They both agree that salvation is by grace, through faith, and not from ourselves: "it is the gift of God—not by works, so that no one can boast" (Eph. 2:8–9). *Mercy's minimum wage is always greater than merit's maximum compensation!* That is why the landlord responds to the early workers—the "firsts," with a gentle rebuke, "I am not being unfair to you, friend. Didn't you agree to work for a denarius? Take your pay and go. I want to give the one who was hired last the same as I gave you. Don't I have the right to do what I want with my own money? Or are you envious because I am generous?" (Matt. 20:13–15).

"Biblical questions," writes Dale Bruner, "are altar calls, asking hearers to admit wrongs." The landlord's first question

---

16   Helmut Thielicke, *The Waiting Father: Sermons on the Parables of Jesus* (New York: Harper & Row, 1959), 124.
17   Bruner, *Matthew*, 2:321.

("Can't I do what I want with my own money?") "asks a *theological question* about the sovereignty of God." The second question ("Are you mad because I am good?") asks an *anthropological question"*about the sinfulness of the self-righteous.[18] It is all too easy for us to act like the elder son, resentful of the father's love, wishing that our younger brother had never come home. God's grace may be hard for us to fathom and even at times appreciate, but shouldn't we rejoice that we serve the God of all grace and mercy?

A father who is not given to charismatic experiences recently shared with me the following. He was climbing one of his favorite mountain trails. It was midweek, and no one was around for miles. He said the silence was loud. Suddenly he heard God speaking to him. He literally heard a voice say to him, "This is where you gave up on your son." Years ago he had climbed that same trail with his son and his son's friend, and by the end of the day he was so disgusted with his son that he stopped praying for him. That was the day he gave up on him. His wife continued to pray for their son, but he was so deeply troubled and disappointed with his son that he stopped caring and praying for him. Years passed, and his son came to know the Lord in a profound and meaningful way. Now, he and his son worship and serve in the same church and their relationship is the best it has ever been. But it wasn't until he heard the voice of God confronting him on that lonely mountain trail that he felt the pain of his own resentment and

---

18   Bruner, *Matthew*, 2:321.

the hardness of his heart. He said he wept and wept, with the realization of what he had done.

The early workers, who grumbled and accused the landlord of being unfair, may have been like the believers in the church of Ephesus who lost their first love. The sovereign Lord of the church commends the church at Ephesus for their deeds, hard work, and perseverance. They were vigilant against wickedness, victorious in their defense of the truth, and vital in their faith. What's left, we might ask? What church would not be pleased with this strong commendation? As John Stott writes, "Its members were busy in their service, patient in their suffering, and orthodox in their belief. What more could be asked of them?"[19] "Yet," Christ says, "I hold this against you: You have forsaken the love you had at first" (Rev. 2:4). Hidden in their strengths, which were many, was a weakness that was deadly. The church at Ephesus had everything but the most essential thing. They had lost their first love for Christ. What they lacked was a true passion for God.

It is not enough for us to be known by our deeds; we need to be known for our devotion to God. Defending the faith is important, but never as a substitute for loving God. Jesus said, "By this everyone will know that you are my disciples, if you love one another" (John 13:35). Loving the Lord Jesus is always first and foremost. Everything follows from this central commitment. Without it we are susceptible to pride, and we

---

19 John R. W. Stott, *God's New Society: The Message of Ephesians* (Downers Grove, IL: InterVarsity, 1979), 21.

begin to calculate what we have done and what we feel God owes us. Hidden in our ministry strengths is a soul-depressing weakness. We are tempted to create a climate of suspicion and defensiveness, with the result that we will be known more for our anger and resentment than for our love and devotion. The primary emotion in a passion for Christ is not hating evil but loving the Lord Jesus Christ.

The danger is that, like the believers at Ephesus, we forget that we are miserable sinners saved by Christ's grace alone. We fail to remember the love of God in Christ. We reduce the faith to practices, rituals, doctrines, and traditions. We hold to true doctrines and faithful traditions, but without a passion for Christ, we lose our first love and we resent our brothers and sisters in Christ because we believe God is giving them a better deal. Christ's prescription is emphatic: "Consider how far you have fallen! Repent and do the things you did at first" (Rev. 2:5). We want to be a church that is so in love with Christ—so impressed with his mercy and grace—that we embrace the latecomers with open arms and hearts!

LATECOMERS

Dale Bruner reminds us that the history of the church is a history of latecomers, sometimes waves of latecomers. Jewish Christians struggled to learn that God's grace extended to Gentile Christians. Roman Catholics and Eastern Orthodox can't afford to look down on latecoming Protestants. Long-time church members must embrace millennial and Gen-Z believers. Fast-growing churches, Bible churches, independent churches, charismatic churches, and megachurches must not look down on slower, smaller churches. Reformed churches, rich in heritage, cannot look down on the emergent church. Mainline churches should be open to newer kinds of churches. Strong Christians should not question the dedication of weaker or seemingly less impressive Christians. And those who are overconscious of being involved in God's work must not speak or think demeaningly of those who are not yet in God's work at all.[20]

The final perspective to be explored is that of the outsiders who have not yet come to Christ. Jesus gave this parable as a warning against spiritual pride. He directed it to disciples like Peter who thought first of their own sacrifices and worried about being shortchanged. But we would be remiss if we did not acknowledge the very positive message this parable holds for the outsider, the person who is still standing around unemployed in God's kingdom work. The message of this parable is that today is the day to respond to God's call. We want to be a church of old-timers and latecomers. The invitation still stands, right up to the last hour: "Come to me, all you who are weary and burdened, and I will give you rest. Take my yoke upon you and learn from me, for I am gentle and humble in heart, and you will find rest for your souls. For my yoke is easy and my burden is light" (Matt. 11:28–30). Remember the first will be last and the last, first because mercy's minimum wage is always greater than merit's maximum compensation.

---

20 Bruner, *Matthew*, 2:318.

✤19✤

THE TWO SONS

MATTHEW 21:28–32

The parable of the two sons is more radical than you may think at first glance. It is sobering to be reminded that our initial "yes" to Jesus can become over time a passive "no" to God's kingdom work. There is no hint in Jesus's teaching of a laid-back kingdom work ethic. Instead of slacking off, Jesus seems intent on kicking it up a notch. You recall that the Lord was not very sympathetic to Jeremiah: "If you have raced with men on foot and they have worn you out, how can you compete with horses? If you stumble in safe country, how will you manage in the thickets by the Jordan?" (Jer. 12:5). We remember Jesus saying, "No one who puts his hand to the plow and looks back is fit for service in the kingdom of God" (Luke 9:62). Clearly, there is kingdom work for us to do, and our lives will be significantly diminished without it and greatly enriched by it.

BINARY LOGIC

Jesus told the parable of the two sons in the temple courts in the midst of escalating tension between himself and the religious leaders. Jesus was on a collision course with the powers that be, and he knew how it was going to end. He was heading to the cross. This pattern of escalating tension remains true today for all believers. The cost of discipleship is real. Faithfulness to Christ in a hostile world seldom results in a life of ease. Following Jesus's triumphal entry into Jerusalem and the temple cleansing, the Pharisees and teachers of the law were outraged. They were furious that he received praise fit for a king. They were plotting Jesus's death as the crowds were shouting, "Hosanna to the Son of David!" The whole city was asking, "Who is this?" while the religious leaders were thinking, "Who does he think he is?" Think of it. The best religious minds in the country were focused on stopping Jesus. They confronted him, saying, "By what authority are you doing these things? . . . Who gave you this authority?" (Matt. 21:23).

Jesus's authority was based on who he was in himself in relationship to his heavenly Father. He had no title or office or institutional clout. His wisdom, teaching, and compassion defined his authority. His unique claim did not depend on the pressure to prove himself to the powers that be. He shows no impulse to win their approval. He exercised his authority in complete freedom from institutional control and traditional authorities because of his relationship with the Father. "My Father is always at his work to this very day, and I too am working. . . . Very truly I tell you, the Son can do nothing by himself; he can do only what he sees his Father doing, because whatever the Father does the Son also does" (John 5:17, 19).

The authority of Jesus stands over and against every human strategy designed to subvert the will of God. Jesus remained unapologetic. He said, "First let me ask you a question. You answer my question and I'll answer yours. About the baptism of John—who authorized it: heaven or humans?" (Matt. 21:24–25 MSG). This is at the heart of every issue: God's will or our will. Jesus's frames it as a simple case of binary logic. There are only two possibilities. We have to choose between what is either good or bad, true or false, right or wrong. The chief priests and elders refused to yield to Jesus's simple logic, because they would either have to admit that John was sent from God or they would have to face the outrage of the people. Jesus had them in a bind, so the religious leaders feigned ignorance. "We don't know," they said. Today they would form committees and claim they needed more time to study the issue. In any case, the religious leaders who were out to get Jesus sidestepped the issue. They chose to hide their unbelief in ambiguity and indecision. Feigned neutrality thinly veiled their resentment and anger.

Jesus responded with a parable that connected the dots and drew a conclusion that even the religious leaders could not deny. The meaning of the parable is this: in our relationship with God, the emphatic "no" that becomes a "yes" is better than the enthusiastic "yes" that becomes a "no." There are no "fence sitters" in the kingdom of God. It is either a "yes" or a "no" to God. Religion often obscures this simple binary fact, but Jesus always demands it. The precedence for this can be found in other binary texts, such as when Joshua said to the children of Israel, "choose for yourselves this day whom you will serve, whether the gods your ancestors served . . . or the gods of the Amorites. . . . But as for me and my household, we will serve the LORD" (Josh. 24:15). Or, when Elijah on Mount Carmel said, "How long will you waver between two opinions? If the LORD is God, follow him; but if Baal is God, follow him" (1 Kings 18:21).

With that said, there is a place for *both/and* thinking in a Christ-centered worldview. Certain biblical truths should be held in positive tension. For example, we believe in the total depravity of humankind *and* in the evidence of God's image even in the vilest sinner. We accept God's unconditional, sovereign control and election of all people *and* we affirm the freedom and responsibility of each individual to respond to God. We believe in God's salvation for the elect through Christ's atoning sacrifice on the cross *and* we believe in the universal invitation of the gospel, that whosoever will may come. We believe in the irresistible grace of God *and* in the freedom of choice to reject as well as to accept the gospel. We believe in the perseverance of the saints *and* we strive to remain faithful to the end. We hold these truths in tension because of our commitment to Christ and his word.

No one emphasized the either/or alternative more than Jesus. We might prefer an indecisive "maybe," or a kind of middle-of-the-road *whatever* response, but Jesus did not give us that option. He concluded the Sermon on the Mount with a series of either/or alternatives: two ways (broad and narrow), two teachers (false and true), two pleas (words and deeds), and two foundations (sand and rock). Jesus filled out this final image with a parable about two kinds of builders: one who builds on the rock and one who builds on the sand. Jesus ended the Sermon on the Mount with clear, binary logic contrasting wisdom and foolishness.

THE NO THAT BECAME A YES

Jesus uses this same binary, either/or logic in a simple relational parable. He began, "What do you think? There was a man who had two sons." Jesus's simple line "Son, go and work today in the vineyard" bears special meaning. Like the father sending his sons to work, God commands all people to carry out his will. But even beyond that, the Son of Man sees himself in this parable. The vineyard is a metaphor for the people of God, and the Father has sent the Son to work the harvest.[1] Like the son who said "yes" but ultimately disobeyed, some people promise to work but they do not perform, while others who refuse to work initially end up obeying.[2] The analogy of the father/son relationship corresponds to our relationship with God the Father. The plot of the parable turns on this relationship: "Yet to all who received him, to those who believed in his name, he gave the right to become children of

---

1 Snodgrass disagrees: "The vineyard is not Israel, which would make no sense; rather it stands for God's purposes generally. To work in God's vineyard is the equivalent of being engaged with God's purposes" (Klyne R. Snodgrass, *Stories with Intent: A Comprehensive Guide to the Parables of Jesus* [Grand Rapids: Eerdmans, 2018], 274.)
2 Craig L. Blomberg, *Interpreting the Parables* (Downers Grove, IL: InterVarsity, 1990), 188.

God—children born not of natural descent, nor of human decision or a husband's will, but born of God" (John 1:12–13).

The vineyard is a metaphor for God's chosen people and signifies the nature and character of the work we are called to do. Jesus's organic models of growth clearly suggest that the expansion of the kingdom of God is not left to human strategies. The mustard seed reality of the kingdom of God is consistently demonstrated (Mark 4:34). What the world deems small and insignificant has the potential of growing great, not because of anything we do, but because of what God does. In the parable of the seed and soils, God is sovereign and the good seed reproduces abundantly (Mark 4:20). Jesus's church-growth strategy is never an excuse for sloth, but always a reminder that God is responsible for the growth. As planters and harvesters, we are part of the process, but the real growth remains a divine mystery, not a human enterprise. "I planted the seed," wrote the apostle Paul, "Apollos watered it, but God has been making it grow. So neither the one who plants nor the one who waters is anything, but only God, who makes things grow" (1 Cor. 3:6–7). Jesus's models of growth call us to pray: "Ask the Lord of the harvest . . . to send out workers into *his* harvest field" (Matt. 9:38, emphasis added). The cost for such growth is high, but not in the cost-effective ways that we are in the habit of measuring today. The truth of the matter is that "unless a kernel of wheat falls to the ground and dies, it remains only single seed. But if it dies, it produces many seeds" (John 12:24). Jesus said this not only to explain his death, but also our ministry. "Anyone who loves their life will lose it, while anyone who hates their life in this world will keep it for eternal life. Whoever serves me must follow me; and where I am, my servant also will be" (John 12:25–26). If we look to Jesus, the founder and finisher of our faith (Heb. 12:2), we will not be tempted to feel that the kingdom of God lies in our initiatives, methodologies, and budgets. But we will pray for people who are called by God to come alongside and participate in this labor of love for Christ and his kingdom.

The parable poses a question: Which is better, a yes-out-of-a-no or a no-out-of-a-yes? *The emphatic no that turns to a positive yes is better than the enthusiastic yes that turns to a passive no.* The outward "yes" that really meant "no" is a thinly veiled description of the scribes and Pharisees. Whereas the outward "no" that becomes a true "yes" is another way of saying, *the last will be first and the first last.* The parable is a sober warning against anyone who says "yes" to the tenets of the faith, but hardly lifts a finger for Jesus's kingdom work. Their initial, enthusiastic "yes" may be impressive to others, but to God it is a non-committal, passive "no." Conversion doesn't mean much if it doesn't lead to transformation. Faith apart from faithfulness is really not faith at all. Following this simple parable, Jesus asked the most obvious question: "Which of the two did what his father wanted?" "The first," they answered. Then Jesus drove the message home: "Truly I tell you, the tax collectors and the prostitutes are entering the kingdom of God ahead of you. For John came to you to show you the way of righteousness, and you did not believe him, but the tax collectors and the prostitutes did. And even after you saw this, you did not repent and believe him" (Matt. 21:31–32). Professing believers who admire Jesus are not the same as committed believers who follow Jesus. Only those who are deeply conscious of their need for God's saving grace, and who come to follow Christ, are excited about doing his will.

The parable is radical because a theoretical "yes" to routine church attendance and tithing is really only a cover for spectator passivity. It is the "yes" that means "no" to the call of God. Klyne Snodgrass asks, "How did people ever get the idea that obedience to the will of God is optional?" Like a disgruntled employee, it is possible to quit but not leave. There is no place for the autonomous individual, doing their own thing in their own way, in the body of Christ. The solitary priesthood celebrates the freedom to admire Jesus for the sake of personal satisfaction. But the true holy priesthood follows Jesus for the sake of kingdom-of-God obedience. As Snodgrass writes, the solitary priesthood makes "autonomous choices akin to purchasing an automobile or joining a civic club." But the holy priesthood is submissive to the will of God. The way of Jesus is the way of the cross, the way of sacrifice, the way of love, the way of grace. "Many parables, and especially this one, push for an integrity of life before God."[3]

---

3 Snodgrass, *Stories with Intent*, 275.

❧20❧

THE TENANTS

Matthew groups three parables together to underscore the religious leaders' resistance to Jesus: the parable of the two sons, the parable of the tenants, and the parable of the wedding banquet. Matthew arranged these parables to reinforce the universal scope of the gospel and to intensify the consequences of rejecting Jesus, the Messiah, the Son of David, the Son of God. These parables are based on the Old Testament, and they point to the fulfillment of God's covenant prophesies to Israel. They show explicitly how Jesus anticipated Israel's rejection and how he used this rejection for God's glory. The promises to Israel are not superseded nor suspended; they are fulfilled in a wonderful and unexpected way.

PROPHETIC TRUTH

Jesus lays out the explosive truth of his messianic coming under the cover of parables. These stories echo the deep meaning of the prophets and the Psalms, but on the surface they could be taken more lightly. The people loved them, finding them intriguing and insightful, maybe even a little entertaining. Luke describes the crowd hanging on every word (Luke 19:48). The religious leaders knew exactly what Jesus was doing, but they feared a popular uprising if they tried to arrest Jesus publicly. His friendly, subversive speech was popular on the surface but provocative below the surface. Jesus told the parable of the tenants after his overt occupation in the temple when he threw out the money changers and the sellers of sacrificial animals (Matt. 21:12–17). He was committed to preaching the gospel of grace and the justice of judgment.[1]

"This parable encourages the church with four of the most important truths of the gospel," writes Dale Bruner:

> (1) the long-suffering love of God, illustrated by the many sendings of the landlord (the parable could be called "The Parable of the Many Sendings"); (2) the incredible sinfulness of the human race, illustrated by the representative resistance of the landlord's servants to the landlord's many sendings; (3) the centrality and finality of the sending of the Son at the dramatic center of the story; and (4) the urgency and awfulness of the judgment that comes upon the opponents of the sendings, not only in the past but also in our own present and future (Matthew 21:44). These four truths almost spell out the content of the

---

1   N. T. Wright, *Jesus and the Victory of God: Christian Origins and the Question of God*, vol. 2 (Philadelphia: Fortress, 1996), 414–21.

gospel, but a fifth truth makes this parable unique: it teaches in vivid language (5) the transfer of the kingdom of God from Israel to a mysterious "nation" (Matthew 21:43). This transfer is one of the Gospel's most influential convictions.[2]

THE VINEYARD

Jesus's supporting text for the parable of the tenants, or as Ken Bailey prefers, the parable of the noble vineyard owner and his son, is Isaiah 5. The imagery of the vineyard echoes the full message of the prophet Isaiah. Jesus used a powerful image that invoked the decisive impact of the prophet's message.[3] Most of the Old Testament references to God's vineyard are negative and refer to judgment. When Jesus was walking from the upper room to Gethsemane shortly before he was arrested, he brought up the metaphor of the vine again, this time positively. On the way, Jesus and the disciples may have passed by the temple. Above the gate in stone relief were golden vines with grape clusters as big as a man. The evening shadows may have obscured the image, but Jesus's metaphor invoked these deep prophetic roots. The vine was the iconic symbol of Israel, used by the

---

2   Frederick Dale Bruner, *Matthew: A Commentary*, vol. 2, *The Churchbook*, Matthew 13–28 (Grand Rapids: Eerdmans, 2007), 377.

3   Richard C. Trench, *Notes on the Parables of Our Lord* (Trenton, NJ: Revell, 1953), 201. Trench writes, "The image of the kingdom of God as a vine-stock, or as a vineyard, runs through the whole Old Testament (Deut 32:32; Ps 80:8–16; Isa 27:1–7; Jer 2:21; Ezek 15:1–6; 19:10; Hosea 10:1)."

prophets to indict Israel. Hosea charged that even though God made Israel fruitful, she persisted in worshiping other gods (Hos.10:1–2). Isaiah declared, "The vineyard of the Lord Almighty is the nation of Israel"; on a fertile hillside, Yahweh planted only the choice vines and did everything possible to care for his crop, but his vine only produced bad fruit (Isa. 2:1–7). Jeremiah accused this "choice vine" of becoming "a corrupt, wild vine" (Jer. 2:21). Ezekiel likened Israel to a useless vine and lamented that wood from a vine was good for nothing but to be burned (Ezek. 15:1–5).

The psalmist used the vine to tell the story of Israel from Exodus to judgment: "You transplanted a vine from Egypt; you drove out the nations and planted it. . . . Your vine is cut down, it is burned with fire; at your rebuke your people perish." But then the psalmist unexpectedly shifts his focus from the depressing story of the vine to the messianic hope of the Son of Man: "Let your hand rest on the man at your right hand, the son of man you have raised up for yourself" (Ps. 80:8–17). The indictment of the prophets and the hope of the psalmist are answered in the one who says, "I am the true vine." This is the seventh and final "I am" saying of Jesus in the gospel of John.[4] Jesus used these descriptive images drawn from the Old Testament to paint a messianic self-portrait free from nationalistic and political triumphalism. The comparison

---

4   "I am the bread of life" (6:35); "I am the light of the world" (8:12); "I am the gate of the sheep" (10:7); "I am the good shepherd"(10:11); "I am the resurrection and the life" (11:25); "I am the way and the truth and the life" (14:6).

is straightforward: Israel persists in being the false vine; Jesus is the true vine. The prophets used the image of the vine to indict Israel, but Jesus used the image to comfort his disciples. Jesus invites us—his followers—to be rooted and grounded in him, to be at home with him.

A review of the Old Testament imagery of the vine helps us realize how much meaning lies behind Jesus's opening statement, "There was a landowner who planted a vineyard. He put a wall around it, dug a winepress in it and built a watchtower" (Matt. 21:33). The owner of the land did everything necessary to secure success. Four verbs describe the work of the vineyard owner: he planted, constructed, dug, and built. He made the big investment and did all the heavy lifting. The farmers only had to work the land and collect the harvest. Therefore, it was only reasonable that the landowner should gain from his investment and collect his fruit. But when he sent his servants to "collect his fruit," the renters reacted like a gang of criminals. Against all rational reason and good moral sense, they seized the landowner's servants: "they beat one, killed another, and stoned a third" (Matt. 21:35).

Thielicke attempts to get behind the rationale of the wicked tenants' incomprehensible action. He concludes that they must have "claimed everything as their own: their capacity to work, their output, and finally the whole scene of their work and their life, namely, the vineyard itself. In the end they even take credit for sunshine, rain, and good climate: 'Ah, we are the ones who produced this good wine!'"[5] Thielicke argues that the secular person does much the same thing when he or she takes credit for their gifts and resources. The modern Western person claims to have no need of the God hypothesis. They are shaped by a social imaginary that assumes human self-sufficiency and self-actualization. Ironically, the wicked tenants make tragic sense in a secular age that has developed an entire worldview around being alone in the universe.

We imagine, as Jesus talked, the crowd reacting to the horror of the beatings, killings, and stonings of these defenseless, innocent servants. Who in their right mind would do such a thing? However, no one in the moment, including the disciples, grasped that Jesus was replaying salvation history. Israel's long history of rejecting the word of the Lord delivered by the prophets is remembered in this parable as an inexplicable and irrational tragedy. Yet even more incomprehensible than the escalating human atrocity is the "patience, longsuffering, risk-taking, compassion, and self-emptying" of the vineyard owner![6]

The center of the story lies in the voice of the vineyard owner, who against all the evidence, continues to believe, "They will respect my son" (Matt. 21:37). Luke tells the story with the vineyard owner asking, "What shall I do? I will send my son, whom I love; perhaps they will respect him" (Luke 20:13). He's out of options, so "finally" he sends his son—not another

---

5 Helmut Thielicke, *The Waiting Father: Sermons on the Parables of Jesus* (New York: Harper & Row, 1959), 103.

6 Kenneth E. Bailey, *Jesus through Middle Eastern Eyes: Cultural Studies in the Gospels* (Downers Grove, IL: InterVarsity, 2008), 410.

servant, but his very own son (Mark 12:6). Given the fate of the servants, what father would do that? But the Father did the unthinkable and sent his one and only Son. "He ventured a new beginning," writes Thielicke. "If God had wanted merely to retaliate and to react to what we do, there would have been no rainbow over the Flood and we should never have been able to celebrate Christmas or New Year's or Easter."[7]

The tenants are as hard-hearted as they could be. When they see the son coming, they intentionally devise a premeditated course of action. They entertain the unthinkable—murder. They openly discuss killing the son: "This is the heir. Come, let's kill him and take his inheritance." Then they deliberately carry out their premeditated plan. "So they took him and threw him out of the vineyard and killed him" (Matt. 21:38–39). Their depraved and perverse attitude and action recalls Israel's ancient history when Joseph's brothers deliberately faked his death and sold him into slavery (Gen. 37:3–4). One wonders if any of the disciples picked up on this. Christians hearing this story today recall the author of Hebrews comparing the discarded carcasses of sacrificial animals outside the gate to Jesus's self-sacrifice through crucifixion "outside the city gate to make the people holy through his own blood" (Heb. 13:11–12).

With the son of the vineyard owner dead, Jesus asked the crowd, "Therefore, when the owner of the vineyard comes, what will he do to those tenants?" The crowd responded, "He will bring those wretches to a wretched end . . . and will rent

---

7 Thielicke, *Waiting Father*, 112.

the vineyard to other tenants, who will give him his share of the crop at harvest time" (Matt. 21:40–41). Jesus responded to the crowd by citing Psalm 118:22–23 to explain how the Lord will transcend the horror of this tragic rejection and bring about salvation. In Psalm 118, Israel is the stone that is rejected, but here the stone that is rejected is the Anointed One who has come—Jesus. The one telling the story is the one being rejected by the very leaders who ought to be embracing the heir to the kingdom of God.

PSALM 118

Psalm 118 declares that Israel is the load-bearing foundation for the kingdom of God. This is the fulfillment of God's covenant promise to Abram: "all peoples on earth will be blessed through you" (Gen. 12:2). This is the fulfillment of Isaiah's prophecy, "See, I lay a stone in Zion, a tested stone, a precious cornerstone for a sure foundation; the one who relies on it will never be stricken with panic" (Isa. 28:16). But the stone stands not only for Israel, but the One who comes in the name of the Lord, to bring salvation and to bless the house of the Lord. This carefully orchestrated harmony in the psalm between Israel and her representative is missing in Jesus's use of Psalm 118 in the parable of the vineyard and the wicked tenants.

Jesus confronted Israel's leaders, in what must have been an exasperated tone of irony, "Have you never read in the Scriptures: 'The stone the builders rejected has become the cornerstone; the LORD has done this, and it is marvelous in our eyes'" (Matt. 21:42; Ps. 118:22–23). In Psalm 118, Israel is rejected by the likes of Babylon, Persia, Egypt, and Samaria, but in the parable of the tenants, it is Israel's own leaders who have rejected their rightful representative, their God-anointed Messiah. Peter makes this very point in his trial before the Sanhedrin. He quotes Psalm 118 and declares, "Jesus is 'the stone you builders rejected, which has become the cornerstone,'" adding, "salvation is found in no one else, for there is no other name under heaven given to mankind by which we must be saved" (Acts 4:11–12).

The apostles develop the typology of Psalm 118 in keeping with Jesus's own interpretation. The confession of Christ is the rock upon which the church is built (Matt. 16:18), as well as all who come to him, "the living Stone—rejected by humans but chosen by God and precious to him—you also, like living stones, are being built into a spiritual house to be a holy priesthood, offering spiritual sacrifices acceptable to God through Jesus Christ." Peter adds, "Now to you who believe, this stone is precious. But to those who do not believe, 'The stone the builders rejected has become the cornerstone'" (1 Peter 2:4–7). Paul alludes to Psalm 118 when he refers to "Christ Jesus himself as the chief cornerstone. In him the whole building is joined together and rises to become a holy temple in the Lord. And in him you too are being built together to become a dwelling in which God lives by his Spirit" (Eph. 2:20–22). The often repeated call to worship "This is the day the LORD has made, let us rejoice and be glad in it" (Ps. 118:24; cf. Isa. 25:9) is embedded in a theology of salvation that depends absolutely on the gospel of grace. Our rejoicing depends on Jesus, the rock of our salvation.

The psalmist describes the whole congregation erupting in praise, shouting, "Lord, save us!" (Ps. 118:25). There was a similar emotional outburst when Jesus entered Jerusalem on the Sunday before Passover riding a donkey. Jesus intentionally identified himself with Zechariah's well-known prophecy (Zech. 9:9), and the enthusiastic crowd entered into the drama. The people paved the way for Jesus with their coats, and they cut down palm branches to lay on the path. They shouted, "Hosanna!" adding in their excitement, "to the Son of David" (Matt. 21:9; see Mark 11:9–10, Luke 19:38; John 12:13). This left little doubt as to Jesus's special identity, and it drew the ire of some of the Pharisees in the crowd. They admonished Jesus, "Teacher, rebuke your disciples!" But Jesus responded, "I tell you, if they keep quiet, the stones will cry out" (Luke 19:39–40).

Year after year Israel reenacted the festal procession at the feast of the Passover. It was a joyous time of celebration and thanksgiving. They rehearsed the blessings of God and looked forward to the Son of David who promised to set things right and bring about the kingdom of God. Derek Kidner writes, "What those who took part in such a ceremony could never have foreseen was that it would one day suddenly enact itself on the road to Jerusalem: unrehearsed, unliturgical and with explosive force. In that week when God's realities broke through His symbols and shadows (Heb. 10:1), the horns of the altar became the arms of the cross, and the 'festival' itself found fulfillment in 'Christ our Passover' (1 Cor 5:7)."[8]

Dale Bruner calls Matthew 21:43 one of the most important verses in the gospel, because "it says nothing less momentous than that the kingdom of God will be taken away from Israel and given to a new 'nation,' which is usually understood as the church of both Jews and Gentiles."[9] This is correct as long as we explain that the kingdom is being taken away from people who have rejected the good news of the Messiah—the One who has come and whom God sent. All of the covenant promises are now being fulfilled in a wonderful way, so that the true Israel and the true Jews remain at the center of God's salvation and kingdom promise. This new creation is a transformed Israel of both Jews and Gentiles who produce the fruit of God's kingdom. Anyone who does not accept Christ, the load-bearing foundation stone, will be broken to pieces and crushed. Bruner writes, "The rejection of Jesus's teaching means a shattering fall today and a pulverizing judgment tomorrow."[10] The chief priests and the Pharisees sensed that Jesus was talking about them in his parables. The thin veil of ambiguity was not fooling them, but they were afraid of the crowd.

The gospel is good news to Jew and Gentile alike. All the promises made to Israel, the covenant people of God, are

---

8   Derek Kidner, *Psalms 73–150: An Introduction and Commentary* (Downers Grove: IL: InterVarsity, 1973), 415.

9   Bruner, *Matthew*, 2:381.

10 Bruner, *Matthew*, 2:384.

fulfilled in Jesus Christ. The Messiah has finally come, and he has brought salvation to the nations. The parable of the vineyard owner and wicked tenants sets up the parable of the wedding banquet. Jesus intended the first parable to help people understand the second.

❧ 21 ❧

THE WEDDING BANQUET

MATTHEW 22:1–14

The previous parable's theme and audience remain the same for the parable of the wedding banquet. Jesus's target audience for this parable is the religious establishment: the chief priests, the elders of the people, and the Pharisees (Matt. 21:23; 22:41). It is likely that Jesus shared variations of specific parables in different settings. The parable of the wedding banquet follows closely the parable of the great banquet (Luke 14:15–24), and even in that earlier version, the image of a wedding feast was on Jesus's mind (Luke 14:8). We see in this parable hints of the apostle John's focus on the marriage supper of the Lamb. The wedding theme framed his ministry from Cana in Galilee (John 2) to the last supper (Matt. 22:29). The consummation of salvation is compared to a royal wedding banquet that gathers the family of God from everywhere in true and lasting fellowship.

ROYAL WEDDING

The first thing to be understood is that the kingdom is about the king.[1] The rule and reign, the order and the peace, the political reality and the social condition all center in a person—the king. This is true of the apostle John's picture of the kingdom of God in heaven (Rev. 4–5), and it is true in Jesus's parable of the wedding feast. The action taken by the king is on behalf of his son, who is the reason for the wedding banquet. Throughout the parable, the king's action revolves around the son, but the king is in complete command. He is the subject who prepares the wedding banquet and sends out the servants with the royal invitation to subjects. He reacts in anger when his servants are mistreated and killed and sends the army to destroy the rebels. Then, the king sends out the servants again to gather all the people they could find. It is the king who notices and questions the man without wedding clothes and summarily orders his judgment. The king is responsible for all the action. True to Jesus's self-description, the son is a picture of willed passivity: "Very truly I tell you, the Son can do nothing by himself; he can do only what he sees his Father doing, because whatever the Father does the Son also does. For the Father loves the Son and shows him all he does" (John 5:19–20).

---

1   Helmut Thielicke, *The Waiting Father: Sermons on the Parables of Jesus* (New York: Harper & Row, 1959), 183.

INVITATION

The invitation comes in two parts, an initial "save-the-date" invitation, so everyone knows what's coming, and then a final come-to-the-feast invitation that lets everyone know that the dinner is ready.[2] The recipients of the king's first general invitation had accepted and responded with their RSVP, but now when the time comes to attend the royal wedding banquet, they refuse to come.[3]

The key word throughout the parable is "call" (Matt. 22:3, 8, 9, 14). The king's invitation stands for the call of God. It is an open invitation to enter into the joy of discipleship. It is not a dutiful call to work nor a mournful call to grieve. It is a celebratory call to rejoice. Those who are called should be honored and overjoyed that they have been included in the invitation. If you were an African living in northern Ghana, you would know exactly what Jesus meant in the parable when the king says, "My oxen and fattened cattle have been butchered, and everything is ready. Come to the wedding banquet" (Matt. 22:4). An abundance of meat is a symbol in many cultures of a special provision and celebration. Who in their right mind would turn down a lavish feast with friends on the joyous occasion of a royal wedding?

---

2 Craig S. Keener, *Matthew: The IVP New Testament Commentary Series* (Downers Grove, IL: InterVarsity, 2011), 323. Keener writes, "Papyri testify to the practice of double invitations, both among upper classes and in regular village life."

3 Frederick Dale Bruner, *Matthew: A Commentary*, vol. 2, *The Churchbook*, Matthew 13–28 (Grand Rapids: Eerdmans, 2007), 386.

There is a sacramental cast to all of life. Christians ought to be focused on "life's positive richness," a richness that is life-affirming, rather than life-rejecting, and that revels in the beauty, truth, and love derived from the divine nature.[4] Harry Blamires describes the Christian mind's positive view of life:

> A living Christian mind would elucidate for the young a finely articulated Christian sacramentalism which would make sense of, and give value to, the adolescent's cravings towards the grandeur of natural scenery, towards the potent emotionalism of music and art, and towards the opposite sex. A living Christian mind will not be content to refer to these things only in cold abstract terms which annihilate wonder and transmute them into bloodless modes of experience, unrecognizable as the stuff of passion and exaltation.[5]

We should dwell on "the tremendous blessedness" of the invitation to the wedding feast.[6] Again, this is not a summons to report for duty or a call to fulfill an obligation.[7] The theme

---

4   Harry Blamires, *The Christian Mind* (London: SPCK, 1963), 173.

5   Blamires, *Christian Mind*, 175

6   Thielicke, *Waiting Father*, 184.

7   Missionary statesman Lesslie Newbigin agrees: "There has been a long tradition which sees the mission of the Church primarily as obedience to a command. It has been customary to speak of 'the missionary mandate.' This way of putting the matter is certainly not without justification, and yet it seems to me that it misses the point. It tends to make mission a burden rather than a joy, to make it part of the law rather than part of the gospel. If one looks at the New Testament evidence one gets another impression. Mission begins with a kind of explosion of joy. The news that

of the call runs through salvation history. All believers are called to salvation, service, sacrifice, and simplicity. To be called of God means that we are chosen, predestined, adopted, redeemed, forgiven, and marked by the promised Holy Spirit. We are all called "to live a life worthy of the calling [we] have received . . . so that the body of Christ may be built up until we all reach unity in the faith and in the knowledge of the Son of God and become mature, attaining to the whole measure of the fullness of Christ" (Eph. 4:1, 12–13).

Jesus's call to holistic, *joyful* discipleship challenges the cultural pressure to compartmentalize life. When each sphere of life, including family, work, friends, recreation, entertainment, and hobbies all have their own separate agendas and tribal worldviews, the Christian is faced with the negative tension of sorting through an array of conflicting priorities and values. The call of God is meant to fix our focus on Christ the center, who is Lord of all. He is Lord over our personal spiritual devotional life and our so-called "secular" work life. There is no sphere of life where Christian ethics and Christian spirituality do not apply. We are Christ's disciples in the boardroom or in the sanctuary or around the family dinner table or on the playing field. We are meant to live all of life "worthy of the calling" we have received. Whenever the apostles spoke of being called of God, they refer to all Christians inclusively.

---

the rejected and crucified Jesus is alive is something that cannot possibly be suppressed. It must be told. Who could be silent about such a fact?" (Lesslie Newbigin, *The Gospel in a Pluralistic Society* [Grand Rapids: Eerdmans, 1989], 116).

For the gifts and the *calling* of God are irrevocable.

—Romans 11:29

I press on toward the goal for the prize of the upward *call* of God in Christ Jesus. Let those of us who are mature think this way.

—Philippians 3:14–15

Therefore, holy brothers, you who share in the heavenly *calling*, consider Jesus, the apostle and high priest of our confession, who was faithful to him who appointed him, just as Moses also was faithful in all God's house.

—Hebrews 3:1–2

Therefore do not be ashamed of the testimony about our Lord, nor of me his prisoner, but share in suffering for the gospel by the power of God, who saved us and *called* us to a holy *calling*, not because of our works but because of his own purpose and grace, which he gave us in Christ Jesus before the ages began.

—2 Timothy 1:8–9

To this end we always pray for you, that our God may make you worthy of his *calling* and may fulfill every resolve for good and every work of faith by his power, so that the name of our Lord Jesus may be

glorified in you, and you in him, according to the
grace of our God and the Lord Jesus Christ.
                                —2 Thessalonians 1:11–12

Therefore, brothers, be all the more diligent to make
your *calling* and election sure, for if you practice
these qualities you will never fall.
                                —2 Peter 1:10 (see 1 Peter 2:9)

For consider your *calling*, brothers and sisters: not
many of you were wise according to worldly standards, not many were powerful, not many were of
noble birth. But God chose what is foolish in the
world to shame the wise; God chose what is weak in
the world to shame the strong; God chose what is
low and despised in the world, even things that are
not, to bring to nothing things that are, so that no
human being might boast in the presence of God.
                                —1 Corinthians 1:26–29

To each as the Lord assigned, and to each as God
has *called*—let him walk. This is my directive in all
the churches.
                                —1 Corinthians 7:17[8]

---

8 I am drawing on Ken Bailey's translation of 1 Corinthians 7:1. Ken E.
   Bailey, *Paul through Mediterranean Eyes: Cultural Studies in 1 Corinthians*
   (Downers Grove, IL: InterVarsity, 2011), 211. Bailey offers a helpful ex-
   planation of the text: "Paul is talking about *the calling/assignment of God*

God's call opens up the fullness of the gospel to all believers. We have been "called to belong to Jesus," "called to be his holy people," "called to be free," and called to be one body (Rom. 1:6, 7; Gal. 5:13). We are all called to one hope, one Lord, one faith, one baptism (Eph. 4:1–5). We have all been called to suffer for Christ, and we have all been called to peace (1 Peter 2:21; Col. 3:15). Paul's challenge is our challenge: "I press on toward the goal to win the prize for which God has called me heavenward in Christ Jesus" (Phil. 3:14). To be called is to be blessed, chosen, predestined, redeemed, saved by grace, and rooted and established in love.

THE WEDDING BANQUET

When Jesus told this parable, he invoked the prophets and anticipated the apostles. The prophet Isaiah used wedding imagery to express deep communion with God: "I delight greatly in the LORD; my soul rejoices in my God. For he has clothed me with garments of salvation and arrayed me in robes of righteousness, as a bridegroom adorns his head like a priest, and as a bride adorns herself with jewels" (Isa. 61:10), and "As a young man marries a young woman, so will your Builder marry you; as a bridegroom rejoices over

---

and telling the entire church that there is no special cultural identity required for discipleship in the kingdom of God. . . . He tells his readers that regardless of their ethnic origins (Jewish or Greek) there is an 'assignment,' a 'calling' from the Lord tailored to who they are that does not require becoming someone else. From Constantine onward, the times and places where this vision of Paul has not been honored are legion." All Scripture passages but 1 Corinthians 7:17 (author's translation) are from the ESV; emphases added.

his bride, so will your God rejoice over you" (Isa. 62:5). Through the prophet Hosea the Lord said, "I will betroth you to me forever; I will betroth you in righteousness and justice, in love and compassion. I will betroth you in faithfulness, and you will acknowledge the LORD" (Hos. 2:19–20). The apostle Paul directly linked Genesis 2:24, "For this reason a man will leave his father and mother and be united to his wife, and the two will become one flesh," with Christ and the church, calling it a profound mystery (Eph. 5:31–32).

Throughout salvation history, the wedding symbolized the joyous communion of God and his people. The wedding invitation goes out, "Blessed are those who are invited to the wedding supper of the Lamb!" (Rev. 19:9). "For the wedding of the Lamb has come, and his bride has made herself ready. Fine linen, bright and clean, was given her to wear." The "fine linen stands for the righteous acts of God's people" (Rev. 19:7–8). The followers of the Lamb are transformed by the grace of Christ. They are freely given what they need to fully enter into the joy of the King. The bride of Christ becomes holy because she has been made holy.

THE GREAT REFUSAL

The servants deliver the second invitation to the guests who have already responded positively to the initial general invitation. The previously invited guests are a privileged group "who symbolize the chief priests and elders/Pharisees who, like the 'sons of the kingdom' in Matthew 8:12, are expected to share in the feast."[9] But this time, the king's follow-up invitation is met with indifference, followed by outright rebellion. There is no explanation for this behavior: "They paid no attention and went off—one to his field, another to his business" (Matt. 22:5). There is no real answer given as to why, but the reaction is shared by farmer and merchant alike. If we had been in the audience, we might have heard an audible gasp. The people must have thought, "Who would do this?" "Who wouldn't want to be an honored guest at the wedding feast of the king's son?" But if we can't explain the apathy, how could we possibly explain the atrocity? The king's servants are seized, abused, and killed.

Jesus tells the story as if he were reporting facts. He doesn't say what his audience is thinking, that to react this way to the king's invitation is ludicrous. It is outrageous! It has no basis in reality. Robert Capon laments, "Score a sad point, therefore, for the unhappy truth that the world is full of fools who won't believe a good thing when they hear it. Free grace, dying love, and unqualified acceptance might as well be a fifteen-foot crocodile, the way we respond to it: all our protestations to the contrary, we will sooner accept a God we will be fed to than one we will be fed by."[10]

Helmut Thielicke observes that initial indifference to the gospel is always a passing reaction on the way to outright

---

9   R. T. France, *Matthew: New International Commentary* (Grand Rapids: Eerdmans, 2007), 824.

10 Robert Farrar Capon, *Kingdom, Grace, Judgment: Paradox, Outrage, and Vindication in the Parables of Jesus* (Grand Rapids: Eerdmans, 2002), 457–58.

hostility. It is "a profound mystery of the kingdom of God" that "one can never take a passive attitude toward the message of Christ. Eventually one must actively oppose it." Thielicke continues, "Here is the root of all of Israel's hostility to the prophets and here too is the root of all the fanaticism and radicalism of modern anti-Christians. . . . One cannot live in continuing tension with the message of Christ." Thus, "to say no to Christ in the attitude of tolerance . . . is merely a passing calm." Thielicke reaches an ominous conclusion: "Anybody who knows the secret of the kingdom of God knows that one day the storm will break loose again. One need not even conjure up the example of the Third Reich (which also began so tolerantly!) to know the course these things take."[11]

The great paradox confronting the church is that this gospel of peace in Christ, which is designed to destroy the walls of hostility, actually provokes hostility. The old paganisms and the new messianisms fight against the church with everything they have.

Never mind that the meat is roasting in the barbecue pit— the enraged king sends his army to wipe out the murderous rebels and burn their city down. Hyperbole is the storyteller's friend, and Jesus enjoyed using it. The account is a thinly veiled reference to the final judgment of God. Bruner explains that as Matthew recounted Jesus's parable, he was fully aware that "the unremitting hostility of official Israel to the coming of Jesus was the great spiritual and intellectual enigma of the

---

11 Thielicke, *Waiting Father*, 188–89.

early church," even as the church through time has wrestled with "the equally unremitting hostility of the leading classes of all times and places to the living God."[12]

The king's reaction represents the Lord's judgment against Israel for rejecting the Messiah. The initial audience, the chief priests, and the elders of the people rightly understood Jesus's indictment against them. The early church read the parable in the light of Rome's burning of Jerusalem and the desecration of the temple (see Matt. 23:38; 24:2).

The king is not through. In spite of the insanity that required judgment, grace prevails. So now he sends out a third and final invitation. This time the target is anyone who can be found. These recipients represent the opening up of the gospel mission to the Gentiles. The king says, "The wedding banquet is ready, but those I invited did not deserve to come. So go to the street corners and invite to the banquet anyone you find" (Matt. 22:8–9). The open invitation is meant for "all the people they could find, the bad as well as the good." This amazing grace knows no barrier. The wedding hall fills up with all kinds of people. Imagine all the joy and energy in the room. Imagine the extraordinary array of diversity experienced in this gathering. Nothing like this had ever happened before. The parable could end here, or so it seems. Jesus has covered a lot of ground: the joyous good news, the call of God, Israel's elite's rejection, the Gentile mission, and God's amazing grace. But it doesn't end here; there's more to the story.

---

12 Bruner, *Matthew*, 2:388.

The king then comes to see the guests. He sees a man out of the corner of his eye who probably was too busy eating hors d'oeuvres to notice the king's attention. The king approaches and asks, "How did you get in here without wedding clothes, friend?" And as Jesus tells the story, "The man was speechless" (Matt. 22:12). What should we make of this? The man's failure to say anything in his defense implies that there is no excuse. There was nothing he could say. Augustine speculated that the royal host provided wedding attire for everyone, but according to R. T. France, there is no convincing evidence in the wedding customs of the day that account for this possibility.[13] Joachim Jeremias claimed that wedding clothes were not special, just clean. Soiled clothes were an insult to the host.[14] There was no need for a tuxedo, just a shower and clean clothes, but this man refused to do even the most basic thing. Apparently, he thought he could get away with it. He was just being his slovenly self. He accepted the invitation on his terms. France writes,

> The symbolism is of someone who presumes on the free offer of salvation by assuming that therefore there are no obligations attached, someone whose life belies their profession: faith without works. Entry to the kingdom of heaven may be free, but to continue in it carries conditions. Even though

---

13 France, *Matthew*, 826.
14 Joachim Jeremias, *The Parables of Jesus* (London: SCM, 1972), 187.

this man belongs to the new group of invitees, he is one who produces no fruit, and so is no less liable to forfeit his new-found privilege than those who were excluded before him. As the parable of the sower has reminded us, there is many a slip between initial response to the word of God and ultimate fruitfulness.[15]

We can come as we are, but we cannot remain as we were. Faith and faithfulness are joined together. Thielicke writes, "We seat ourselves at the banquet table without a wedding garment when we allow our sins to be forgiven but still want to hang on to them. We do this, in other words, when we say to ourselves, consciously or unconsciously, 'This is great stuff; a man can remain in his sins without worrying, since this God of love can never be really angry; he shuts both eyes; he will let it pass.'"[16]

Drawing on multiple sources, Bruner writes, "A wedding garment in the context of Matthew's Gospel is not passive, imputed (Pauline) righteousness; it is active, moral (Matthean) righteousness; it is doing God's will; it is evidence of repentance by a law-abiding discipleship. But neither this nor any wedding garment is a dreary legalism. . . . The wedding garment of personal righteousness was *not* necessary in order to be *invited* to the party—both good and bad

---

15 France, *Matthew*, 827.
16 Thielicke, *Waiting Father*, 190.

were invited—but the garment of personal righteousness is necessary to *stay* in the party."[17]

Ordinary faithfulness, the faithfulness expected of every believer, is the clothing prescribed for the bride of Christ (Col. 3:12; Eph. 6:11–17; Rom. 13:14; Rev. 21:15).[18] But this wedding guest managed to import the world's indifference and self-centeredness into the very gathering of joyful wedding guests. It would have been better for him if he had shunned the invitation altogether. The king told his attendants to bind him up and throw him into hell. Judgment has the last word. It is "judgment that falls like a thunderclap on the refusal of grace, and that, in the process, defines the true nature of hell." It is the "nowhere that is the only thing left for those who will not accept their acceptance by grace."[19]

We may be startled to read that the Father "cuts off every branch in me that bears no fruit" (John 15:2). We are disturbed to find that these diseased branches are in Christ. External religion alone offers no assurance of salvation. We are

---

17 Bruner, *Matthew*, 2:390 (emphasis original).
18 See Douglas Webster, *Follow the Lamb: A Pastoral Approach to The Revelation* (Eugene, OR: Cascade, 2014), 229. In Revelation 21, "keeping your clothes on" is important. The staccato imperative, "Keep your clothes on," may strike us as a bit odd at first. But clothing is an important metaphor throughout the Revelation. It signifies purity and righteousness. To their shame, many in the church in Sardis had soiled their clothes, but a few had not, and Christ promised, "They will walk with me, dressed in white, for they are worthy" (Rev. 3:4). Nakedness signifies exposure and shame. To be clothed in compassion, kindness, humility, gentleness, and patience is the best defense against falling for evil. To put off the old self and to put on the full armor of God is the best way to be prepared for any and every eventuality in a world that opposes the Christian.
19 Capon, *Kingdom, Grace, and Judgment*, 464.

not going to get away with showing up at the wedding banquet in our old, worldly work clothes. We can be baptized, regular church attenders, and attentive to sermons, but in the absence of life-changing, saving faith, we are just going through the motions. We can embrace the ritual and the tradition and cultivate religious habits yet not know Christ. Make-believe Christians are deadwood (Matt. 22:1–14). Judas is our prime example of being close to Jesus but as far removed from real faith and trust in Christ as a person can be. Judas died on the vine. Klyne Snodgrass writes, "Often NT scholars seem to try to protect Jesus from any description we do not like, particularly anything that has to do with judgment. However, which of Israel's prophets ever lacked a message of judgment?—and Jesus certainly came as a prophet."[20]

The parable ends with one final twist, a surprise zinger, a provocative one-liner that grabs our attention: "For many are invited [called], but few are chosen" (Matt. 22:14). Jesus strikes a sober note. Many are invited, but only a few make it to the party. This truth is expressed in the Sermon on the Mount when Jesus challenged his hearers to enter through the narrow gate. "For wide is the gate and broad is the road that leads to destruction and many enter through it. But small is the gate and narrow the road that lead to life, and only a few find it" (Matt. 7:13–14). This is the truth illustrated in the parable of the sower where the seed falls on the path, on the

---

20   Klyne R. Snodgrass, *Stories with Intent: A Comprehensive Guide to the Parables of Jesus* (Grand Rapids: Eerdmans, 2018), 318.

rocky ground, and among the thorns, but the seed that falls on good soil is fruitful (Matt. 13:1–23). And this is the truth found in Jesus's Sermon on the End of the World when he said, "Many will turn away from the faith and will betray and hate each other" (Matt. 24:10). Snodgrass offers this concluding perspective on the two banquet parables (Luke 14; Matthew 22): "Both parables teach that we cannot have the kingdom on our own terms. The invitation of grace brings with it demand. At stake is the issue of a person's identity. It is not enough to wear the right label ('the invited one'); rather, the kingdom must shape identity so that one has a whole different set of concerns. . . . The invitation to God's table is sheer grace, but it is never cheap grace. The parable is not about mission, but it becomes a basis for reflection about mission."[21]

---

21 Snodgrass, *Stories with Intent*, 323.

❧22❧

THE FEAR-OF-THE LORD PARABOLIC

MATTHEW 24:42–25:46

The Sermon on the End of the World concludes with four parables: the parable of the faithful and faithless servants (see Luke 12:42–48), the parable of the ten virgins, the parable of the talents, and the parable of the sheep and goats. Jesus left the temple for the last time, having delivered a scathing denunciation and warning against the religious leaders. He was hot—agitated, accusatory, fierce in tone and temper. He burned with anger against the teachers of the law and the Pharisees for their hypocrisy, showy piety, and hostility to the revelation of God. Like Isaiah, Jesus pronounced seven woes (Isa. 5:8–6:5). He called them names: "You hypocrites!" (Matt. 23:13, 15, et al.). "You snakes! You brood of vipers!" (Matt. 23:33). He blamed them for the blood of the prophets, from the blood of righteous Abel to the blood of Zechariah. His parting words were, "For I tell you, you will not see me again until you say, 'Blessed is he who comes in the name of the Lord'" (Matt. 23:39).

I'm not sure how the disciples understood this blistering prophetic rebuke or whether it even sunk in, because as Jesus was leaving the temple, "his disciples came up to him to call his attention to its buildings" (Matt. 24:1). I imagine that the temple's stonework was the last thing on Jesus's mind. One wonders who among the disciples tried to impress Jesus with the architectural marvel of the temple. Was it an attempt to distract Jesus, because he was so angry? Maybe it was a group effort, or maybe it was Peter. Remember it was Peter who had wanted to construct three shelters on the Mount of Transfiguration. You will recall that it was Peter's "big idea" that was interrupted by the voice of the Father saying, "This is my Son, whom I love; with him I am well pleased. Listen to him!" (Matt. 17:5). Given what Jesus had just finished saying in the temple courts, any attempt to get Jesus to notice "how the temple was adorned with beautiful stones and with gifts dedicated to God" (Luke 21:5) was bound to fail. Instead, Luke reports that Jesus noticed a poor widow giving her offering of two very small copper coins. Jesus made an example of her. Her act of worship provided a teachable moment. "Truly I tell you," he said, "this poor widow has put in more than all the others. All these people gave their gifts out of their wealth; but she out of her poverty put in all she had to live on" (Luke 21:3–4).[1]

---

1 Pentecost will prove that the disciples have undergone a transformation. Peter and John are now more interested in a lame man that the beautiful buildings (Acts 3:4–6). What could be more beautiful than the temple? What could be more amazing than the gate called

THE OLIVET DISCOURSE

Jesus delivered the Sermon on the End of the World while seated on the Mount of Olives overlooking the temple.[2] He prepared the disciples for the trouble that was to follow: spiritual deception, political upheaval, social disasters, persecution, and tribulation. His message wove together two themes: no-fear-apocalyptic and fear-of-the-Lord parabolic. Jesus preached a complex sermon with truth-slanting simplicity. He drew on his Old Testament sources: Daniel's abomination that causes desolation; Isaiah's description of the day of the Lord; Zechariah's mourned and martyred messiah; and Noah's evil age of complacency before the cataclysm. Jesus developed the scope and the sequence of salvation history. Jesus unfurls a picture of the end that is all encompassing. His scope could not be greater: "Nation will arise against nation" and "the gospel of the kingdom will be preached in the whole world as a testimony to all the nations" (Matt. 24:7, 14). Angels will "gather his elect from the four winds, from one end of the heavens to the other" and "all the peoples of the earth will mourn" (Matt. 24:31, 30). And "all the nations will be gathered before him, and he will separate the people from one another as a shepherd separates the sheep from the goats" (Matt. 25:32). The most obvious complexity of the sermon lies in the sequencing of the events. Jesus merges immediacy

---

Beautiful? The answer: a poor lame beggar on his feet walking, jumping, and dancing—praising God.

2 Douglas D. Webster, *Text Messaging: A Conversation on Preaching* (Toronto: Clements, 2010), see 107–24.

and longevity into a single stream of urgency. The sermon causes us to see events as God sees them, in the present tense.

Added to the complexity of this message is the intensity of Jesus's last sermon. There is nothing laid back about Jesus's message; both the complexity and the intensity contradict our conventional sermonizing. From his opening, "Watch out," to his closing, "Then they will go away to eternal punishment, but the righteous to eternal life," everything is extreme (Matt. 24:4; 25:46). The coming of the Son of Man is like lightning, the sun will be darkened, and the stars will fall from the sky.

Extremism invades Jesus's parables as a communicational strategy. This is no bland recital of interesting nuggets of truth. The fate of the wicked household servant is gruesome: "cut him to pieces and assign him a place with the hypocrites, where there will be weeping and gnashing of teeth" (Matt. 24:51). The useless servant in the parable of the talents is thrown outside, "into the darkness, where there will be weeping and gnashing of teeth" (Matt. 25:30). In the last judgment, the apathetic, the indifferent, the clueless, the unresponsive, and the selfish will be told, "Depart from me, you who are cursed, into the eternal fire prepared for the devil and his angels" (Matt. 25:41).

Jesus's sermon is filled with intense concern for his disciples. He does not want them to fall away. His first concern is deception. Christians are in danger of deception from tricksters who claim to be little messiahs or God's special representatives. These deceivers are not broadcasting, "I am the messiah," nor impersonating Jesus, but they are drawing attention to themselves and claiming to fulfill the role and title that belongs exclusively to Jesus.[3] These are the heroic Christians Jesus warned about in his Sermon on the Mount: "*Many* will say to me on that day, 'Lord, Lord, did we not prophesy in your name and in your name drive out demons and in your name perform many miracles?' Then I will tell them plainly, 'I never knew you. Away from me, you evildoers!'" (Matt. 7:22–23, emphasis added).

Jesus's number-one concern and the greatest danger facing Christians comes from within Christendom. Ironically, professing Christians pose the greatest threat. Jesus warns, *Don't be deceived. Keep your theological sanity.*[4]

Jesus's second concern is fear. Cycles of upheaval and centuries of pain and plague and political chaos will be routine. There will be massive social upheaval: wars, famines, earthquakes, family breakdown, and financial meltdowns. Jesus comforts, *Do not be afraid. Take it in stride. Keep your emotional stability.*[5]

His third concern is apostasy. Extreme persecution, martyrdom, universal hatred, and intense animosity will take its toll on the church. "Many will turn away from the faith and will betray and hate each other" (Matt. 24:10). False teachers will deceive many and many believers will succumb to

---

3 R. T. France, *Matthew: New International Commentary* (Grand Rapids: Eerdmans, 2007), 902.

4 Frederick Dale Bruner, *Matthew: A Commentary*, vol. 2, *The Churchbook*, Matthew 13–28 (Grand Rapids: Eerdmans, 2007), 482.

5 Bruner, *Matthew*, 2:482.

wickedness and "the love of most will grow cold, but whoever [singular] stands firm to the end will be saved" (Matt. 24:13). Jesus's bottom line is this: *Do not give up. Preach the gospel of the kingdom. Keep the faith.*

These three concerns, deception, fear, and apostasy, are overcome by discernment, love, and faithfulness. This motley minority of real Christians, hated by the world and even by *many* professing and "successful" Christians, will *successfully* preach the gospel of the kingdom to the world as a testimony to all nations. According to Jesus, this is how it will be right up to the end. These are the ongoing dynamics that the body of Christ will face in every generation.

The climax of the first movement of this apocalyptic symphony is the destruction of temple. The first cycle of deception, fear, and apostasy will end in AD 70 when Rome destroys the temple, but the cycle of deception, fear, and apostasy will be repeated over and over again. Jesus warns the first generation of disciples that the *end* of the *beginning of the end* will be cataclysmic. Jesus draws on the language and themes of Daniel, Isaiah, and Zechariah to describe the destruction of the temple and its impact on the worldwide body of Christ.

The message for believers today is this: what the first generation of Jewish Christians faced is paradigmatic for future generations of disciples. The "great distress, unequaled from the beginning of the world until now—and never to be equaled again" (Matt. 24:21), becomes a theme running through church history. Jesus warns believers that they will face false messiahs and false prophets who perform great signs and wonders, but they must not fall for the deception. Don't be fooled. Don't be deceived. The coming of the Son of Man will be as obvious as lightning. Jesus warns believers of great social upheaval, but there is no reason to panic. God is in control. Jesus concludes this section with an apocalyptic description of the worldwide success of the mission of God: "And he will send his angels [messengers] with a loud trumpet call, and they will gather his elect from the four winds, from one end of the heavens to the other" (Matt. 24:31).

Understanding all of this does not require special insight or secret knowledge. It is as simple and straightforward as recognizing that spring is coming in the green tender twigs of the fig tree (Matt. 24:32). Anyone who implies otherwise is a false prophet leading people astray. In his Sermon on the End of the World, Jesus prepares not only the first disciples but also the *last* disciples for his coming. Jesus dampens speculation and ramps up readiness. His sermon calls for commitment, not curiosity; patient endurance, not complacency.

The fact that the first and the last generations of believers are in view is underscored by Jesus in three ways: (1) No one knows, not even the Son of Man, when the final end will come. Only the Father knows. (2) Noah's age is typical of the end of the age. Everything will go on as normal. People will be eating and drinking, marrying and giving in marriage right up to the end. (3) No one will be expecting the Lord's return when it comes. Everyone will be doing their regular work and in their normal routine; "people who seem so similar at work will be shown [to be] dramatically dissimilar at the Judgment."[6]

THE FEAR-OF-THE-LORD

The Word of God says, "The fear of the LORD is the beginning of wisdom" (Prov. 9:10). Biblical scholars tell us that the fear-of-the-Lord is a bound phrase. We miss the meaning of fear-of-the-Lord when we look up "fear" and "God" in the dictionary and then piece them together for a definition. Fear-of-the-Lord means living our lives in the presence of God moment by moment, with all the awe, obedience, humility, love, and courage that such living requires. It is a common and comprehensive term for referring to the way we live the spiritual life. Eugene Peterson calls it "the stock biblical phrase for the way of life that is lived responsively and appropriately before who God is, who he is as Father, Son, and Holy Spirit."[7]

These four parables are fear-of-the-Lord parables for two reasons. First, they teach us what the fear-of-the-Lord is. David prayed, "Come, my children, listen to me; I will teach you the fear of the LORD" (Ps. 34:11). The fear-of-the-Lord is like no other fear. Earlier in the psalm, David praised God, saying, "I sought the LORD, and he answered me; he delivered me from all my fears" (Ps. 34:4). In the same psalm, David contrasts "all my fears" with the fear-of-the-Lord. To be delivered from our fears is to embrace the fear-of-the-Lord. This is what John

---

6 Bruner, *Matthew*, 2:527.
7 Eugene H. Peterson, *Christ Plays in Ten Thousand Places: A Conversation in Spiritual Theology* (Grand Rapids: Eerdmans, 2008), 41.

meant when he said, "perfect love drives out fear" (1 John 4:18). In the wilderness, Moses distinguished between being afraid and the fear-of-the-Lord. He said to the people, "Do not be afraid. God has come to test you, so that the fear of God will be with you to keep you from sinning" (Exod. 20:20). In the early church, Luke reports that Barnabas helped Jerusalem Christians overcome their fear of Saul even as he describes them living in the fear-of-the-Lord (Acts 9:26, 31). Second, these three parables put the fear-of-the-Lord in us. Jesus was deadly earnest when he taught that the consequences of self-ishness, thoughtlessness, and uselessness are devastating. He made it clear that we could lose our souls over these matters.

THE PARABLE OF THE FAITHFUL AND FAITHLESS SERVANTS

Jesus likens the coming of the Son of Man to a midnight break-in. Fear is the emotive element embedded in this metaphor. It is a good kind of fear that is meant to get our attention and keep up our guard against danger. The purpose behind this metaphoric break-in is preparedness. Jesus designed the parable to produce an attitude of readiness in his disciples. It may strike some believers as incongruous that Jesus would compare the glorious coming of the Son of Man to a burglary. To make his point, Jesus drew a parallel between home security and eternal security. He did this to cultivate a healthy fear of what is expected of his followers. Even so, Jesus promised to never leave us nor forsake us. We can count on it that "all things work together for good to those who love God and are called according to His purpose" (Rom. 8:28 RGT). But God's faithfulness is no excuse for our faithlessness. Jesus holds us accountable and challenges us to meet our vulnerabilities with vigilance. Stay alert. Be on guard.

The master entrusts all his household servants to a faithful and wise servant "to give them their food at the proper time. . . . But suppose that servant is wicked and says to himself, 'My master is staying away for a long time,' and he then begins to beat his fellow servants and to eat and drink with drunkards" (Matt. 24:45, 48–49). If you are tracking with Jesus, you are asking yourself the significance of providing food at the proper time or in season. Jesus's admonition to Peter, "feed my sheep," comes to mind (John 21). We need gospel truth delivered in a timely fashion. Dale Bruner explains, "'The food' means revelation; 'in season' means relevance."[8] When the master returns and discovers that this faithless servant has been acting more like an abusive master than a faithful steward, he will be judged severely. The verdict is unbelievably harsh. "He will cut him to pieces and assign him a place with the hypocrites, where there will be weeping and gnashing of teeth" (Matt. 24:51). Jesus isn't fooling around. Faithfulness until he returns, no matter how far off, is expected, and those who insist on faithlessness will suffer eternal consequences.

---

8 Bruner, *Matthew*, 2:538.

THE PARABLE OF THE TEN VIRGINS

Jesus likened the coming kingdom of heaven to a wedding ceremony with ten bridesmaids.[9] The role of these young women in the ceremony may have been to escort the bridegroom in a torchlit procession.[10] In the Old Testament, the coming of God is likened to the bridegroom coming for his bride (see Psalm 45; Isa. 61:10; 62:4–5). Jesus equated his coming to the coming of God (Luke 4:18–21; Matt. 11:4–6; Luke 7:22–23). The coming of the kingdom of God is simply analogous to the coming of the bridegroom. Some ancient allegorical interpretations of the parable tried to make every aspect of the parable mean something. For example, the virgins represent the church, and the two types of virgins symbolize Gentiles and Jews. The number ten stands for the completeness of the church, and the oil represents the Holy Spirit. But most interpreters today deny an allegorical interpretation.[11] Jesus never intended these correspondences, and Matthew gives no hint to their validity.

---

9   Snodgrass refers to "insufficient information about first-century Palestinian weddings" to be overly concerned about the details of this parable. "If the virgins wait at the groom's house, they are part of his clan, and he is probably escorting the bride to his home after a banquet at the bride's home. If they are at the bride's house, they are her friends and wait with her for the coming of the groom. They will go out to meet him when his approach has been announced and escort him to the house. Either option is possible, but the former seems more likely. . . . Questions of realism cannot be the determining factor in interpretation. . . . The primary question is whether the parable functions as a narrative development with sufficient plot and resolution that hearers would be carried along. That is the case here" (Klyne R. Snodgrass, *Stories with Intent: A Comprehensive Guide to the Parables of Jesus* [Grand Rapids: Eerdmans, 2018], 513).

10 France, *Matthew*, 947.

11 Snodgrass, *Stories with Intent*, 515.

The focus of the parable is straightforward. It is on the readiness of the disciples, rather than on the delay of the second coming of Christ. Faithfulness to the end is the concern (Matt. 24:37–51; Mark 13:34–37; Luke 12:35–40; 21:34–36). Five of the bridesmaids were foolish and five were wise. The thoughtful bridesmaids are a picture of long obedience in the same direction.[12] They have the reserved energy to go the distance. Their lamps will remain lit. They have the "oil" of disciplined, discipled faith in Christ. They are prepared for either a long delay or an immediate return of the bridegroom. The thoughtless bridesmaids, on the other hand, are flighty and unprepared for the midnight entrance of the bridegroom. The foolish bridesmaids are a picture of shallow faith—maybe even excited and enthusiastic faith, but without depth and obedience. They represent distracted, overly dependent, and irresponsibly weak believers who may say, "Lord, Lord" and even feel emotional about the faith but are not receptive to the Jesus way. They are thoughtless, and the Lord comes down hard on them. "Truly I tell you, I don't know you." In the parable of the faithless servant, the Lord comes sooner than expected; in the parable of the ten virgins, he comes later than expected.[13] Jesus's bottom line: "So stay alert. You have no idea when he might arrive" (Matt. 25:13, MSG). Readiness cannot be achieved by "last-minute adjustments" but depends on "long-term provision."[14]

---

12 Eugene H. Peterson, *A Long Obedience in the Same Direction: Discipleship in an Instant Society* (Downers Grove, IL: InterVarsity, 1980).

13 Bruner, *Matthew*, 2:547.

14 France, *Matthew*, 947.

THE PARABLE OF THE TALENTS[15]

If we're thinking that the next parable, the parable of the talents, is about money, we've got it all wrong. It is not about positive thinking or the prosperity gospel or the "law of increase." It is all about being an agent of the kingdom, being faithful to the gospel. We live in between the first coming of Christ (John 1:14) and the second coming of Christ (John 14:3). We live in the "now and not yet" (see 1 John 3:2–3). This parable does not tell us how to obtain salvation, but how to live out our salvation (Phil. 2:12–13). The parable of the talents is all about being *faithful* and has nothing to do with being *successful*. Ken Bailey writes, "A British journalist once asked Mother Teresa how she kept going, knowing that she could never meet the needs of all the dying in the streets of Calcutta. She replied, 'I am not called to be successful; I'm called to be faithful.'"[16]

A very wealthy master entrusted his wealth to his three servants and then left on a journey. This is like our Master,

---

15 Luke's version of this parable (the parable of the ten minas) sets the stage for Palm Sunday and Jesus's triumphal entry into Jerusalem (Luke 19:11–27). The parable of the ten minas counters the people's expectation that the kingdom of God was going to appear immediately. The kingdom of God had drawn near in Jesus, but the consummation of the kingdom was sometime in the future. The parable becomes a prophecy and the prophecy (Zech. 9:9) becomes a parable. Jesus is the nobleman, and the parable is based on the political history of the day. The story fits the saga of Archelaus, who went to Rome after the death of his father, Herod the Great, hoping to be made king. As in the parable, a delegation of Jews followed him to Rome seeking to persuade Caesar Augustus to give him only half of his father's kingdom. The parable, especially in Luke's Palm Sunday setting, works prophetically because it anticipates Jesus's second coming.

16 Kenneth E. Bailey, *Jesus through Middle Eastern Eyes: Cultural Studies in the Gospels* (Downers Grove, IL: InterVarsity, 2008), 409.

the Lord Jesus, who entrusts his wealth—the gospel—to the church in this interim period before he comes again. By most accounts, these three individuals were given a huge amount of capital to invest.[17] If a single talent was worth six to ten thousand denarii, as some scholars have suggested, and a denarius was worth a fair day's wage, then the sum of money is vast—"the equivalent of approximately a whole lifetime of wages."[18] The hyperbolic amount of money gets our attention. People like Warren Buffett or Bill Gates come to mind. But the investment is not about money; it is about whatever talent the Lord has given to us for the sake of the gospel. The meaning of *talent* has mission written all over it. For the followers of Jesus Christ, *talent* means the opportunity to live and preach the gospel of grace.

Klyne Snodgrass insists that the parable is analogical, not allegorical. "Rather than allegorizing this parable," he insists, "we need once again to understand how the analogy works. Given the assumption of an interval necessitated by the coming death of Jesus, the analogy works easily."[19]

The parable sets up a comparison between the two servants who invest what they have received, and the third who buries his talent. *Receiving* underscores the grace that precedes the

---

17 Snodgrass, *Stories with Intent*, 528, 536. Snodgrass writes, "A talent in the ancient world was a monetary weight of approximately 60–90 pounds. . . . Depending on the metal in question, the value of the talent was equivalent to 6000 days' wages for a day laborer (roughly twenty years' work), so the man given five talents was given an enormous sum" (a mina [Luke] was worth about three months' wages of a day laborer).

18 Bruner, *Matthew*, 2:547.

19 Snodgrass, *Stories with Intent*, 540.

work, followed by three aggressive action verbs that emphasize the effort. Two servants immediately *moved out, went to work*, and *won* more money. The third servant went off, "dug a hole in the ground and hid his master's money" (Matt. 25:18). Instead of moving out, he retreated. Instead of going to work, he dug a hole. Instead of winning more, he hid what he had. When the master returned to settle the accounts, the two servants are commended for gaining a profit. The servant who had received five talents was proud of his success: "Master, *you* entrusted me with five bags of gold. See, *I* have gained five more." The five-talent servant is brimming with confidence and joy. R. T. France comments, "Here is a joy in work that should not be depressed by a heavy-handed spirituality. Jesus wants disciples to feel good about their work."[20]

Both productive servants receive identical words of praise: "Well done, good and faithful servant! You have been faithful with a few things; I will put you in charge of many things. Come and share your master's happiness!" (Matt. 25:23). Bruner writes, "Human beings have been created to be goal-and-praise-oriented. The single great goal of Christians can be to hear their Lord's 'Wonderful!' spoken to their life work at the Judgment. We cannot live without laying up treasures *somewhere*—so we can lay them up in heaven."[21] The two servants used the first-person personal pronoun "I" as it should be used, in a confident, well-earned declaration. They share

---

20 France, *Matthew*, 947.
21 Bruner, *Matthew*, 2:557.

the right kind of pride in the master's work and they seek the master's reward.

The negative force of the parable of the talents falls on the third servant who squanders the opportunity to invest his master's talent. He blamed the master for this: "Master," he said, "I knew that you are a hard man [*sklēros*], harvesting where you have not sown and gathering where you have not scattered seed. So I was afraid and went out and hid your gold in the ground. See, here is what belongs to you" (Matt. 25:24–25). The freedom and joy of the first two servants to go quickly and invest everything testify against the third servant's assessment of the master. The first two servants lived life unhindered. They took their whole investment and put it to work to please the master. How was the third servant able to conclude that the master was harsh and unreasonable if it wasn't simply in his own imagination? He imposed his own harsh standards on any and all investment strategies. He fell victim to his own pessimistic conservatism and projected his paranoia onto the master. He responded to the opportunity as he would act if he were the master. He refused to acknowledge the investment as a gracious trust. He saw it only as a dangerous liability. He experienced the opportunity of abundance as a burden, not a grace. We can be thankful that the master is not anything like the third servant.

In Luke's version of the parable of the ten minas, the third servant's critique of the king sounds similar to today's critique of religion. The gospel of Jesus Christ is blamed for the harsh and demanding burden of religion. Helmut Thielicke, the post–World War II German Lutheran pastor, concluded that the third servant who imposed his strong and twisted view on the master wanted to be left alone. He is a picture of today's self-centered individual who wants to preserve what he already has. He prides himself on his Christian tradition, with its baptisms, weddings, funerals, and beautiful repertoire of church music. He loves the organ and liturgy. He wraps his religion in his chosen tradition and preserves it for himself. He prides himself on his "balance" and is careful not to go overboard. Thielicke writes: "There are really only two ways to take a thing seriously. Either you renounce it or you risk everything for it. There is no third choice. The kind of Christian who is merely conservative and those who want only the Christian 'point of view'—these people want this third choice, which doesn't exist. Throw your Christianity on the trash heap, or else, let God be the Lord of your life; let him be that in dead earnest; let him be someone from whom you receive each day meaning and comfort, a goal for your life, and marching orders, but don't wrap him up in your handkerchief! You can only curse him or fall on your knees."[22]

Some biblical scholars believe that the third servant is like the Pharisees who labored under a false and self-imposed view of God's grace-less rigidity. The Pharisees were unwilling and unprepared to do anything with the gospel but bury it under their self-righteous rules, regulations, and traditions. They succeeded in crucifying Jesus and *burying* him. Other

---

22 Thielicke, *Waiting Father*, 145.

scholars reason that the disciples are Jesus's main concern. Jesus holds his followers accountable for living flat out for the gospel. Snodgrass writes, "We do not need to allegorize the talents or other aspects of the parable to know how the analogy works. The talents do not stand for anything other than the great value of the kingdom and the significant responsibility it brings. As a master rewards or punishes his servants for their productivity during his absence, so Jesus will hold his followers accountable for their productivity in the kingdom during his absence."[23]

The third servant's containment strategy recalls C. S. Lewis's image of the casket: "There is no safe investment. To love at all is to be vulnerable." *To really invest your life, your time, your energy, and your resources in Christ is to be vulnerable.* To live the Jesus way is risky business. If you want to keep your heart intact, if you want to play it safe, then you don't want to risk anything, much less your all. Lewis's advice for the bury-it-in-the-ground type servant is to protect your heart: "Wrap it carefully round with hobbies and little luxuries; avoid all entanglements; lock it safe in the casket or coffin of your selfishness."[24]

"Look, here's your money!" Did the third servant honestly think the master would be pleased? One gets the impression "of a bad conscience wrapping itself in 'good' theology."[25] And in this case the so-called "good" theology is heretical in

---

23 Snodgrass, *Stories with Intent*, 535.
24 C. S. Lewis, *The Four Loves* (San Diego: Harvest Books, 1960), 121.
25 Bruner, *Matthew*, 2:561.

the worst way, because it *sounds* right. But the third servant's theology is really false. His bad theology is presumptuous and pretentious. He imposed his twisted view on the gracious master. Sacrilege can go up as well as down. Obsequious piety is offensive to God, ranking right up there with blasphemy. If he thought he was honoring the master by burying the master's money, he was mistaken. No matter how well-intentioned his risk-free strategy was, he had diminished the investment and insulted the master. He had done nothing to show for the gift of the master. It would have been better if he had never received the money in the first place.

"You wicked, lazy servant!" the master exploded, as he barked out his orders, "So take the bag of gold form him and give it to the one who has ten bags. . . . And throw the worthless servant outside, into the darkness, where there will be weeping and gnashing of teeth" (Matt. 25:26, 28, 30). "This parable is unique," writes Bruner, "in attacking *humility*."[26] This is the kind of humility that is false in every way. It is the showy pious humility that confidently knows where the gospel is buried, whether in creed or doctrine or tradition or sermon. It is the response that is a nonresponse. It never embraces the gospel, never risks anything for the sake of the gospel. This is the humility that prides itself on grace but knows nothing of the costly grace that demands one's all. The first two servants share in their master's happiness, but the self-preoccupied and self-pleasing third servant is cast out into utter darkness.

---

26 Bruner, *Matthew*, 2:561.

Jesus's scary story hits home. The third servant in Jesus's parable of the talents was oblivious to his danger. He never saw the judgment coming. He was caught off guard.

Jesus is telling this parable because he is concerned about our faithfulness. Without question, the disciple's faithful response to the gospel rests on God's grace and mercy. We know that whatever responsibility and accountability is called for is based entirely on God's grace. But it is impossible not to hear the strong voice of the prophets in Jesus's challenge to his disciples to live into the gospel with everything they have. "Jesus's parables—and certainly this one—do emphasize moral responsibility and carry an unavoidable threat of judgment," writes Snodgrass. "Prophets use strong language, and this language functions to shock, arrest, and force consideration. If the kingdom is about anything, it is about accountability to the will of the Father."[27] Professing believers who are selfishly, thoughtlessly, and fearfully unfaithful will face extreme consequences. Jesus isn't kidding. We can assent to a few ideas about Jesus and then go on about our life as if nothing has changed, but there's literally hell to pay. To believe is to obey and to obey is to believe, and if we don't believe and obey, Jesus is clear about the consequences.

Unlike the selfish servant, authentic followers of Jesus are committed to the household of faith. We proclaim *Christ*, admonishing and teaching everyone with all wisdom, so that we may present everyone fully mature in Christ. To this end *we*

---

27 Snodgrass, *Stories with Intent*, 536.

strenuously contend with all the energy Christ so powerfully works in *us* (Col. 1:28–29). Unlike the silly bridesmaids, we are committed to the long obedience in the same direction. *We* are confident that he who began a good work in *us* will carry it on to completion until the day of Christ Jesus (Phil. 1:6). Unlike the useless servant, we are committed to investing the gospel in every and any way we can. We want to put the gospel to work in everything we say and do. "I don't know about you," Paul urges, "but I'm running hard for the finish line. I'm giving it everything I've got. No sloppy living for me! I'm staying alert and in top condition. I'm not going to get caught napping, telling everyone else all about it and then missing out myself" (1 Cor. 9:26–27 MSG).

THE PARABLE OF THE SHEEP AND GOATS

The Sermon on the End of the World (Matt. 24:1–25:46) concludes with a parable about the final judgment. Jesus ended his last sermon with a vivid, visual metaphor and a powerful admonition. He thrust an either/or decision before his disciples with no in-between state. No middle ground. We are either in or out, accepted or rejected, blessed or cursed. Jesus's sermon recalls Moses's last sermon: "Take to heart all the words I have solemnly declared to you this day" (Deut. 32:46). The Sermon on the End of the World ends where it began, by drawing attention to people in need and to the people who are called to meet those needs. Jesus commended the poor widow for her sacrificial giving (Luke 21:1–4). The invisible people who are ignored and overlooked by the world become the center of attention. Jesus expects us to see those in need with the eyes of faith.

Jesus described the process of separation in parabolic terms. Snodgrass suggests, "One could say that we have a two-verse analogy and that the rest is explanation."[28] Jesus framed the decisive decision of life by painting a simple pastoral scene. It is like a shepherd separating the sheep from the goats. On an initial visit to northern Ghana, I was surprised to learn that the sheep and goats looked very similar. I guess I expected plump white wooly sheep and lean, spotted goats, but in Ghana, to my untrained eyes, all the sheep and goats looked alike. Of course the Ghanaian shepherds didn't have any troubled distinguishing them, and like the Ghanaians, the Lord knows the difference between sheep and goats. Two groups stand before the Son of Man when he comes in all his glory. He is the King and he will say to those on his right, "Come, you who are *blessed by my Father*, take your inheritance, the kingdom prepared for you since the creation of the world" (Matt. 25:34, emphasis added). But to those on his left, he will say, "Depart from me, you who are cursed, into the eternal fire prepared for the devil and his angels" (Matt. 25:41).

Like the previous parables, Jesus is concerned with "faithful living in anticipation of the coming parousia."[29] The gathering of all the nations "depicts the eschatological judgment of all persons."[30] The meaning of the parable depends on the

---

28 Snodgrass, *Stories with Intent*, 543.
29 Snodgrass, *Stories with Intent*, 554.
30 Snodgrass, *Stories with Intent*, 555.

identity of the "least of these brothers and sisters of mine." Are they needy people in general or are they fellow disciples? Does the parable focus on humanitarian effort or does it focus on the body of Christ. Snodgrass observes that Matthew uses the language of "brothers" and "little ones" elsewhere for disciples. Jesus says, "Anyone who welcomes you welcomes me, and anyone who welcomes me welcomes the one who sent me. . . . And if anyone gives even a cup of cold water to one of these little ones who is my disciple, truly I tell you, that person will certainly not lose their reward" (Matt. 10:40, 42). Jesus reassures the disciples that salvation and judgment depend on the recognition of the body of Christ.[31] But with that said, the mission of the church as the body of Christ is to evangelize the world and to love our neighbor. Jesus isn't interested in a talking-head Christianity. Jesus's words in the Sermon on the Mount (Matt. 7:21–23) deserve to be placed side by side with this passage: "Not everyone who says to me, 'Lord, Lord' will enter the kingdom of heaven, but only the one who does the will of my Father who is in heaven. Many will say to me on that day, 'Lord, Lord, did we not prophesy in your name and in your name drive out demons and in your name perform many miracles?' Then, I will tell them plainly, 'I never knew you. Away from me, you evildoers!'" (Matt. 7:21–23).

Matthew stresses Jesus's emphasis on responsibility, but his focus on the work of righteousness is completely consistent

---

31   Snodgrass, *Stories with Intent*, 555.

with salvation by faith alone.[32] The parable of the sheep and goats is in harmony with the apostle Paul's proclamation: "For it is by grace you have been saved, through faith—and this is not from yourselves, it is the gift of God—not by works, so that no one can boast. For we are God's handiwork, created in Christ Jesus to do good works, which God prepared in advance for us to do" (Eph. 2:8–10). As mentioned earlier, the Reformers insisted that we are saved by faith alone, but saving faith is never alone. True faith in Christ is always accompanied by the works of Christ. We not only have faith *in* Jesus, but we demonstrate the faith *of* Jesus. Beatitude-based living begins with grace but does not lack works: "Blessed are the merciful, for they will be shown mercy" (Matt. 5:7); "Blessed are those who hunger and thirst for righteousness, for they will be filled" (Matt. 5:6).

Those on the right are *not* commended for performing great signs and wonders (Matt. 24:24). They are commended for feeding the hungry, giving water to the thirsty, hospitality to the stranger, clothes to the needy, care for the sick, and friendship to the imprisoned. Moreover, they do this naturally, automatically, routinely. They don't give it a second thought—or maybe I should say that when they see someone in need, they give it a second thought and a third thought, until they help meet that need. Need-meeting in the name of Jesus is who they are. It is no pious big deal. They follow Jesus, and this is what disciples who are saved by grace through faith do with their lives. The

---

32　Bruner, *Matthew*, 2:568; see Matt. 13:10–17; 11:25–27; 15:13; 16:17.

gospel of Jesus Christ plays itself out in ten thousand ways in the daily routine of ordinary selfless concern for the other. Life is marked by the principle of the cross. The description reminds us of Jesus's "who is my neighbor" parable.

There is something beautiful about the ignorance of those on the right: "Lord, when did we see you hungry and feed you, or thirsty and give you something to drink? When did we see you a stranger and invite you in, or needing clothes and clothe you? When did we see you sick or in prison and go and visit you?" (Matt. 25:37–39). This is an ignorance that runs contrary to the presumption of works righteousness. It fits with "so-that-no-one-can-boast" salvation by grace through faith. Because of Jesus Christ, the righteous care for the needy and they do so without showy piety or inflated spirituality. This is a beautiful picture of faithful discipleship and the priesthood of all believers. Those who are saved by the "gift of God" are earnestly engaged in kingdom work. Everybody in Christ is involved in meeting real needs. The sermon begins with Jesus's disciples asking *when* will the temple be destroyed. But the sermon ends with Jesus's disciples (those on his right) asking *when* did we see you in need. Jesus has moved his disciples, then and now, from curiosity about the end to compassion for those in need until the end. Instead of speculation, "When is the end?" the emphasis is on action, "How then shall we live?" King Jesus identifies with the poor and oppressed. Snodgrass writes, "A person is not a disciple of Christ on the basis of ancestry, ritual act, or liturgical confession. One is a disciple in actually following Jesus's compassion and obedience to the will of the Father. This is not works-righteousness; acts of mercy are not done as a means to an end, but are expressions of knowledge of God's love" (see 1 John 2:7–11).[33]

It is ironic that the exegetical debate about this parable should be over the identity of the "least of these," as if Christian compassion is somehow directed principally to Christians. Didn't Jesus say, "Love your enemies and pray for those who persecute you" (Matt. 5:44)? Didn't he condemn the Pharisees for loving only their own kind? Jesus gave living water to the Samaritan woman at the well, and in the upper room he offered the bread and the cup to Judas. He prayed with the thief on the cross. Jesus defined the least of these as the least of these. Everyone is a potential brother or sister in Christ. James said it well: "Religion that God our Father accepts as pure and faultless is this: to look after orphans and widows in their distress and to keep oneself from being polluted by the world" (James 1:27).

The holy naivete of those on the right is beautiful for its lack of self-preoccupation and pretentiousness. In Christ, they follow the Jesus way and serve regardless of whether the person is deemed important or not in the eyes of the world. Christ's disciples can do no other. The inexcusable ignorance of those on the left, however, is maddening. Those on the right are "blessed by my Father," but those on the left only have themselves to blame for being cursed. Their disregard of needy people is consistent with their failure to follow Christ.

---

33 Snodgrass, *Stories with Intent*, 562.

What we do for others we do for Christ; what we don't do for others, we don't do for Christ. Those on the left are big talkers. They are the super-Christians who "perform great signs and wonders" (Matt. 24:24). They are like the wicked steward who abused the household staff. They are like the five bridesmaids, unprepared for the coming of the bridegroom who replies to their excuses, "Truly I tell you, I don't know you" (Matt. 25:12). They are like the worthless one-talent servant who blamed the master for his failure to invest. Those on the left have earned their well-deserved judgment entirely on their own. They may speak of the Lord with a confident and familiar air. They are comfortable with church lingo and a show of piety. Matthew makes sure that Jesus's conclusion to the Sermon on the End of the World highlights the problematic church. Some professing believers may claim big things for God, but in reality they come off looking and acting like the Pharisees. Jesus was intent on warning the disciples not to become like the Pharisees, whom he had condemned a few hours before when he left the temple for the last time.

Four parables bring the Sermon on the End of the World to a resounding conclusion. Faithfulness to the end proves faith from the beginning and faithlessness always ends in judgment. Jesus used a faithless and abusive servant-manager to prove that he was serious about disobedience. Five irresponsible bridesmaids who are left out of the party drive the message home. And a one-talent, wicked, and lazy servant ends up cast out "into the darkness, where there will be weeping and gnashing of teeth" (Matt. 25:30). The binary logic of the sheep and goats defines the difference between God's blessing and God's curse: "Then they will go away to eternal punishment, but the righteous to eternal life" (Matt. 25:46). All four parables are designed to get us ready. In simple, straightforward terms Jesus calls for discernment, resilience, readiness, and obedience. He warns his followers to remain honest stewards, responsible attendants, eager investors, and compassionate ministers. The message is clear: don't become fearful, complacent, lazy, or indifferent to the needs around you. Wake up. Keep watch. Stay alert. Be prepared. Invest in God's kingdom work. Make the most of your ministry opportunities! Amen. Jesus is Lord.

APPENDIX:
PREACHING THE PARABLES

Like a prism refracting light into a rainbow of colors, God's word splits the light of truth into a multimedia presentation of clear prose, true stories, passionate poetry, powerful visions, defining precepts, and provocative parables. For those willing to listen to God's word on its own terms, the message is powerful and penetrating. This is why it is so important to pay attention to the Jesus way—to learn from the Master how to communicate the gospel faithfully and fruitfully. Our task is not to interpret the Bible as much as it is to be interpreted by the Bible.

Jesus's parables push past our defenses and open us up to the impact of the gospel. The preacher in Hebrews wrote, "For the word of God is living and active. Sharper than any double-edged sword, it penetrates even to dividing soul and spirit, joints and marrow; it judges the thoughts and attitudes of the heart" (Heb. 4:12 NIV1984). Nowhere is this truer than in Jesus's parables. Since much is hidden from our eyes, and "nothing in all creation is hidden from God's sight" (Heb. 4:13), it makes sense to listen to Jesus's friendly, subversive speech with open ears, an open mind, and an open heart. Someday we will give an account of how we preached and lived the gospel (Heb. 4:13). "Whoever has ears, let them hear"

(Matt. 11:15). Ten reasons for using parables doesn't come close to capturing their dynamic impact, but I'm convinced that tapping into Jesus's communication strategy is important and rewarding for today's preachers.

1. Jesus used parables to teach in difficult situations. Parables challenge us to pay attention to the truth of God. They are simple, vivid stories, often drawn from ordinary life. They picture truth in profound and meaningful ways. Parables may either unsettle or inspire, but they do not lecture. They draw us into the drama of God's will and invite us to respond. Parables avoid reducing life to a list of points. The twists and turns of Jesus's parables evade our mental and emotional roadblocks. His friendly, subversive speech refuses to confuse truth with technique. Like Jesus, we preach the parables to get around people's defenses and to penetrate their minds with the gospel.

Parables are the Bible's version of going to the movies. They help us to visualize the impact of God's truth in our real life situation. As role-playing models, parables are a significant element in God's pedagogical strategy. They set us up to see ourselves and God's message in a new light. Just when we thought the message was for someone else, Jesus tells a story that pivots and penetrates our lives.

2. The parables are never just a story; they are always the gospel told slant. Jesus intended for all of his stories to shine a light on our fallen human condition and God's redemptive provision—the gospel of grace. Preachers are not telling moralistic tales to challenge their parishioners to try harder! They are preaching redemptive stories grounded in God's grace to inspire disciples to take up their cross and follow Jesus. The parables call for a way of life based on the principle of the cross—my life for yours. It is precisely because Jesus's parables penetrate and provoke that they call into question a preacher's shallow habits of amusing anecdotes and entertaining human interest stories. Parables show how story and message interface for the sake of proclaiming the gospel. They call into question any communicational strategy that is not rooted in the gospel.

3. Jesus's parables have a history of meaning rooted in the Old Testament. They are drawn from the Pentateuch, the Psalms, and the Prophets. To the unsuspecting listener, Jesus's stories may lack depth, as if he were just winging it; but to those who know better, the parables are deeply rooted in the Old Testament. These are the stories that never fall flat on the page with stick figure stereotypes and pedantic points, as if they were made up on the fly. There is always a canonical shape to Jesus's parables. If we want to grasp the true meaning of the parables, we have to explore and come to terms with their biblical depth. Jesus's method of incorporating stories and types, grounded in Scripture and tied to salvation history, provides the preacher with the necessary understanding for preaching the parables today. The way we preach Jesus's parables ought to be embedded in the great drama of the Bible. The gospel writers draw out the Old Testament meaning and encourage preachers to pay attention.

4. The most important thing to remember about preaching the parables is that Jesus is telling the story. The teller of the tale transcends the tale. *Who* is telling the parable of the good Samaritan or the parable of the lost sons makes all the difference in the world. Jesus gave his parables with a messianic edge, and so should we. When we preach the parables, we should never assume his place in the parable, nor should we forget who is telling the story. But we can never preach his parables apart from the reality of Christ's life, death, and resurrection. Preachers are always looking for the tension in the text, the fault line between the fallen human condition and God's redemptive position. In the parables, this fault line comes in the juxtaposition of human need and God's grace. If we identify the tension in the text, we will discover the passion of the passage and only then will we see ourselves and the gospel as Jesus intended. His parables were unavoidably offensive, and they remain that way today. They run counter to the prevailing ethos of culture, whether secular or religious, whether first century or twenty-first century. Jesus challenged the status quo by preaching messianic fulfillment through the parables, and he gave us a model for doing the same.

5. The second most important thing to remember when we are preaching the parables is that Jesus had to die to tell these stories. If we keep these truths uppermost in our minds, we will have a biblical advantage in interpreting the parables. The apostles compiled their gospel accounts in the conviction that the epicenter of God's gracious redemption was the death, resurrection, and ascension of Jesus Christ. This is why it is absolutely critical to let the biblical context shape our understanding of the parables. When the writers shaped their gospel accounts, they did not plug in the parables at random. The parables are intentionally situated in the narrative flow. There is nothing haphazard about the placement of the parables in the gospels. They find their pedagogical purpose in a context intended by Jesus, inspired by the Spirit, and recognized by the apostles.

6. The way Jesus used parables calls into question any and every effort to manipulate the hearer. The notion that any response from the listener is better than no response at all is mistaken. It is one thing to tell the truth slant to get past people's defenses and quite another thing to override their thinking and manipulate their emotions. The parables give the preacher a creative strategy designed to cause people to think in new ways. But they were never intended to override the listener's thinking. The gospel writers never imply that Jesus was a communicational genius. His purpose was to deliver the authoritative word of God-in-person. Manipulators and propagandists have to look away from Jesus to find their inspiration. The performance-preacher who holds his audience in the palm of his hand and who spins his stories to solicit laughter or tears will not find in Jesus a serviceable model. If we want to preach and teach like Jesus, the parables are a helpful guide. They are tutorials in friendly, subversive communication. There is no fanfare, no wild gestures, no displays of ego, no grandstanding. The style and substance of the parables are perfect for the humble representative of the Father's authority. The medium of Jesus's parables is a conversation, not a performance by an actor on a stage. But make no mistake—Jesus was never boring. The passion and pace of his delivery commanded attention. He never talked down to people in clichés or in cartoon-bubble speech. Parables are one of the reasons we cannot imagine Jesus speaking in a pompous, condescending way. His speech was penetrating, not pedantic; persuasive, not pandering. His message was always compelling, convicting, and authoritative, but never bombastic or bullish. Jesus knew his audience well and respected them as thinking beings. He appealed to their heart through their mind. His quick transitions, story twists, vivid images, and sharp applications model effective communication for today's preacher. We need to become more like Jesus if we expect to call people to follow Jesus.

7. Jesus's teaching method assumes the sovereignty of God from beginning to end. The power of persuasion remains with the Father to draw people to himself. The Danish Christian philosopher Søren Kierkegaard insisted that Christians distinguish between worldly persuasion and divine authority. Disciples listen to Jesus not because he was a genius but because he was the Son of God. In his 1847 essay "Of the Difference between a Genius and an Apostle," Kierkegaard explained it this way: a genius is born; an apostle is called. A genius adds to the accumulated understanding and science of humanity, but an apostle proclaims the wisdom of God, not found in the nature of things. A genius's insights are quickly assimilated and superseded by new breakthroughs, but the apostle's proclamation remains true through time. A genius is measured by intelligence, inventiveness, and innate abilities, but an apostle is identified exclusively by divine authority. We do not listen to an apostle "because he is clever, or even brilliantly clever" but because his message comes from God. Authority is not measured in "the profundity, the excellence, the cleverness of the doctrine."[1]

8. *The earthy quality of the parables resists grandstanding and invites a conversation that transforms.* Jesus's communicational strategy encourages a "come let us reason together" dialogue (Isa. 1:18). Kierkegaard lamented the artificial style of preachers in his day. He wrote, "Yet, nowadays, it is seldom, very seldom, that one hears or reads a religious discourse which is framed correctly. . . . If one had to describe Christian discourse as it is now heard with a single definite predicate, one would have to say it was *affected* . . . the whole train of thought is affected."[2] Kierkegaard argued that we must not accept the truth of God because it is "clever or profound or wonderfully beautiful, for this is a mockery of God."[3] Jesus is not a dazzling orator or a brilliant communicator wooing his audience. He is simply proclaiming God's word—telling the truth slant—and inviting a response: "Whoever has ears, let them hear" (Matt. 11:15).

---

1   Søren Kierkegaard, *The Present Age; and Of the Difference between a Genius and an Apostle* (New York: Harper Torchbooks, 1962), 96.
2   Kierkegaard, *Of the Difference*, 101–3.
3   Kierkegaard, *Of the Difference*, 104.

9. Pastors who preach Jesus's parables become parables in the process. In *The Art of Pastoring*, David Hansen distinguishes between pastor as symbol and pastor as parable. He reasons that "being a symbol of God is an exceedingly weak pastoral role" because "symbols reinforce what people already believe."[4] Pastors who become symbols stand before the people like the American flag or the Queen of England. By virtue of their position or office, they simply mirror back to the people their hopes and dreams. Instead of being a catalyst for meaningful discipleship, pastors who become symbols meet and placate people's expectations. As we have seen, Jesus used parables to reveal the truth indirectly, provocatively, even subversively. Pastors who embrace the pedagogy of the parables take on the parabolic character of the parables *in person*. Instead of confirming people's preconceived ideas of the religious life, they provoke reflection on the meaning and practice of the Christian life.

10. The parables and the sacraments serve as object lessons of God's grace. Preaching Jesus's parables sets the context for the celebration of the sacraments. Word and sacrament come together beautifully. Baptism and the Lord's Table are an extension and fulfillment of the gospel preached in the parables. Like the parables, the down-to-reality of God's supernatural grace is manifest in the redemptive cleansing of baptism and

---

4   David Hansen, *The Art of Pastoring: Ministry without All the Answers* (Downers Grove, IL: InterVarsity, 1994), 131.

in the hospitality of the Table. "In all its activities, especially the Lord's Supper," writes Kevin Vanhoozer, "a local church in its corporate life 'puts on' the spectacles of reconciliation in Christ, and not only acts out but also becomes a parable of the kingdom of God."[5] The divine methodology of parables and sacraments confirm in concert *mercy over merit*.

---

5   Kevin J. Vanhoozer, *Hearers and Doers: A Pastor's Guide to Making Disciples through Scripture and Doctrine* (Bellingham, WA: Lexham, 2019).